Mind, Heart, and Soul

in the Fight against Poverty

Mind, Heart, and Soul

in the Fight against Poverty

Katherine Marshall
Lucy Keough

THE WORLD BANK
Washington, D.C.

Contents

BOXES

TABLE

Foreword

No challenge to the global community has higher importance or greater urgency than the fight against poverty. And nothing is more central to that fight than working together, particularly in new and dynamic partnerships.

The continuing suffering of almost half of the people alive in the world today—who live daily with poverty, disease, and hunger, who have few opportunities, little access to the most basic services, and muffled hope for a better future—is a scandal. Millions of people who have seen their lives improve in the past decades are testimony to the key fact that poverty can be overcome, but the numbers of those who have yet to see progress are greater still.

The global community has, most dramatically in the formal commitment of the leaders of all nations to the Millennium Declaration in 2000, committed itself to changing this picture. This commitment is inspirational, and still more inspirational is the commitment to measure and judge progress continuously by keeping the light shining on the specific and tangible Millennium Development Goals. There are no grounds for complacency, however, as we are still far from achieving the goals though the year set for their achievement—2015—is fast approaching. We have far to go.

The central mission and purpose of the World Bank is to work toward a world "free of poverty," and our programs and staff efforts are all directed to this end. However, we are keenly aware that many others, above all the people who struggle each day to improve their lives, are equally engaged and committed to the same endeavor. The work we all do is directed, more and more, to a common end, and there is today a much keener appreciation than even a decade ago that we hold many values and goals in common.

Different institutions and sectors have their roles to play in working on the global challenges of the Millennium Development Goals, and diversity, local initiative, and creativity are essential to success. Nonetheless, there is much evidence that the overall sum of efforts often achieves less than it ideally should. A central reason is that many are poorly informed about what others do, misapprehend their efforts, or even work consciously in different directions. We are therefore looking more and more to thoughtful and creative ways to bring greater coherence, knowledge, and creative partnerships to the overall development agenda and action, so that indeed the sum of efforts adds up to the sum of real progress that we seek.

The vast and complex array of institutions that are organized with faith in God or with spiritual goals at their center share with the development institutions a commitment to addressing the problems of poverty. The critical role of faith institutions in the historic development and current provision of both education and health services is a central example, but so too are the remarkable roles that these institutions play in countries and regions wracked by conflict, their capacity to influence land use, and perhaps less remarked, their significant role in directing investment of financial assets. The most troubling issue facing humanity today may well be the HIV/AIDS pandemic, and here faith communities have critical roles to play, both in raising awareness about the complex practical and ethical issues around the pandemic and in working from global to community levels to combat it.

Where faith and development institutions have combined their efforts and work to common ends, remarkable results have been achieved. The experience suggests two conclusions: first, that the engagement of faith communities in the fight against poverty is vital to success in achieving the Millennium Development Goals; and second, that there is great scope for new and different forms of partnership that work to the respective strengths of the different communities. Yet these efforts are too little known and the lessons, good and bad, have engendered too little reflection.

This book recounts a series of experiences that involve common efforts of institutions from different sectors and realms, especially faith institutions, working to fight poverty and improve the lives of poor communities. The cases cover different regions of the world, and they range widely in terms of sectors and types of intervention. What all have in common is that shared objectives brought uncommon partners to work together and to achieve results that had eluded the institutions working by themselves. It offers practical lessons and inspiration, and we hope it will lead the way both to more analysis of such uncommon partnerships and to new and creative ways to combat problems and work to common objectives with new means and in new combinations.

James D. Wolfensohn
President
World Bank

Acknowledgments

This book is about remarkable successes by institutions and individuals that have been little sung in the development literature. While there have been, from time immemorial, inspirational and bold efforts by faith communities to respond to the challenge of poverty, and, increasingly, programs that have joined the efforts of faith and development institutions, the documentation of these stories is quite rare. This book represents a first effort by the World Bank to explore such experience across different sectors. It has thus taken the form of a series of narratives, based largely on interviews, some field work, and review of existing documentation with new eyes.

The book reflects a team effort, under the leadership of Katherine Marshall and Lucy Keough, working over a two-year period in 2002–04. The material was initially assembled as an "inventory" of experience in faith and development collaboration in preparation for a meeting of leaders of faith and development institutions in Canterbury, England, in October 2002. The World Faiths Development Dialogue has been a close partner in the endeavor. In the culling process, Hope Neighbor and Sandra Hackman provided extensive editorial support.

A large team of people, inside and outside the World Bank, contributed to this work, and we gratefully acknowledge their creativity, diligence, and inputs. From outside the Bank, we offer special thanks to

Emily Fintel (Avina Foundation), Dominique Peccoud (International Labour Organisation), Kathy Bartlett (Aga Khan Foundation), Faouzi Skali (Fez Festival), Canon Richard Marsh (Canterbury Cathedral), and Kathryn Poehtig (St. Lawrence University). Within the Bank, the team included Richard Anson, Jairo Arboleda, Samuel Choritz, Olivia Donnelly, Christine Dragasic, Mary Hawkins-Arthur, Tara Karacan, Anjali Kaur, Rebecca Ling, Yao Odamtten, Kelli Mullen, Monica Ploch, Leonid Sevastianov, Mariana Todorova, and Anthony Whitten. Where individuals took a direct part in drafting early versions of a specific case, their role is acknowledged, but we stress that this was a team effort overall and all material was substantially pruned and edited for this volume. Book design, editing, and print production were coordinated by the Bank's Office of the Publisher.

We are most grateful to the United Nations Population Fund and the Aga Khan Foundation for agreeing to our use of edited versions of case study materials they prepared.

Abbreviations and Acronyms

ABC	Abstinence, Be Faithful, and Responsible Use of Condoms (Uganda)
ACP	AIDS Control Program (Uganda)
AFSC	American Friends Service Committee
AIC	AIDS Information Center (Uganda)
AIDS	Acquired immunodeficiency syndrome
AKF	Aga Khan Foundation
AMIA	Argentine Israelite Mutual Aid Association
ANC	African National Congress
ARC	Alliance of Religions and Conservation
ARLPI	Acholi Religious Leaders' Peace Initiative
ARMM	Autonomous Region of Muslim Mindanao (Philippines)
ARV	Antiretrovirals, an HIV drug therapy
ATD	Aide à Toute Détresse (Aid to All Distress) Fourth World Movement
AUSJAL	Asociación de Universidades Confiades a la Compania de Jesús en America Latina
AVINA	Foundation working in Latin America
BNPP	World Bank–Netherlands Partnership Program
CBO	Community-based organization
CDC	Centers for Disease Control and Prevention (USA)
CDF	Comprehensive Development Framework
CDPMM	Consortium for Development and Peace Magdalena Medio (Colombia)
CFSI	Community and Family Services International (Philippines)
CINEP	Center for Research and Popular Education (Colombia)

CODLA	Centro Ocupacional de Desarrollo Laboral
DFID	Department for International Development (United Kingdom)
DIRGD	Guatemala Interreligious Dialogue on Development
DREAM	Drug Resource Enhancement against AIDS and Malnutrition (Run by Community of Sant'Egidio)
ECOPETROL	National oil company (Colombia)
EIFDDA	Ethiopian Interfaith Forum for Development Dialogue and Action
FAEPTI	Family AIDS Education and Prevention through Imams Project
FGC	Female genital cutting
G7	Group of Seven (leading industrial nations)
GDP	Gross domestic product
HACI	Hope for African Children Initiative
HIPC	Heavily indebted poor country
HIV	Human immunodeficiency virus
ICRC	International Committee of the Red Cross
IDA	International Development Association
IDB	Inter-American Development Bank
ILO	International Labour Organisation
IMAU	Islamic Medical Association of Uganda
IMF	International Monetary Fund
INEB	International Network of Engaged Buddhists
LRA	Lord's Resistance Army
LTTE	Liberation Tigers of Tamil Eelam
MCC	Mennonite Central Committee
MDGs	Millennium Development Goals
MNLF	Moro National Liberation Front
MRC	Madrasa Resource Center
NACWOLA	National Community of Women Living with HIV/AIDS (Uganda)
NATO	North Atlantic Treaty Organization
NEIAP	Northeast Irrigated Agriculture Project (Sri Lanka)
NFP	Not-for-profit
NGO	Nongovernmental organization
PAG	Participatory action group
PCI	Communist Party of Italy
PFP	Policy Framework Paper
PPA	Planned Parenthood Association
PRSP	Poverty Reduction Strategy Paper
REACH	Reproductive, Educative and Community Health Program (Uganda)

RRR	Framework for Relief, Rehabilitation, and Reconciliation (Sri Lanka)
SPCPD	Southern Philippines Council for Peace and Development
SZOPAD	Special Zone of Peace and Development
TASO	The AIDS Service Organization (Uganda)
TRO	Tamil Rehabilitation Organization (Sri Lanka)
UAC	Uganda AIDS Commission
UNAIDS	Joint United Nations Programme on HIV/AIDS
UNDP	United Nations Development Programme
UNESCO	United Nations Educational, Scientific, and Cultural Organization
UNFPA	United Nations Population Fund
UNHCR	United Nations High Commission for Refugees
UNTAC	United Nations Transitional Authority
USAID	United States Agency for International Development
USAID CORE	USAID Communities Responding to the HIV/AIDS Epidemic
USO	Oil Workers' Union (Colombia)
VCT	Voluntary counseling and testing
VDP	Village development plan
VSP	Village social profile
WCC	World Council of Churches
WCRP	World Conference on Religions for Peace
WFDD	World Faiths Development Dialogue
WWF	World Wildlife Fund, Worldwide Fund for Nature

CHAPTER 1

Separate or Common Worlds?

Faith and Development Partnerships for the New Millennium

The worlds of faith and development might seem, at first glance, natural allies in efforts to combat poverty, to fight for social justice, and to improve the daily lives of the world's poor and marginalized people. The connections between these two worlds, however, have been fragile and intermittent at best, critical and confrontational at worst. Why?

Religion, faith, and spirituality are discussed and debated with energy in every corner of the contemporary world. Libraries are full of learned texts about religion; bookstores devote large sections to spiritual topics; and political discourse turns often around the role of religion, its motivational force, and its potential divisive repercussions. It is a rare instance where a faith institution is not a defining marker of the space and character of a community. Charles Kimball, a scholar of religion, opened a recent book by holding that "religion is arguably the most pervasive and powerful force on earth."[1] Whether it is "the" or "a" central force, recognition is growing that religion in today's world plays many critical roles. Above all, it is pivotal in the daily lives of most of the world's people. Faith-based organizations are important players in many spheres of development, with broadly and deeply established roots as key, and sometimes sole, providers of social services—notably health and education—and community mobilizers.

Against this backdrop, one topic has received strikingly limited attention: the relationship between faith and economic and social development. The two worlds have remained largely separate for important reasons. The primary concern of faith leaders and institutions is people's spiritual well-being, over a long time horizon, while development institutions have tended to focus on the material, in the here and now. The vocabulary and approach of spirituality often—though not always—seem inimical to the technical, hard-nosed economic and financial approaches of development practice. Most domains of public policy also assume a separation of state and church, particularly official development institutions such as the World Bank, which by mandate must work with and through member states. The result is that the world of religion has been largely unacknowledged and often unseen among many development practitioners, both in writing and on the ground.

However, propelled by a divergent set of impetuses, the links between faith and development have become much more apparent. Whether concerning developing-country debt, socially responsible investment, preservation of land and natural resources, management of social services, or gender roles as a key facet of the HIV/AIDS pandemic, development and faith institutions find themselves working in the same fields, sometimes as allies, sometimes in apparent opposition.

In the development world, awareness that multifaceted and complex processes underlie economic and social change has risen markedly. What at one time seemed a distinct and relatively simple process of linear, predictable, and manageable progress is now more clearly seen as a complex kaleidoscope of social change that takes different forms in different parts of the world. Each development challenge—whether ensuring stability in the financial sector, boosting food crop production, or reducing infant mortality—depends critically on human motivations and institutions, often at a grassroots level. Likewise, the missions and lives of religious leaders, as shepherds of a "flock," might once have seemed relatively straightforward, and geared more toward spiritual well-being. More recently, however, the need to foster community and temporal well-being is now also widely accepted as falling within the purview of religious leaders and organizations, and sometimes challenges traditional beliefs and previously accepted notions of social change.

The walls that appear to divide the realm of the faith community from the secular and pragmatic world of economics crumble, faced with the gamut of issues that fall under the heading of social justice. "Globalization" has also brought, among countless other changes and challenges, a realization of the profoundly complex links among phenomena often viewed as distinct. The barriers that appeared to separate nations—rich and poor—now seem mere chimeras, so porous that wise observers everywhere highlight the bonds that link humankind.

A central thread runs through this quest for development solutions: the common responsibility of the global community, and thus of both institutions and individuals within it, to address the travesties that stand in the way of a more just world. These include the persistence of widespread and deeply rooted poverty and the violence that threatens individual lives and global security. Both are central to the mission and tangible work of the two worlds of development and faith, and we will need the engagement and active intervention of both these worlds to make progress.

Prompted by a positive sense of common concern and sharp differences on specific topics, this volume seeks to document a range of collaborative efforts between faith and development institutions. In different places, formats, and degrees, faith and development institutions have engaged in programs and dialogue around poverty and social justice. The partnerships range from a development dialogue born of a 1998 meeting called and chaired by James D. Wolfensohn, president of the World Bank, and George Carey, then Archbishop of Canterbury, to the work of the Community of Sant'Egidio, a Catholic lay organization, with AIDS patients in Mozambique and the commitment of Buddhist and Christian organizations to work for peace and disarmament in Cambodia. What is central to these and other stories in this book is the richness of the partnerships, and the potential for dynamic alliances, between organizations and worlds that have heretofore often viewed one another with apprehension.

To suggest that these engagements have dissolved the many layers of misunderstanding, differing perceptions, and outright disagreements over development priorities and work that have separated faith and development institutions would be a utopian dream. Nonetheless, it is heartening to see and hear, from leaders and communities in far-flung regions, a commitment to work together to fight poverty and advance justice, reflecting common purpose and respect for the motives of others.

MILLENNIUM GOALS AND CHALLENGES

The central challenge for the global community—to ensure a decent life and opportunities for all people—took tangible form in the Millennium Declaration of World Leaders in September 2000 and the ensuing Millennium Development Goals (MDGs). The declaration reflects an inspirational agreement—termed by some a "covenant"—that the global community will unite to eliminate the scourge of poverty in a finite time frame. The declaration is historic in its stirring commitment and near universal support among the world's heads of state. The MDGs reflect an effort to translate this covenant into concrete goals, with an apparatus for measuring progress and results (see box 1.1). As World Bank President James Wolfensohn often says, this overall agreement is so unambiguous and the commitments so specific that "there is no place to hide."

BOX 1.1
THE MILLENNIUM DECLARATION AND THE
MILLENNIUM DEVELOPMENT GOALS

From the Declaration:
"We will spare no effort to free our fellow men, women and children from the abject and dehumanizing conditions of dehumanizing poverty, to which more than a billion of them are currently subjected. We are committed to making the right to development a reality for everyone and to freeing the entire human race from want....

"We solemnly reaffirm, on this historic occasion, that the United Nations is the indispensable common house of the entire human family, through which we will seek to realize our universal aspirations for peace, cooperation and development. We therefore pledge our unstinting support for these common objectives and our determination to achieve them."[2]

The Goals:

1. **Poverty and hunger:** Reducing global poverty and hunger lie at the core of the Millennium Development Goals. The targets: reduce by half the proportion of people living on less than US$1 a day in low- and middle-income countries—from 28 percent in 1990 to 14 percent in 2015, and halve the proportion of people who suffer from hunger during the same period.

2. **Education** is development. It creates choices and opportunities, reduces the twin burdens of poverty and disease, and gives people a stronger voice in society. For nations, it creates a dynamic workforce and well-informed citizens able to compete and cooperate globally, opening doors to economic and social prosperity. The target: by 2015, children everywhere, boys and girls alike, will be able to complete a full course of primary schooling.

3. **Gender equality:** Women have an enormous impact on the well-being of their families and societies, yet discriminatory social norms, incentives, and legal institutions prevent them from realizing their potential. While the status of women has improved, gender inequalities remain pervasive. The target: eliminate gender disparity in primary and secondary education by 2005, and in all levels of education no later than 2015.

4. **Infant and child mortality:** More than 10 million children die each year in the developing world, the vast majority from causes preventable through a combination of good care, nutrition, and medical treatment. Mortality rates for children under five fell 19 percent over the past two decades, but those rates remain high in developing countries. The target: reduce the under-five mortality rate by two-thirds between 1990 and 2015.

5. **Maternal mortality:** Worldwide, more than 50 million women suffer from poor reproductive health and serious pregnancy-related illness and disability. And every year more

(Box continues on the following page.)

BOX 1.1 (continued)

than 500,000 women die from complications of pregnancy and childbirth. Most of these deaths occur in Asia, but the risk of dying is highest in Africa. The target: reduce the maternal mortality ratio by three-quarters between 1990 and 2015.

6. **Preventable disease:** HIV/AIDS, tuberculosis, and malaria are among the world's biggest killers, and all have their greatest impact on poor countries and poor people. These diseases interact in ways that make their combined impact worse. Effective prevention and treatment programs will save lives, reduce poverty, and help economies develop. The targets: halt and begin to reverse the spread of HIV/AIDS and the incidence of malaria and other infectious diseases by 2015.

7. **The environment** provides goods and services that sustain human development, so development must sustain the environment. Better natural resource management increases the nutrition and income of poor people. The targets: integrate the principles of sustainable development into country policies and programs and reverse the loss of environmental resources, halve the proportion of people without sustainable access to safe drinking water and basic sanitation by 2015, and significantly improve the lives of at least 100 million slum dwellers by 2020.

8. **Global partnership:** This goal calls for an open, rule-based trading and financial system, more generous aid to countries committed to reducing poverty, and debt relief for developing countries. This goal draws attention to the problems of least-developed countries, landlocked countries, and small-island developing states, which have difficulty competing in the global economy. It also calls for cooperation with the private sector to address youth unemployment, ensure access to affordable, essential drugs, and distribute the benefits of new technologies.

Source: www.developmentgoals.org

The MDGs offer a common framework for action. They do not belong to a single institution, region, sector, or nation but rather strive to link the entire global community. Therein lies their unique strength. The goals establish 2015 as a critical point for weighing progress, and the situation as of early 2004 is worrying, even discouraging. While progress in many regions and sectors shows what can be attained, most of the goals are not being achieved, especially in the poorest countries. The call is to redouble efforts and to reflect more deeply on what needs to be accomplished in the decade ahead.

While not an explicit focus of this volume, the MDGs provide a backdrop to it. Each of the book's sections treats issues related directly or tangentially to the MDGs, including partnerships around poverty, four specific MDGs, and work for peace. The breadth of the challenge of the MDGs and the sobering assessment of where we stand now call for new partnerships and new approaches.

Although the goals enjoy wide support among donors and governments, they are less well-known—and agreed upon—on the ground. This is critical because nongovernmental organizations (NGOs), faith institutions among them, are playing a growing role in development. The range of organizations working on poverty-related questions means that such work has become highly creative, diverse, and often rooted in unique local contexts. Counterbalancing these strengths are difficulties in coordinating these efforts and the risk that development institutions will not listen to this fragmented but important constituency. In this environment, existing institutions, current programs, and old ways of working cannot achieve the required change. What is needed is a commitment to the goals of the MDGs developed through spirited debate across organizations large and small, and a recognition that achieving them will require the full engagement of both faith and development communities.

MIND, HEART, AND SOUL (AND HANDS)

The wisdom and practical insights that have emerged through dialogue about poverty, and the inspirational but formidable challenges posed by the MDGs, suggest the need for new and enhanced partnerships that combine different faculties and perspectives. These may be characterized as mind, heart, soul, and, of course, hands.[3] Each is needed to face contemporary development challenges, and faith and development leaders cannot properly address any one challenge if we do not bring each element to bear.

The need to bring the resources of the mind to the fight against poverty is clear and straightforward—efforts to look critically at assumptions and learn from experience are essential weapons in our arsenal. Just as important is the need for imagination in defining new solutions and recognizing new applications for more traditional solutions. The rigorous analysis of problems and options, and concentrated and creative efforts to learn from experience and chart new paths, are "core competencies" of development institutions.

What is the role of heart in the development challenge? In highlighting the importance of heart, we point to the passion and commitment that drive the daily lives and work of both faith and development institutions. Fighting poverty has a technical dimension, but even more it requires a capacity to respect and care for fellow human beings. By explicitly emphasizing the notion of heart, development practitioners also highlight the need for a deep and sustained effort to keep the fight against poverty at the center of the agenda, to ensure that neither numb acceptance nor indifference take hold. We need to keep alive the picture of poverty as it is: a stain on the world's conscience, especially for those of us fortunate enough to live in the ostensibly developed world.

And soul? By referring to soul—which development institutions have traditionally invoked infrequently—we highlight the need to delve into the core values that give purpose to our work. In looking to the soul as a dimension underpinning action, we seek inspiration from the wisdom of the ages from all corners of the world, which informs so much of religious and cultural tradition and teachings. Soul also suggests a concern for the spiritual dimensions of life beyond the material, and a perspective on the far horizons of time and meaning. Qualities much in demand in development work—humility, courage, and conviction—are often described as spiritual, of the soul. In development discussions, two central dimensions of this concept emerge. The first is an awareness of the common values that link many if not most cultures, often with deep roots in religious teachings and traditions. The strongest common link may be the Golden

Rule—do not do unto others what you would not have them do unto you—but other common values include prohibitions against lying, stealing, and murder.[4] Many of these values are embodied in the Universal Declaration of Human Rights. The second dimension is the constant quest for excellence in an effort to give meaning to life and contribute to the community.

We are convinced also that hands are important, symbolizing the central reality that the work of development and the fight against poverty are above all about translating ideas and passions into action. There is a time and place for reflection, a time and place for caring, but there is also a time for doing, with commitment and consistency. Lord Carey of Clifton (formerly Archbishop of Canterbury) defines the central essence of the ancient concept of covenant as the willingness and determination to carry promises and verbal commitments to practical reality.[5]

No definable or visible barriers distinguish or separate mind from heart, soul, and hands. They blend together in motivation, word, thought, and deed. And while, by tradition, many people would identify the world of development most closely with the work of the mind and the hands and the world of faith with heart and soul, this is a false characterization and a false distinction. No single capacity or tendency is the exclusive province of any single partner, tradition, culture, or region. And nowhere is the combined application of mind, heart, soul, and hands more urgently needed than in the fight for social justice in the twenty-first century.

THE BOOK

This book represents a collection of creative partnerships that link development and faith institutions in working to improve the lives of people in many different regions of the world, across many sectors. The book's central purpose is to demonstrate the richness of these partnerships, with mind, heart, soul, and hands together of central importance to the stories. The volume illustrates the high ceiling for initiative and numerous dynamic alliances between unlikely partners. The examples range from global interventions directed principally to promoting dialogue and mutual learning to specific community-level action occurring at certain places and times. These are in many senses case studies, though they may more properly be described as stories. They hark back to one of the special gifts the world of faith offers: its genius for communicating through story and inspiration.

The book touches on the challenges that may arise in such partnerships as well. A principal difficulty of these initiatives is weak evaluation, with practitioners hard-pressed to "show results." Progress on this front will be indispensable to making the initiatives more broadly appealing, and to clarifying their strengths and weaknesses.

The case studies—or stories—in this volume stem from background work done for a meeting of development and faith leaders in October 2002 in Canterbury, England. In preparing for the meeting, participants steered us toward numerous anecdotes of development and faith partnerships, but we found precious little documentation about them. What existed was difficult to find, rarely collected in any one publication, and rarer still in the annals of official development organizations. Within the World Bank, for example, documents rarely addressed the role of faith institutions, much less explored the lessons from that experience. To begin to remedy such gaps, we (as organizers of the Canterbury meeting) prepared several case studies, and a team from the World Bank worked to draw insights from them. This volume includes edited versions of some of those cases as well as others relevant to the struggle to bring faith into the dialogue and practice of development organizations, to encourage a closer focus on development tradeoffs by the world of faith, and to foster greater communication between the two worlds.

The book is organized into three parts. The first part addresses questions around the definition and interpretation of poverty, emphasizing approaches that help explain the related challenges. Chapters in this part highlight work between official development organizations and faith institutions; work by NGOs, some of which is faith based, that puts pressure on official development organizations; and work by organizations that have folded faith and development into a coherent model for program and thought.

The book's second part takes four of the MDGs—on HIV/AIDS, maternal and child health, children's education, and the environment—as the starting points, highlighting partnerships that promise to increase both the scale and the quality of action toward achieving those goals. The need to promote broader awareness and programming around the goals—among actors ranging from small NGOs to the largest development organizations—serves as a subtext. The initiatives highlighted in these chapters must be built upon, and their approaches used by a wider range of development organizations, if we hope to achieve the goals.

The third part explores cases of common engagement between faith and development institutions in situations of conflict. The work of religious organizations during and immediately after armed conflict is perhaps the most visible in the development arena, and some of the most intuitively appealing. Cleansing and rebirth are central tenets of many faiths, and central, too, to the process of healing and forgiveness critical to lasting peace. These chapters illustrate the depth of partnerships needed to resolve conflict and sustain peace, with a few addressing the underlying causes that government-led, military-heavy, peace-building processes too often neglect.

This collection of case stories illustrates the richness of many different forms of partnership and points to the benefits that accrue when different types of institutions join forces to address a common problem. Of course, this collection is preliminary and by no means comprehensive. The central purpose is to stimulate the worlds of faith and development to explore their common interests, to listen better to each other, to communicate with more hope and less reserve, to work together on a more even footing, and to realize that a just world is not a singular aim, but shared.

NOTES

1. Kimball 2003, p. 1.
2. United Nations Millennium Declaration, September 8, 2000.
3. This framework owes a debt to Klaus Schwab, executive chair and founder of the World Economic Forum, who highlighted the need for head, heart, and soul as a framework for partnerships at the 2004 Davos annual meeting.
4. An exhibition at the International Monetary Fund in September 2002 highlighted the common elements of the global ethic drawn from many faith traditions, as elaborated by Hans Kung, the distinguished Swiss theologian; the core of the exhibition is published in a pamphlet titled "World Religions, Universal Peace, Global Ethic."

5. Statement at Canterbury meeting of leaders of development and faith institutions, October 2002.

REFERENCE

Kimball, Charles. 2003. *When Religion Turns Evil: Five Warning Signs.* San Francisco: Harper.

PART I

Faith Perspectives
and the
Understanding
of Poverty

Introduction

A strong common thread that links virtually all faith traditions is compassion and concern for those who suffer. Much thinking about poverty over human history has reflected the work of theologians and faith practitioners, and many social programs—including education, health, social assistance, emergency interventions, and peacemaking— have close ties, past and present, to faith institutions.

Likewise, the central mission of the World Bank is articulated in the statement that greets visitors to the headquarters as they first enter the complex: "Our dream is a world free of poverty." The World Bank and most other institutions whose core mission is to support and promote international development aim to keep their primary and constant focus on the goal of working with and supporting the world's poorest men, women, and children. This focus on poverty, present over many decades, is heightened with the contemporary focus on the framework of the Millennium Development Goals.

But what do we understand when we use the term *poverty*? What are its causes, its manifestations, its dynamic, its pathology? The answers to these questions are by no means simple, and without a clear consensus about the causes and nature of poverty, it is hardly surprising that there is less agreement still about what should be done about it and by whom.

The World Bank's dialogue with leaders of faith institutions has taken as its point of departure the exploration of how the different traditions and institutions understood poverty, and from there what should be done to counter its causes. It was apparent from the outset that this entailed a highly complex process, going to the roots of different traditions with issues and insights woven throughout the history of religious texts and practice. It involved a major part of the history of intellectual and practical work of the development institutions.

Discussion of what was meant by *poverty* was thus the central focus of the first meeting of faith leaders led by James D. Wolfensohn and George Carey (then Archbishop of Canterbury) in February 1998. The results were three: first, the emergence of a stronger common sense of shared mission, concerns, and field of action in the calling to work with and support poor communities; second, much greater awareness of the complex and varied differences of perspective among faiths, within faiths, and between faiths and development institutions about poverty; and third, a consensus that this topic called for, even demanded, much more dialogue.

The exploration of perspectives on poverty after 1998 may be characterized as conscious intellectual work complemented by specific actions undertaken by development and faith institutions, particularly working together, to deepen their respective understanding of poverty. A major endeavor was centered on the World Bank's traditional practice, undertaken every 10 years, to dedicate the "flagship" annual research and advocacy exercise, the *World Development Report*, to the topic of poverty. As part of a broadening process of consultation and engagement, a special effort was undertaken by the World Faiths Development Dialogue (WFDD) to consult with representatives of major faith traditions about both the topic of poverty and their assessment of the World Bank's work in this area. This consultation, which yielded a rich series of insights, is summarized in a booklet published by the WFDD.[1] The WFDD has pursued this work, primarily in the form of consultations with a growing network of committed individuals coming from every continent, and in specific work focused on the Poverty Reduction Strategy Paper (PRSP) process. Likewise, within the World Bank, the past six years have seen an intensive focus on expanding and deepening the understanding of poverty. A major focus of this work was the global survey exercise that reached some 60,000 people in poor communities across the globe, led by Deepa Narayan, and reflected in a three-volume series titled *Voices of the Poor*[2]; subsequent work is concentrating on a major thrust of the findings—the imperative of translating into reality the goal of empowering poor communities;[3] and, perhaps most important, the elaboration of a fundamental change in policy and practice to focus more directly and effectively on poverty issues, best reflected in the developing PRSP process.[4]

This process is the focus of chapter 2. At least to some degree, all PRSP exercises have engaged faith institutions.

A major impetus for reflection has been specific events and debates. The most remarkable example has been the Jubilee Campaign on Third World Debt, which is the focus of chapter 3. A remarkable effort, rooted in a provocative effort to promote dialogue around globalization issues, is the Fez Colloquium called "Giving Soul to Globalization," described in chapter 4.

Much reflection has also been undertaken by faith institutions. An example of this work is a consultation about Christian perspectives on poverty, led by the Rev. Michael Taylor, in association with the World Council of Churches (WCC).[5] The continuing and remarkable work of the Fourth World Movement (Aide à Toute Détresse or ATD Quart Monde) is described in chapter 5.

In addition to the efforts by the World Bank, other development institutions have also invested major efforts to learn more about poverty, in many instances with an explicit focus on the perspectives and partnership of faith institutions. One striking example is the major Ethics Program launched by the Inter-American Development Bank (IDB) in collaboration with the government of Norway and the IDB's member governments. This ambitious program grew from a series of consultations with leaders of different faith traditions, involving the IDB's president directly, and came to focus on the linked issues of social capital and ethics.[6] This experience is outlined in chapter 6.

A particularly interesting illustration of reflections on differing approaches to a practical issue with many poverty dimensions is the dialogue launched by the International Labour Organisation with the World Council of Churches (WCC). It is summarized in chapter 7, "The Significance of Decent Work—Faith Insights into an International Priority."[7] While decent work has become an important part of international human rights and development agendas, it is also a point of departure. In this sense, it is like the other global partnerships and institutions under the umbrella of the eighth MDG: the decent work agenda is an end in terms of labor rights, but more critically a means by which we work as communities, nations, and international networks to achieve the MDGs that come before it.

Finally, specific pilot exercises to promote faith and development collaboration undertaken by the WFDD in 1999–2002 in Ethiopia,

Guatemala, and Tanzania also have yielded both intellectual and on-the-ground experience of how faith communities experience poverty issues. Chapter 8 briefly highlights these three country experiences.

The basic caveat of this collection of cases applies in this section: What is presented is a set of stories that illustrate dimensions of the common effort to understand poverty better and to seek new avenues to address it. The examples are by no means comprehensive nor are they designed to present a systematic representation of thinking and work under way. They do, nonetheless, reflect a fascinating set of thoughtful and engaged efforts at analysis and action and offer many insights that have relevance for future work.

NOTES

1. WFDD 1999.
2. Narayan and others 2000.
3. Narayan 2002.
4. For more information on the PRSP process see the World Bank Web site: www.worldbank.org/
5. Taylor 2003.
6. For a description of the IDB's work in this area see www.iadb.org
7. The results are published as *Philosophical and Spiritual Perspectives on Decent Work*, edited by Dominique Peccoud, and are described in chapter 7.

REFERENCES

Narayan, Deepa, ed. 2002. *Empowerment and Poverty Reduction: A Sourcebook.* Washington, D.C.: World Bank.

Narayan, Deepa, Raj Patel, Kai Schafft, Anne Rademacher, and Sarah Kock-Schulte. 2000. *Voices of the Poor: Can Anyone Hear Us?* New York: Oxford University Press.

Peccoud, Dominque, ed. 2004. *Philosophical and Spiritual Perspectives on Decent Work.* Geneva: International Labour Office.

Taylor, Michael. 2003. *Christianity, Poverty and Wealth: The Findings of "Project 21."* London: Society for Promoting Christian Knowledge, and Geneva: World Council of Churches.

WFDD (World Faiths Development Dialogue). 1999. *Poverty and Development: An Interfaith Perspective.* Oxford, U.K.: WFDD. Available at www.wfdd.org.uk

2

Beyond "Consultation without Participation"?
Faith Institution Engagement with the Poverty Reduction Strategy Paper Process

Multilateral development banks and other official development institutions have in recent years sought much more actively, and through a variety of means, to reach out to a broad range of civil society institutions, religious organizations among them. Experience in outreach has been uneven, and there is considerable reflection ongoing about lessons learned and next steps. The effort poses many complex challenges. For those institutions whose basic governance structures revolve around governments as shareholders and governors, approaches to civil society reflect to a considerable degree the approaches and views of member governments. Further, one of the few points of unanimous agreement is the difficulty even of defining civil society, let alone outlining coherent and consistent ways to engage their undisputed wealth of insight, engagement, and talent.[1] Civil society actors rarely speak with a common voice, nor can they be seen to represent seamlessly the society in which they operate. Members of civil society often stress a lack of economic fluency that shrinks the common

This chapter was drafted by Hope Neighbor, and it is based in large part on the WFDD reports on consultations about PRSPs.

ground on which they and development agencies might communicate. Faith organizations face particular challenges in integrating their perspectives into the dialogue and operations of large aid organizations, though the experience does vary widely by country and region, depending in large measure on traditions and laws governing state–civil society relations.

This chapter explores recent experience of the interface between faith institutions and "mainstream" development agencies through a specific vehicle and formal process. It describes an exercise designed to elicit feedback from a group of faith institution representatives, coming from different faith traditions and parts of the world, about their experience of engaging with governments and the World Bank and International Monetary Fund (IMF), with Poverty Reduction Strategy Paper (PRSP) consultations as a basis for the discussion.

PRSP PROCESS—THE BACKDROP

As background, the PRSP is a strategy developed largely by the World Bank and the IMF to elaborate explicit strategic frameworks that are to guide growth and poverty reduction in a client country.[2] The PRSP is a government-led document that outlines a comprehensive strategy for growth and poverty reduction. By design, the PRSP aims to pull the priorities and analyses of the different actors working under the general umbrella of "development" onto one page, making their efforts more complementary and, one hopes, coherent. During PRSP development, a series of consultations are held with influential figures and organizations in a given country. Consultation can range from a steering committee made up of government, academic, and NGO representatives to a series of "town hall meetings" with local officials and townspeople throughout a country. The underlying principle of PRSP consultations is to adopt growth and development strategies that make economic sense while trying to ensure that the policies and programs envisioned are also compatible with the hopes and aspirations of a country's people. There is no rigid formula for consultation. In practice, the quality of consultation and the depth of its influence varies considerably from country to country.

Once the PRSP is finalized, the World Bank and the IMF assess its strength as the basis for providing loans and credits to that country. In this sense, the PRSP is circumscribed by the limits of World Bank and IMF assistance and approach.

The participation of civil society is thus seen as essential and central to the design of a PRSP. The PRSP process is relatively new, introduced formally only in 1999, but the nature and depth of participation varies. It is thus evolving, and many of the early PRSP exercises were conducted under tight deadlines, as interim exercises that entailed quite limited participation from the broad civil society of the country concerned. Major efforts are taking place now both to broaden participation and to hone this participation so that it is effective both in eliciting a wide range of views and experience and in forging the understanding and consensus about the strategy that is so critical to success. The overall PRSP process has been the subject of several formal evaluation efforts and much commentary; no effort is made here either to summarize or assess the overall experience.

The topic examined here is the specific experience of faith institutions as part of the evolving PRSP process. There is no explicit approach or policy on engagement of faith groups in the PRSP processes, and indeed there has been no global discussion of the issue nor specific effort to canvass or evaluate experience. This is largely because the PRSP processes are designed and led by government leaders in the countries concerned and thus vary widely, both by country and over time. However, the general expectation has been that faith institutions would be part of the overall participation process in each country.

WFDD CONSULTATION WITH FAITH LEADERS ON THE PRSP EXPERIENCE

The World Faiths Development Dialogue (WFDD) organized a specific consultation about faith group experience with a set of PRSP participation processes.[3] This was focused on a four-day meeting in Canterbury, England, in July 2002, which involved individuals from 15 countries[4] where PRSP consultations had already taken place, and from several different faith traditions. The consultation was led by the director of the WFDD, Michael Taylor, and included representatives of the World Bank as observers (the IMF was invited to participate but could not be present). A second objective of the meeting was to help gain a better understanding, against the light of the PRSP challenge, of how the faith groups involved framed their vision and work on poverty, and how they saw government strategies to deal with poverty reflected in the PRSP.

Visions of Poverty

At the July Canterbury workshop, the first task set to the faith group was to report on the nature of poverty in their respective countries. One of the interesting elements was not only the variation in poverty in the absolute but also the manner in which poverty was described. Although many in the group referred to the numbers and share of the population living on less than US$1 a day, the focus was much more on contextual information and qualitative description. Faith participants emphasized again and again their vision of poverty as a complex phenomenon, with the importance of freedom and a satisfying life more central to their presentations than gains in income or improvements in social indicators.

The faith presentations, almost without exception, highlighted the importance they attached to the nuances of poverty as a persistent and central theme. In Albania, the poor quality of basic services such as education, health, water, and sanitation was seen as a problem that was equally as thorny and significant as the fact that one in three Albanians lived in poverty.[5] The Albanian participant underscored disproportionately high rates of poverty in families with children. In Albania, over 40 percent of families with three or more children live in poverty, compared to 25 percent of all families living in poverty.[6] He spoke of an increasing number of children living in the streets, a fact and growing trend that had not been picked up by household-based survey instruments. As he presented the situation and its overarching cause, the increase in poverty and vulnerability in Albania was linked to its extensive internal and external migration, which had weakened social cohesion, and traditional family and community-based safety nets, over time.

Along similar lines, the Ethiopian participant described his country's poverty across sectors, reciting a litany of human development statistics that place Ethiopia among the planet's least developed countries. The presentation alluded to the intertwined roots of poverty. While agriculture employs 89 percent of the work force[7] and provides just over half the country's gross domestic product (GDP),[8] Ethiopia has not yet attained food security.

Participants from other countries focused on life satisfaction much more than growth. Aspirations of largely Buddhist Sri Lankans differ from those of people living in countries tightly focused on economic growth, argued one representative, who commented: "The middle path, path to the human liberation in Buddhism, guides people for a simple, happy and content life."

An interesting theme was the suggestion of several present that opportunities rival wealth in importance. The participant from Tanzania emphasized the importance of rights in alleviating poverty, citing social well-being and the rights to security, justice, freedom, and a peaceful life. This participant had seen an erosion in the effectiveness of instruments of law and order, as well. In Zambia, opposition parties were seen as weak, so "only the church speaks out." Catholic social teaching served as a source of inspiration for Zambians. Its focus on human dignity laid down a challenge to the "economic growth equals development" shorthand. The Zambian participant remarked, "If growth does not benefit the human being, then it is not development at all."

Generally speaking, the group described their sense that there were marked differences in perceptions of poverty between faith groups on the one hand and government and international development agencies on the other. While the latter seemed always firmly oriented toward economic growth, the former have a range of viewpoints on poverty and consider it a more complex, less growth-oriented question. For a dialogue between these actors to be fruitful and of substance, greater acknowledgment of the different points of departure in addressing development questions is necessary. How can development agencies and governments constructively integrate faith groups' perspectives on "poverty reduction" into their programs and policies, when many faith groups do not view poverty reduction as the central question in the creation of more fulfilling, sustainable lifestyles? This question of reconciling views on poverty has central importance to the work of development agencies.

These nuances and differences in perception and emphasis also have importance in an instrumental sense. With an estimated 200,000 imams in Bangladesh,[9] 450,000 religious people working for the Orthodox Church alone in Ethiopia,[10] and 78 percent of Ghanaians[11] attending a religious institution at least once a week, religion is enormously important in guiding the choices of billions of people. Religion influences viewpoints on individual agency and collective responsibility. It profoundly shapes development agendas and people's willingness to be involved in them. In this sense, understanding faith is central to developing policies that will say —and do—something meaningful about poverty.

Faith Institutions' Contributions to PRSPs

While the group, and particularly the international agency representatives, wrestled with the variations and subtle nuances of different faith groups' perspectives on poverty, the faith participants at the Canterbury consultation quickly turned to the practical issues emerging from their direct experience and their history of work in *service delivery*. They saw this as their primary contribution to the design of poverty strategies, their potential role in execution, and the justification for a seat at the table.

It was here that the wide variations in experience, largely by country but also, to some degree, by faith tradition, emerged in the discussion. A common theme, across virtually all the countries represented, was a concern that structural and semantic differences could and did prevent their knowledge and perspective from being given its due. Beyond this general concern about marginalization and not being heard, several reported much more specifically on individual country legal frameworks that actually barred or limited their participation in the PRSP process. In several instances, relationships with government were either too antagonistic or too accommodating, with the consequence of diminishing faith groups' participation in the PRSP.

The diversity of actual experience and level of engagement of the faith institutions represented in service delivery to the poor was striking. The Albanian Islamic Community serves as an umbrella organization for the Islamic NGOs working in Albania. A US$79 million investment by Islamic organizations in social service delivery from 1992–2000 was reported, representing a significant share both of overall service levels and of growth and change. The participation of faith communities in Sri Lanka's development process had grown consistently since the late 1970s. This included providing secular education and vocational training to the poor; assisting displaced children; maintaining primary schools; providing partial financial and material support to schoolchildren; and offering logistical support for community development programs, within religious institutions. In Cameroon, faith communities support hospitals and health clinics throughout the country. Throughout the 15 countries represented at the Canterbury consultation, the discussion highlighted how uniformly the faith groups' history of involvement in social service delivery was long and deep.

While most participants differentiated faith groups' service delivery work from that of international NGOs or development agencies, they reported that some of their counterparts in civil society organizations had, in effect, accepted or acceded to the dominant, growth-oriented framework. The participant from Ethiopia remarked, "A great majority of [faith-based organizations] have not been engaged in systematic learning about how to apply their spiritual tradition in their development endeavors. Instead they, presumably unconsciously, follow the current fad of mainstream development practices and operate within their conceptual and philosophical frameworks which are essentially materialistic."

Within the faith community, then, there is a considerable plurality of views on how to attack poverty, and from which point of view. Government and international development agencies were perceived to share the singular view that poverty would be reduced through growth alone.

While faith groups from those countries participating in the WFDD workshop have had decades of experience in service delivery, their degree of influence in government on these and related issues was described in terms that highlighted the wide variations in practice, perceptions, and relationships. Their depth of experience would be a critical, though not central, element of government's willingness to take faith institutions' perspectives into account during the PRSP consultations.

Legal and Organizational Issues

The diversity of experience in faith groups' participation and influence in the PRSP process was striking. In a few cases, basic constitutional and legal arrangements had a material role in faith groups' participation in PRSP consultations. In Albania, for example, the representative argued that faith groups had been explicitly excluded from civil society consultation at the level of the constitution,[12] though they were deeply and directly involved in many aspects of the development process. In Zambia and Malawi, by contrast, religious institutions, and Christian churches in particular, have been at the heart of strategic discussions from well before the birth of the PRSP process and are formally recognized in this role by the government.

Beyond legal restriction or facilitation of their role, faith groups' prior relationship to governments heavily influenced government willingness to take their perspectives, or those of civil society organizations in general, into account. Half of the WFDD participants reported that governance issues had affected faith institutions' willingness to participate in national dialogue on development. In Guatemala, Mozambique, Sri Lanka, and Zambia, faith institutions had distanced themselves from government because of the perception of high and contagious public sector corruption. In 1992, Catholic bishops in Malawi wrote an open letter condemning the government of then-President Hastings Kamuzu Banda, sparking mass demonstrations and contributing to the suspension of humanitarian aid; Malawi's electoral system and administration changed two years later. In Ethiopia, sector policies in theory build in collaboration between government and religious organizations but in practice, "the former tends to regard religion as at best irrelevant to the life and transformation of society." The Ethiopian participant to the WFDD consultation characterized faith organizations' diminished role in governance debates as "giving blessings and witnessing the events." The Honduran Catholic Church's activism in the Jubilee 2000 campaign had resulted in debt relief worth US$556 million in 2000.[13] In Cameroon, the government's human rights abuses were highlighted with the acknowledgment that religious institutions had been hesitant to speak out against them.

The group described a consistent pattern of faith organizations taking positions, either implicit or explicit, on poverty and governance. In many countries, however, these positions placed faith groups in at least partial opposition to government. This in turn gave rise to a degree of mistrust, or at least apprehension, in the relationships between the two groups. The Cameroonian participant commented, "This marginalization of civil society is explained, among other things, by the fact that the Cameroonian government still considers NGOs as competitors, not partners."[14]

In anticipating upcoming PRSP consultations, then, the general view expressed was that faith organizations could offer comparatively deeper perspectives in the sectors in which they delivered services, given their acute understanding of the composition and weak links of those sectors. They were well aware, however, that legal or historical arrangements might reduce the influence that they would have on the PRSP design, irrespective of the merit of their contribution. The discussions also highlighted that the PRSP design consultations would need to allay faith groups' skepticism about the ability of governments and donors to consider alternative messages on development.

The group engaged in some common discussion about the significance of the wide variations in approaches to civil society. In some of the countries, the overall atmosphere toward civil society was quite inimical, even hostile; civil society was poorly organized, local government institutions were weak, and the opening of the PRSP process to civil society in itself represented a quite fresh approach, calling for new thinking, new mechanisms, and new means of organization within the broad nongovernmental community, including, often prominently, faith institutions. This was a challenge, and there were few interfaith groups and weak traditions of interfaith consultation on which to build. In other countries, in contrast, and notably in Latin America, the most urgent challenge was seen as building on processes of decentralization to move decisionmaking and service delivery closer to the people and communities affected. This suggested quite different mechanisms for PRSP consultations, notably suggesting that they be tied to, and developed in the light of, the popular participation reforms under way, including the development of local government institutions.

THE PRSP CONSULTATION ITSELF

The picture that emerged was of wide variations in the mechanisms and structure of PRSP consultations across countries. In some countries, such as Uganda, civil society actors were invited to participate at each level of the PRSP development process. In Uganda, the national steering committee guiding the PRSP included civil society actors. Thematic subgroups offered deeper perspectives on critical issues and, finally, large consultative meetings gave other groups and the broader population the opportunity to weigh in on Uganda's proposed Poverty Eradication Action Plan. In other countries, consultation was seen as cursory. The Bangladeshi participant reported a high level of dissatisfaction with the PRSP process and a considerable amount of mobilization to organize a "People's PRSP," to counter the PRSP being rushed through by the government and its implementing partners.

Irrespective of approach, the basic mechanism for consultation was described as a large meeting, facilitated by government or a government subcontractor and drawing in participants from throughout society. Participants range from "average" individuals to representatives of religions, NGOs, associations, or other groups. The tenets of a country's PRSP or a draft PRSP are presented to participants, and discussion is structured to give feedback on its main points.

Over half of the WFDD participants commented specifically on their perceptions and concerns about how useful their engagement had been, and particularly, in this light, how far their comments were considered or incorporated in the final PRSP and the underlying strategic framework that it represented. The balance of the feedback was poor: In the group's view, civil society's views, and those of faith organizations, did not change the substance or structure of the PRSP. As an example, the Ugandan participant applauded the breadth of the consultation, led by OXFAM and the Uganda Debt Network. She noted, however, that viewpoints with which the government did not agree were not included in the final PRSP and reflected the (quite commonly heard) contention that changes in strategy could not be accepted because they would stand no chance of acceptance by the international donor community. The Cameroonian participant observed that government seemed content to have participation; exploring the issues raised within participation was not as important. The language used by facilitators was not understood by the citizen-members of the consultation. In Malawi, the government did not appear committed to changing the substance of the PRSP presented to civil society; in Mozambique, civil society's influence was seen as cursory. Several participants expressed frustration that the PRSP was drafted before the consultations; this increased the efficiency of gathering feedback, but reduced the scope for introducing faith groups' perspectives into the document. It also meant that participants felt, whether real or imagined, that the poverty reduction strategy drafted by government was a fait accompli: limited consultation may have worsened public sentiment more than no consultation at all.

Three themes wove themselves through these narratives of, as one participant put it, "consultation without participation." They included government opinion of civil society, and in some cases faith groups in particular; structural limits of the PRSP; and concern about whether participants to the consultations were able to speak for the poor and marginalized.

Government Opinion of Civil Society, and of Faith Institutions in Particular

The strongest sentiment that came out of the Canterbury workshop was the impression that governments and, to a certain extent, donor agencies were not able to or interested in integrating alternate perspectives into their poverty reduction strategy. This point of view was not uniform, but came out quite forcefully among the participants who saw this as an issue.

In several instances, where strong NGOs and faith groups were seen as rivals to government, only NGOs already toeing the government line were brought into the consultation. When institutions with different views did participate, they felt that their views had been brushed aside. The seriousness with which faith organizations' comments were taken seemed to vary by sector: government was more receptive to messages on health and education, fairly standard areas for religious groups' support, and less open to critique on economic fronts. This can be attributed partly to civil society's relatively low comfort with economic language, and a tendency for hard-nosed economists to discount language that summarizes concepts in terms other than theirs. This issue—strained relationships and confidence between government and civil society, with donor agencies' own biases adding a layer of complexity—placed an enormous drag on vigorous and constructive debate about poverty. It is this lively debate, a positive but counterbalancing perspective to that of government, that will be critical to creating a strong framework for development in many countries. If this debate is central to development, it becomes a central question for international development institutions.

Structural Limits of the PRSP

A difficulty of consultation within the PRSP framework is that it is designed to give feedback *on the PRSP*. The World Bank and the IMF look to PRSPs as blueprints for their assistance, with aid contingent upon agreement on a PRSP. As a strategy, then, the PRSP should be compatible with the development priorities and frameworks for assistance agreed on by the country, the World Bank, and the IMF. Governments are disinclined to consider alternate views of poverty reduction when they expect beforehand that models based on these views will not be approved.

Many actors involved understand clearly the tradeoffs between broadening the scope of consultation and timely completion of the PRSP (important above all because it is tied to international financing). Governments seek to maintain an even flow of development financing. Viewpoints that could eventually be incorporated into a more sensitive, nuanced development strategy will take time to tease out, and additional time means a delay in the donor funding that helps to keep many countries afloat.

Speaking for the Poor

Throughout the consultations, participants raised questions about civil society participants' ability to represent others, and most especially the poor. How effectively can a Maputo-based organization speak to rural poverty, or the Ethiopian elite understand the struggles of the poor who are far removed from them?

SOME CONCLUSIONS

The Canterbury workshop provided an opportunity for faith leaders from 15 countries stretched across the globe to present poverty as they saw it. The understandings that were voiced there built upon years of work with people living in poverty, providing services, and offering spiritual counsel. The vision of how poverty "worked" varied, but was often informed by the philosophical underpinnings of the faiths represented at the consultation. Finally, it was also striking how often the participants did refer to standardized measures of poverty, along income and non-income dimensions.

Observations suggested by the experience include the following:

- *Willingness to listen to faith groups' perspectives,* as those of civil society, is critical. Consultation for consultation's sake was quickly picked up on, generating resentment toward a theoretically "country-owned" strategy for reducing poverty.
- *Well-structured time for consultation,* facilitated by a party in whom both government and civil society had confidence, was roundly appreciated. The facilitation led by the Carter Center in Albania, for example, was reportedly well received. It brought in the participation of multiple stakeholders (though by law not religious organizations), while maintaining the needed focus on Albania's Growth and Poverty Reduction Strategy.
- *Leaving certain questions or areas of inquiry open,* for refinement after the consultations, would alleviate the frustration that the PRSP was virtually finished before the consultation began and that civil society's feedback did very little to change it.
- *Where the poverty reduction strategy was changed, government and donor agencies should make a particular effort to communicate that these changes have been made.* The impression that PRSPs change little as a consequence of the consultation process may be accurate, or skewed by an ineffective strategy for disseminating information. A stumbling block throughout was the failure to disseminate draft or final PRSPs and related documents, with the lack of internet access cited as a frequent problem.

In sum, the 2002 WFDD PRSP workshop in Canterbury gave religious figures from 15 countries a forum to discuss their views on poverty, and to relate this poverty perspective experience to their specific and recent participation in or observation of a PRSP consultation process. The participants expressed considerable uncertainty and ambivalence about the World Bank and IMF roles in the PRSP process, but also curiosity to learn more. They were not constitutionally hostile to engagement with government, but rather disappointed at the form that consultation had taken. Strong examples were proffered, with more frequent dismay at what they perceived as an inability or unwillingness, in the process, to step back to examine the complexion of poverty long term. If not now, within the development of a multiyear poverty reduction strategy, when? Experience with consultation in practice was mixed, but the overarching principle was that constructive, frank debate helps to move understanding—and progress—forward.

NOTES

1. Edwards (2004) provides a rich and thoughtful discussion of both different perspectives on what constitutes civil society and its evolution over recent decades.
2. For information on the PRSP process, see World Bank Web site www.worldbank.org/poverty/strategies.
3. A full account of the consultation is available at www.wfdd.org.uk/programmes.
4. Participants from Albania, Bangladesh, Cameroon, Ethiopia, Ghana, Guatemala, Honduras, Malawi, Mali, Mozambique, Peru, Sri Lanka, Tanzania, Uganda, and Zambia attended the seminar. Representatives from the WFDD, U.K. Department for International Development (DFID), Eurodad, and the World Bank also attended.
5. World Bank 2002a.
6. World Bank 2002a.
7. World Bank 1995.
8. World Bank 2002b. Preliminary estimate.
9. Islam and Al-Khateeb 1995.
10. Personal communication, Patriarch of Ethiopian Orthodox Church, May 2003.
11. Planned Parenthood Association of Ghana 2002.
12. Note that the World Bank country director said that in practice faith representatives had contributed to PRSP consultations in Albania.
13. World Bank 2000.
14. Marshall 2002.

REFERENCES

The word *processed* describes informally reproduced works that may not be commonly available through libraries.

Edwards, Michael. 2004. *Civil Society.* Cambridge, U.K.: Polity Press.

Islam, N., and M. Al-Khateeb. 1995. "Challenges and Opportunities for Tobacco Control in Islamic Countries: A Case Study from Bangladesh." *Eastern Mediterranean Health Journal* 1(2): 230–234.

Marshall, Katherine. 2002. "WFDD Consultation on Faith Community Participation in the PRSP Process." World Bank Development Dialogue on Values and Ethics. Washington, D.C. Processed.

Planned Parenthood Association of Ghana. 2002. "Strengthening the Participation and Implementation of Reproductive Health Services by Religious Institutions." Accra, Ghana. Processed.

World Bank. 1995. *World Development Indicators.* Washington, D.C.

———. 2000. "World Bank and IMF Support Debt Relief for Honduras." Press Release. Washington, D.C. Processed.

———. 2002a. "Albania – Country Assistance Strategy (CAS)." Draft. South East Europe Country Unit. Washington, D.C.

———. 2002b. Development Economics Database. Washington, D.C.

CHAPTER 3

Learning with Jubilee
World Bank Engagement with the Jubilee 2000 Debt Campaign

"I am personally very grateful for the enormous contribution Jubilee 2000 has made to debt relief. While we do not agree on every aspect of how to address this challenge, we salute the coalition for helping to bring this critical issue to the world's attention."
—World Bank President James D. Wolfensohn, April 6, 2000.

The Jubilee 2000 Campaign, which was launched in 1999, spurred knowledgeable debate and massive public support for a moral case for debt relief among poor countries. As the campaign harnessed the political power of millions of credible and informed people, one of its most significant achievements may have been the building of links between high-level officials and grassroots social activists. The resulting deep and intense dialogue between faith and development communities exerted a marked impact on the attitudes of multilateral lenders, and may ultimately influence in important ways the direction of development strategies and relationships between governments and development agencies of developing countries. Intense exchange and sometimes heated debate between the campaign and the World Bank, in particular, led to a

---

Kelli Mullen prepared an early draft of this chapter.

growing conviction that both sides shared much common ground despite significant and continuing differences in perspectives.

ORIGINS OF JUBILEE 2000

The Jubilee Campaign came together as the result of two individuals: Bill Peters (a U.K. government officer) and Martin Dent (a professor for most of his career), both then retired and in their seventies, first developed the idea of linking debt relief to the faith-based concept of jubilee and the new millennium in the early 1990s.[1] Their passion was born of personal experience of witnessing the impact of heavy debt burdens on people in developing countries, though both also cite their Christian faith as a foundation for their activism.

Peters and Dent argued that much of the debt was tainted by historical corruption and inefficiency within developing countries, exacerbated by the self-interested political and economic decisions of creditor countries.[2] Peters and Dent maintained that wealthy creditors had an ethical responsibility to devise a sustainable solution to excessive debt among the world's poorest countries. Their vision was a year of biblical jubilee, when creditors would forgive all debts and developing countries could begin again. The co-founders shared these ideas with faith leaders and social activists throughout the United Kingdom, and the Jubilee 2000 Campaign was founded in 1996. Ann Pettifor, lobbyist for the Debt Crisis Network, helped to launch the global campaign by calling on a network of faith-based NGOs in the Group of Seven (G7) countries, and later throughout the developing world, to mobilize a revolutionary social change movement.

THE MORAL CASE FOR DEBT FORGIVENESS

The Jubilee 2000 campaigners view indebtedness as a transfer of wealth from poor to rich countries that cripples their development prospects. From a faith perspective, these campaigners also see heavy debt burdens as profoundly unjust—even a form of bondage.

The idea of the Sabbath echoes throughout Judeo-Christian scripture as a vehicle for preventing human society from concentrating wealth and power in the hands of a few. In agrarian societies such as biblical Israel, the cycle of poverty began when a family fell into debt, deepened when it sold off land to pay a debt, and reached its conclusion when landless peasants could sell only their labor, essentially becoming slaves. In the Torah, the Sabbath—or seventh year—was intended to extend communal discipline of restraint and restore social, economic, and ecological equilibrium through a year of universal rest. By allowing land to remain fallow, farmers would allow the soil to rejuvenate, and thus to produce higher yields. The Sabbath was also a time of reflection, when scripture directed people to act with compassion for all living things and seek solidarity with their neighbors.

In Leviticus 25, this vision culminates in the Sabbath's Sabbath, occurring every 49 years, when a complete redistribution of wealth and power reverses the cycle of poverty. At this time all debts are forgiven, forfeited land is returned to its original owners, and slaves are freed. The rationale for restructuring the community's assets—which includes a prohibition against lending money for interest—reminds Israel that God is the owner of the land.[3] In the New Testament, Jesus reiterates the call to jubilee, linking forgiveness of monetary and spiritual debts so the excluded can pursue a new start and society can restore equity and harmony.

THE JUBILEE 2000 DEBT CAMPAIGN

The Jubilee 2000 Campaign similarly saw debt forgiveness as giving the poorest people in developing countries, who bear the consequences of massive debts, a voice in development debates. The scriptural roots of debt forgiveness provided a broad-based appeal on which the Jubilee network constructed its campaign.

Organizers first sought audiences in local religious communities throughout the United Kingdom, United States, and other creditor countries, educating congregations on the critical situation facing heavily indebted poor countries (HIPCs). This difficult and painstaking grassroots networking process proved fruitful as it gathered considerable financial and intellectual resources as well as enormous political force. The Jubilee Campaign sought full cancellation of debt for the poorest countries while also recognizing that debt is a component of larger economic issues in developing countries. Campaign organizers thus did not see debt cancellation as a panacea for all the ills of underdevelopment, but rather as a simple and obvious first step toward relieving poverty.

In explaining the extraordinary challenges facing developing countries and the serious impact of heavy debts upon the poor, Jubilee organizers had to help European and American congregations comprehend the complex inner workings of the international financial system. One approach was to relate the message of excessive debt service to the experiences of average Americans and Europeans in contracting more debt than they can handle. This tactic proved successful: congregations took up the cause of debt relief in the jubilee year.

Campaigners eventually collected over 24 million signatures in support of debt forgiveness for highly indebted poor countries. In the United States, Jubilee USA led a letter-writing campaign that sent thousands of postcards to the World Bank, IMF, and the U.S. Treasury. These, along with economic arguments by academics such as Jeffrey Sachs, then of Harvard, attracted the attention of key political and religious leaders—including U.S. President Clinton, Pope John Paul, and the then-Archbishop of Canterbury—along with celebrities such as Bono, lead singer of the Irish rock band U2. Open support by popular and powerful figures created a positive public image for the campaign and rapidly pushed the issues to the forefront of global consciousness.

At the height of the movement, Jubilee affiliates campaigned in more than 60 countries around the world and encompassed a broad cross-section of society, including NGOs, faith communities, and political activists. Members from developing countries recognized their unique voice and formed a separate coalition, known as Jubilee South, during a South–South summit in Johannesburg in November 1999. As a loose network of NGOs throughout the developing world, this group identified common ground in the desire to seek not only debt forgiveness but also greater participation in their countries' development strategies and projects.[4] Involvement with the dynamic campaign in the North inspired members from the South to continue their struggle for economic equality, while northern campaigners drew on compelling stories of poverty and other experiences of the South to inspire their audiences. Overall, the campaign aimed to maintain a delicate balance between respectful dialogue with World Bank officials and active support of a grassroots movement.

For its part, the World Bank had given much thought to the heavy impact of debt servicing on the development prospects of poor countries long before the Jubilee Campaign. Campaigners were therefore able to sustain a persistent dialogue—though it was sometimes fraught with tension and frustration—with the World Bank and other donors. Ultimately, compelling rhetoric combined with often attention-grabbing tactics produced constructive outcomes.

Jubilee campaigners' harshest criticism stemmed from their views of structural adjustment—seen as a one-size-fits-all strategy imposed on developing nations by the World Bank and the IMF. A March 1999 *Newsweek* article quotes Ann Pettifor: "In Tanzania, for example, one child in six dies before the age of 5, but the government spends more on servicing its debt than on primary health care. Money needed for health and education programs goes instead to rich international creditors whose billions have often propped up crooked local elites."[5]

DEBT IN THE POOREST COUNTRIES

Donors and campaigners rarely reached a meeting of the minds on structural adjustment, as the debate drew on images more than on historic analysis of what such programs were designed to accomplish, how they actually unfolded, and where—individually and collectively—they fell short. However, the Jubilee Campaign gained momentum in tandem with mounting efforts by the international community to address the critical worsening of the debt burden among developing countries.

The crisis facing HIPCs differed from that among middle-income countries in the 1980s (which had prompted most thinking and policy reform around debt issues up to that time). Economic growth in most highly indebted countries had been low—less than population growth—over the previous decade. Many HIPCs depended primarily on commodity exports for income, the price of which had proved volatile and often actually fell. A patchwork quilt of measures and programs had developed to deal with parts of the debt burden, including subsidies for interest payments provided by several bilateral donors, debt buy-back programs for commercial bank debt, and a variety of debt swap arrangements. However, these programs offered limited respite, called for enormous investments of time of skilled managers, and came nowhere near offering a comprehensive solution to the overall debt situation. Moreover, nearly 85 percent of the debt of HIPCs was owed to governments and multilateral institutions, and no legal mechanism then existed for rescheduling multilateral loans.

The Paris Club[6] of bilateral donors provided a mechanism for rescheduling debt for a number of countries, including some in the poorest group. However, despite ever-more-favorable reductions of bilateral debt, countries could not exit the loan-rescheduling process. Ann Pettifor described the situation as "aid going full circle," with new loans servicing old loans and only limited funds allocated toward the development projects the loans had originally targeted.[7] An article by a Bank economist painted a grim picture: "Debt stock continued to grow . . . and the situation was exacerbated by accumulating arrears problems within a greater context of decreasing development assistance, stagnating growth, and near total isolation from global capital markets."[8]

As repeated rounds of rescheduling had proven insufficient, creditors realized they would need to cancel loans to make meaningful cuts in debt, while World Bank opinion synthesized around the need to address multilateral debt along with overall debt sustainability. When James Wolfensohn became president of the World Bank in June 1995, one of his earliest acts was to pose demanding and far-reaching questions about the approach to debt and highly indebted countries, prompting much soul searching and analysis within the institution and among its governors.

Thus the Jubilee 2000–inspired movement, combined with support from economists and development scholars and a growing consensus within bilateral and multilateral institutions, from an early period helped to encourage and accelerate alternative mechanisms to relieve the debt of the world's poorest countries. A new phase may be said to have begun when, at the Halifax G7[9] summit in 1995, the G7 countries called upon the Bank and the Fund, albeit in general and tentative terms, to "develop a comprehensive approach to assist countries with multilateral debt problems through flexible implementation of existing instruments and new mechanisms where necessary."[10]

THE FIRST HEAVILY INDEBTED POOR COUNTRY INITIATIVE

The first Heavily Indebted Poor Country (HIPC) initiative, in 1996, linked debt relief with progress on economic reforms, including spending for food security, health, and education. Although Jubilee 2000 and other NGOs initially aimed for full debt forgiveness, definitions of sustainable debt levels for the poorest countries continued to be (and remain to this day) a contested topic within development circles. Other questions persisted around the criteria whereby countries would qualify for debt reduction, including where to draw the line between the poor and the poorest countries. After much debate based on experiences with debt crises among middle-income countries in the 1980s, lenders decided that countries with debt-to-export ratios of 250 percent or more would qualify for the HIPC initiative.

Simply put, to reschedule bilateral and multilateral official debt, a country had to formulate a time-bound program of economic reform. Satisfactory progress at the "decision point"—a midpoint assessment of progress and a commitment to undertake remaining reforms—would yield a limited amount of debt relief. A full assessment at the end of the program, called the "completion point," would release the full amount of debt relief.

Both multilateral and bilateral donors contribute to a trust fund that finances the HIPC program. Although the World Bank had committed US$1 billion as a pledge of future debt cancellation through the International Development Association (IDA), which provides loans and grants on highly concessional terms to the poorest member countries, few countries met eligibility requirements in the early years and progress was slow. Of more than 14 countries eligible in the first three years of the program, only four—Uganda, Bolivia, Mozambique, and Guyana—received debt relief. This record prompted concern within the World Bank, among indebted countries, and within the Jubilee constituency.

Jubilee and NGO observers stepped up demands for greater debt forgiveness, mobilizing large constituencies in donor countries and encouraging NGO involvement throughout the developing world. The campaign also moved discussion from local churches and synagogues to offices, boardrooms, and legislative chambers. The result was a global debate around the HIPC initiative as well as broader development issues. As part of a year-long review of HIPC in 1999, the World Bank launched an interactive Web page and held consultations in Africa, Latin America, the United States, and Europe with representatives of Jubilee 2000 and other NGOs. More than 1,000 pages of concrete proposals informed an enhanced HIPC framework.

ENHANCED HIPC INITIATIVE AND POVERTY REDUCTION STRATEGY PAPERS

Nowhere did consensus among donors, political leaders, and the public on the need for faster and deeper action to address poor countries' debt manifest itself more clearly than in Germany. The catalyst was the coming to power of the Social Democratic Party, reinforced by Germany's hosting of the 1999 G7 meeting in Cologne. Jubilee and other NGOs assembled over 50,000 demonstrators in Cologne who led 100 million more worldwide in a "global chain reaction."[11] The result was a G7 pledge of US$100 billion of support toward deeper and more comprehensive debt relief.

A major review of the HIPC program made it significantly "deeper, broader, and faster." Eligibility criteria shifted from countries' debt-export ratios to nations eligible for IDA loans. In contrast to the original HIPC framework, which based debt reductions on projections of debt stock at the completion point, relief rested on data at the midway decision point. This modification was intended to add greater certainty to the calculations and increase the amount of relief. Finally, the enhanced HIPC initiative reduced the assumed level of sustainable debt from 250 to 150 percent of exports.

The enhanced HIPC initiative also reflected the view that debt relief was not an end in itself, and focused on the need to strengthen links between debt relief and poverty reduction. The World Bank's Comprehensive Development Framework (CDF), which became part of the broad approach articulated by the Bank from the late 1990s, had incorporated this more holistic approach. Henceforth, a country's economic reforms would focus on improving its poverty programs and ensuring the most effective use of the resources of government, donors, civil society, and the private sector freed as a result of debt relief.

Building on the CDF approach and the HIPC experience, the introduction in 1999–2000 of the PRSPs was to provide a central tool to help meet this goal. Under the PRSP process, governments formulate their national poverty reduction strategies, at least in principle, by examining the impact of all other development strategies. This process was designed to include civil society (although consultations would vary considerably from one country to another), and thus to foster greater sustainability of policies and programs designed to alleviate poverty.[12] The PRSP process was directly linked to the provision of concessional financing from the World Bank, and countries would ultimately present their PRSPs to the boards of the World Bank and the IMF for review (but without seeking a formal endorsement—rather, they were to serve as a framework). Countries would submit an interim PRSP—a road map for the full PRSP, including its attendant consultations—at the HIPC decision point.

THE OUTCOME: HIPC DEBT RELIEF

Campaigners viewed these promises of deeper debt relief and the new emphasis on poverty reduction with cautious optimism, continuing to exert political pressure and encourage dialogue while incorporating NGO networks throughout the developing world into the expanding development debate. Policy decisions at the World Bank and other international financial institutions reflected the urgency of debt forgiveness linked with poverty reduction. The World Bank committed to move 20 countries through the HIPC–PRSP process by the end of 2000. By December 2000, 22 countries had completed PRSPs and were at their decision point on HIPC debt relief. The appendix to this chapter highlights some of the issues that emerged in Bolivia, one of the early countries that navigated the HIPC process. It focuses on the role played by the Catholic Church, which was linked to the Jubilee Campaign at different points.

However, the rapid pace of debt relief, once strongly advocated by the Jubilee Campaign, brought unexpected consequences. Early completion points for some countries established debt-to-export ratios before systems were in place to ensure economic stability. For example, shortly after receiving HIPC debt relief, Uganda, an early success story, faced falling commodity prices and thus lower export earnings. Although its debt-to-export ratio had risen, it was too late for HIPC to take this into account. Jubilee campaigners also held that the accelerated timeline sometimes shortchanged input from civil society.

Jubilee organizers generally came to recognize that the World Bank and IMF are increasingly sensitive to the need to focus proactively on the effort to reduce poverty, and that their language had become more inclusive. More so than in the past, the World Bank is seeking to develop and maintain social safety nets and to emphasize expenditures on health, education, social services, and other programs critical to the poor. However, the Jubilee Campaign leaders contend that the actual policy outcomes of the PRSP process differ only marginally from previous policies. While the PRSP process provides a framework for engaging civil society and recognizing the uniqueness of each country, many governments have drawn on well-traveled strategies already applied by multilateral institutions to safeguard concessional lending.

A JUBILEE VISION FOR THE FUTURE

The Jubilee Campaign's call for debt cancellation within the first millennium year captured the attention of millions of people around the world and undoubtedly helped inspire rapid implementation of the enhanced HIPC process. Drawing on moral imperatives inherent in Christianity and Judaism as well as other world religions, the campaign brought together unlikely partners, including liberal inner city Democrats and conservative Republicans in the United States, and trade unions and development agencies such as OXFAM, Christian Aid, and Catholic Agency for Overseas Development in the United Kingdom Jubilee campaigners in the North incorporated the experiences of trade unionists from Mozambique, priests from Zambia, and economists from Ecuador, while campaigners in the South benefited from the unique expertise of their northern partners. Although solidarity did not always guarantee agreement, North and South discovered common objectives. These unprecedented partnerships resulted in a global social movement that altered popular and official views of debt relief and enabled civil society to participate in development decisions.

However, dissatisfied with the policy and project outcomes of the enhanced HIPC–PRSP initiatives, the Jubilee Movement International—successor to Jubilee 2000—continues in its critique of the World Bank and works to mobilize popular support in favor of alternative solutions.[13] For their part, Bank officials acknowledge that the HIPC debt relief and PRSP processes require continual adjustment, but they also see major progress in forging international consensus on the need to combat poverty and provide the necessary resources for doing so.

APPENDIX. BOLIVIA: JUBILEE 2000, NATIONAL DIALOGUE, AND THE CATHOLIC CHURCH

The international Jubilee 2000 movement exerted particular force in Bolivia, where debt had long been a looming obstacle to development. The country had also pioneered many approaches to exorbitant debt, including buybacks, debt-for-nature swaps, and precedent-setting Paris Club arrangements.

Of special interest is the central leadership role played by the Catholic Church in these processes. Bolivia's Catholic Bishops Conference devoted much energy to the Jubilee Campaign, securing important international support, notably from Germany. One result was the Jubilee 2000 Forum, a national debate about poverty led by the Church that included a wide range of civil society organizations. That effort was instrumental in establishing the Law on National Dialogue, which casts the Church in a leadership role in monitoring a national consultation process—known as "control social"—to be held every three years.

The goals of the Bishops' Conference and Caritas, a Catholic NGO, for this process were ambitious from the outset. Designed to track the spending of resources freed by debt reduction, the process then shifted to encompass the goal of ensuring full transparency of all government spending, tracking the absolute level and share of resources actually going to poverty-linked programs, and fighting corruption.

The unique Catholic Church role reflects its dominance in Bolivia: its 500 years of continuous presence, the fact that the great majority of the population is Catholic, the credibility the Church gained by consistently opposing human rights violations and corrupt practices through dark years of dictatorship, and its strong leadership in the Jubilee 2000 movement. Bolivia's constitution guarantees freedom of religion but also recognizes a special status for the Catholic Church. The Church sees itself as politically neutral, thus ensuring some continuity in a system where each new government tends to bring to office a significantly different set of actors and policies. The Church also views itself as a unifying force in a divided nation and as a strong voice for poor communities and social justice.

The role of the Catholic Church in relation to the roles of other civil society and faith groups is the subject of considerable discussion in Bolivia. Other groups recognize the prestige and trust that the Church leadership brings to a fragile and evolving process, but of concern is how effectively an established religion can embrace diverse influences, such as from indigenous groups and women. Fundamentalist elements—both separate Christian "sects," which are growing rapidly in parts of Bolivia, and tendencies within established faiths—also present challenges, and Bolivia has little tradition of formal interfaith dialogue.

Despite nearly 20 years of democratic government and economic reforms, most with strong backing from the international community, Bolivia remains profoundly poor, and the situation appears to be worsening. Jobs are still scarce, and the informal sector encompasses growing numbers of marginalized people. Migration has accelerated, and social disintegration is visible. Violence—within families, communities, and regions—appears to be rising, and several regions are struggling over the distribution of land. The underlying problems are structural and profound, and despite major investments in national dialogue and extensive work on many fronts, long-term strategies for change seem to be weak or lacking. One result is an implicit fatalism that poverty is inevitable—a pitfall recognized by some, but by no means all, church leaders.

The monitoring process now taking shape holds interest for both Bolivia and beyond: How will the country's national dialogue, anchored in civil society, evolve in relation to the National Congress and local elected authorities? What instruments will emerge to ensure effective budget oversight? Can efforts to combat corruption proceed without accentuating mistrust in government? Can diverse civil society organizations find ways to work together to address these challenges?

NOTES

1. The origins of Jubilee are described in several sources, notably a 2002 speech by Bill Peters [Bill Peters, *On Changing the World*, July 2002, Web site of the Jubilee Campaign (www.jubilee2000uk.org) accessed May 4, 2004] and in a

statement by a key campaigner, Ann Pettifor, at SEDOS (Service of Documentation and Study, a Rome-based Catholic Church networking group), February 17, 2000. A summary by the campaign organization is titled "The world will never be the same again ... because of Jubilee 2000."

2. In the late 1970s and early 1980s, the G7 countries supported increasing loans to developing countries. In the words of Margaret Thatcher, "We recognize the particular need for the flows of financial resources to the developing countries to increase, including public, private, bilateral and multilateral resources." With the monetary policies of the Volcker years in the United States and consequent interest rate hikes, servicing their debts became a near impossibility in many countries. See Bill Peters, *On Changing the World*, 2002.

3. Myers 1998.

4. Jubilee South includes members from over 40 countries and 85 organizations in Latin America and the Caribbean, Africa, and Asia-Pacific.

5. *Newsweek* 1999.

6. The Paris Club is an informal group of official creditors, first created in 1956, whose role is to find coordinated and sustainable solutions to the payment difficulties experienced by debtor nations. Paris Club creditors agree in changing the profile of payments on debts due to them. The Paris Club has remained strictly informal. It can be described as a "noninstitution." There are 19 permanent members of the Paris Club, and other official bilateral creditors may participate. Paris Club permanent members are: Australia, Austria, Belgium, Canada, Denmark, Finland, France, Germany, Ireland, Italy, Japan, Netherlands, Norway, Russian Federation, Spain, Sweden, Switzerland, United Kingdom, and the United States of America. It meets in Paris, with a secretariat provided by the French Ministry of Finance. More information can be found at the Paris Club Web site, www.clubdeparis.org

7. Ann Pettifor, SEDOS speech, February 17, 2000.

8. von Trotsenberg 2000.

9. G7 is the term applied to a forum of the world's leading industrial nations, which began to meet in the mid-1970s. The term G8 applies when Russia is included.

10. G7 Halifax summit communique, June 1995, www.g8.utoronto.ca/summit/1995halifax/communique/index.html.

11. Jubilee Campaign 2000, *What We Achieved: First Steps in Debt Cancellation*, http://www.jubilee2000uk.org/jubilee2000/final/what.html

12. The PRSP stands in contrast to the former policy framework paper (PFP), which was meant to reflect a government's overall development policies, including poverty reduction. The PFP was, in theory, a tripartite agreement negotiated among the government, the Bank, and the IMF. However, in practice, IMF and Bank staff usually drafted these documents, and thus they were often seen as imposed on governments and their reforms weak or temporary.

13. The Jubilee Research Web site and organization describe themselves as successors to Jubilee U.K., with a mission to be a "think and do tank," combining analysis and activism (www.jubilee2000uk.org).

REFERENCES

Christiansen, Karin, and Ingie Hovland. 2003. "The PRSP Initiative: Multilateral Policy Change and the Role of Research." Working Paper 216. London: Overseas Development Institute.

Myers, Ched. 1998. "Balancing Abundance and Need." *The Other Side* 34(5): no page numbers available. Available at www.theotherside.org/archive/sep-oct98

Newsweek. 1999. "The Fight to Forgive the Debts of Poor Countries." March 12.

von Trotsenberg, Axel. 2000. "The HIPC Initiative for Poor Countries." In Alfred Herrhausen Society for International Dialogue, *Challenges of the Debt Crisis.* Munich: Piper Verlaug.

CHAPTER 4

The Fez Colloquium
"Giving Soul to Globalization"

What is the scope and purpose of dialogue? This challenge is often posed, perhaps most commonly without words, in response to events where parties engage in the well-known phenomenon of speaking and "preaching," talk past each other, joust with words, and deluge the system with words—spoken and written—to explain and justify a cause. Perhaps on no topic has more been said and written, with less real engagement and communication, than about globalization, its virtues, and its ills. Two apparently radically differing views and approaches to globalization are epitomized in two highly visible annual global events, one organized by the World Economic Forum in Davos, Switzerland; the other by the World Social Forum, initially in Porto Alegre and, in 2004, in Mumbai, India.

For the past four years, an unusual annual colloquium held in Fez, Morocco, has set out to promote a different kind of dialogue, inspired both by a global vision of a multicultural world where differing cultures and perspectives all find a place, and by a conviction that real dialogue requires new and different approaches. This colloquium is juxtaposed with a remarkable festival of global sacred music from all corners of the

---

This chapter benefited from the contributions of Tara Karacan.

world, and brings together and challenges thinkers and doers who expound radically different visions of the world and prescriptions for the future. The Fez Colloquium builds on the metaphor of the bridge, seeking through a more profound understanding, extending well beyond simple facts and values to the world of the spirit, to work toward a richer menu of options and solutions for the future.[1]

THE FEZ FESTIVAL

The acclaimed Fez Festival of World Sacred Music, launched in 1995, celebrates its 10th anniversary in June 2004 as a well established and admired annual music and arts event. The festival takes place in Fez, Morocco, an ancient and glorious city with a rich history and renowned cultural heritage. It draws inspiration from the city's long traditions of cultural harmony and artistic and intellectual excellence, and from the dynamic confrontation of modern and ancient strands in the Fez of today.

The music festival has as its explicit aim the bridging of cultural divides and celebration of diversity, through music and art; its underlying theme is "Giving Soul to Globalization." The artistic program is invariably rich and remarkably diverse. The 2003 bill of fare opened with an oratorio, "Reconciliation," performed by Goran Bregovic (Yugoslavia, Russia, Bulgaria, Morocco, France), and featured artists from around the world, including Gilberto Gil (Brazil); Mohamed Reza Shajarian (Iran); Yungchen Llamo (Tibet); Doudou N'Diaye Rose (Senegal); Sheikh Habboush, The Al Kindi Ensemble, and the Whirling Dervishes (Syria); and the Anointed Jackson Sisters (United States). The 2004 Anniversary program (May 28–June 5) promises to bring together the finest and most challenging artists over the festival's life, with a unifying theme of peace and what is termed "Traces de Lumière" ("Filaments")—referring to the light of both individual and community inspiration.

In addition to the formal concerts, the festival has grown to include a youth program, evening sufi encounters, and concerts in the Fez medina (the old city) for the general public. There are concurrent photographic and film exhibitions. The festival Web site has much additional information (www.fesfestival.com), and compact discs of the festivals are readily available.

The Fez Festival is very much grounded in and run from Morocco but is an international event.[2] It has won wide international acclaim and support, including special recognition by the United Nations, which named the festival and its founding genius, Faouzi Skali, one of its "Unsung Heroes of Dialogue." A Moroccan scholar, anthropologist, and entrepreneur, Skali is also part of Romano Prodi and the European Commission's "Groupe des Sages" (Group of Wise People). The festival comes under the patronage of the King of Morocco and his special adviser, Mohamed Kabbaj.

In March 2004, the Fez Festival embarked on a new and ambitious venture, sponsoring a 17-state tour of the United States, called the "Spirit of Fez." The central theme was peace, and it brought artists, particularly from Muslim, Jewish, and Christian traditions, together in a pageant of peace.

COLLOQUIUM, GIVING SOUL TO GLOBALIZATION

Since 2001, the Fez Colloquium, addressing issues of globalization, has been an integral part of the festival and, like the festival itself, is grounded in the theme "Giving Soul to Globalization." The colloquium sets out to help bridge the gulfs in dialogue separating very different world views, using the inspiration of the music and art and the tangible and audible examples of intercultural exchange that constitute the Fez Festival to stimulate new reflection about global issues. The notion that Fez could be a bridge between diametrically opposed world views—exemplified in the widely separated annual meetings of the World Economic Forum (Davos) and the World Social Forum (Porto Alegre)—was present from the start. Another hope is that the Fez Colloquium will give rise to a continuing "Club de Fez," with various activities and networks extending over the course of the year, between the annual festivals.

The first colloquium, in 2001, began with little fanfare but it concluded on a note of hope, as participants saw that it offered a rare avenue toward different and useful kinds of dialogue on critical and sensitive topics. The dialogue at Fez highlighted the great span in approaches to globalization issues, but also some elements— practical as well as ethical and spiritual— that united even those who represented sharply opposing views. There was a start to communication between some who described globalization as a vampire force, destroying traditional cultures, or as a juggernaut threatening fragile ecosystems, and others who reveled in their hopes for a world where frontiers to opportunity were broken down and prosperity helped to fulfill dreams of a just society. Participants were drawn from all corners of the world, including, for example, Sulak Sivaraksa, an active and engaged Thai Buddhist leader; Thierry de Montbrial, a leading French intellectual; Mexican activist Luis Lopez-Llera; the Reverend James Park Morton of the New York Interfaith Center; Dominique Strauss-Kahn, a former minister of finance of France; and John Lane, author and critic.[3]

The May 2002 colloquium was a more ambitious effort, drawing a wider range of participants and larger audience. Its theme was "Paths to Wisdom," a topic that generated much reflection on common values versus differing perspectives. The colloquium evoked considerable interest both at the festival and in subsequent discussions (including in the media) as a different and important forum for discussion of globalization issues. The World Bank became a partner supporting the colloquium because of the colloquium's promise for offering new insights into understanding globalization debates.

2003 COLLOQUIUM

The 2003 colloquium reflected a third, much more institutionalized event, and it made clear that the Fez process had developed quite strong roots. Under the overall rubric of "Giving Soul to Globalization," the unifying theme in 2003 was "From My Soul to Your Soul: The Art of Transmission." The starting idea was to focus on education and its role in imparting and enhancing cultural values and intercultural harmony. To this notion was added the role of the media and communications in globalization processes, the concept of identity and spiritual citizenship, and our responsibilities to future generations, as well as the social responsibility of corporations.

The format that has evolved for the colloquium is a plenary session every morning for five mornings, based on two panels of speakers. Each speaker makes a short presentation, followed by dialogue within the panel and discussion with the audience. The symposium takes place outdoors, in the courtyard of the Batha Museum under an ancient and glorious fig tree. The beauty of the setting and the musical accompaniment of birds serves as a backdrop that creates an environment that puts participants at ease and shakes them out of habitual patterns of discourse.

The 2003 colloquium had about 60 invited speakers, most international, but also a significant group from Morocco. Because the speakers were numerous, formal presentations were sharply compressed and sharpened. Participants were invited in their personal capacities (not as representatives of institutions), with the aim of bringing together a wide range of perspectives and views, blending activists and thinkers, policymakers and critics. The speakers included (a partial listing to illustrate the range) Swami Agnivesh, an activist on bonded labor from India; Jacques Attali, French man of letters and politics; Patrice Barrat, French journalist with special interest in international dialogue; Bertrand Collomb, chairman of the industrial complex Lafarge, Regis Debray, French intellectual; Peter Eigen, chairman of Transparency International; Gilberto Gil, Brazil's minister of culture; Mario Giro of the Community of Sant'Egidio; Candido Grzybowski, one of the leading lights of the World Social Forum; Mats Karlsson, Swedish, World Bank vice president; Rabbi Matalon from New York; Fatema Mernissi, Moroccan feminist writer and activist; Njoki Njehu, leader of the organization 50 Years is Enough; Jean-Claude Petit, publisher of *La Vie*; Jean-Louis Sarbib, French, World Bank senior vice president; and Sulak Sivaraksa, Thai, engaged Buddhist. The moderators were Faouzi Skali and Katherine Marshall.

Among the topics that sparked particular interest were the ethical responsibilities of the media and its descent into public relations, social action for corporations, changing roles for and expectations from religion, and the role of political leadership in focusing attention on global social justice. The varied group of speakers attracted to the Fez event tend to shed their traditional perceptions of identity and belonging, and speak as humans and brothers and sisters first, creating real mutual trust that takes the dialogue to a new plane.

The colloquium has two unusual features that aim to promote thoughtful and engaged dialogue, which, as always, begins with listening. The first is a daily short musical introduction, generally with a spiritual theme, to set the tone; some artists are part of the music festival, some are unique to the colloquium. These introductions tie the colloquium to the music segment of the festival, and underscore that music breaks barriers that separate us from one another.

The second unusual feature is that each participant is asked to introduce himself or herself with a symbolic object. The range of objects is extraordinary, from elemental symbols of light, earth, and water to more complex symbolic challenges like multipurpose cloth garments, a kaleidoscope, and an analogy made to the echoing music of birds. This device helps to create a discourse with metaphors for different, shorthand views of globalization that highlight far better than standard phrases the images and presumptions each speaker brings. Both musical introductions and symbols as introduction help in the central aim of breaking away in the dialogue from established patterns. They help also to introduce a level of trust and personalization—the symbols often leave behind impressions that words themselves cannot carry.

The colloquium audience is composed largely of people drawn to Fez by the music festival, and is open to the public (for a charge of $100 for the five days). The event has drawn a substantial, loyal audience of several hundred, many returning a second and third year, undeterred by high temperatures that are not the norm but can occur.

Other people come for shorter periods. Such passing participants have included the prime minister of Senegal and a number of Moroccan and French ministers. People have come from all continents, some invited guests but many attracted by the rare combination of musical and intellectual fare. Press interest in the events has increased steadily, some taking off from the musical program (which is widely covered), some specifically focused on the colloquium dialogue.

A feature of the colloquium, commented on in some press reports, is the absence of a specific "stake"—for example, there has never been an effort or move to issue "declarations." However, over the three years of the colloquium there has been a mounting drive to direct the talk to action, to translate the rare and special dialogue of Fez into something more durable and wider in its practical application. This translates into an ongoing exploration of a vehicle for continuing dialogue with some institutional focus.

In sum, there is considerable and growing interest in the colloquium, both in Morocco and internationally.

2004 COLLOQUIUM

The 2004 colloquium will draw its inspiration from the festival theme of "Traces de Lumière" (Traces of Light). It will build on the dialogue of prior years, pressing further ahead toward rendering the insights and spirit of engagement into ideas for concrete action. The colloquium will have three central themes. First, it will explore the light and inspiration that can be drawn from a few individuals who have truly, through action, ideas and courage, made a difference perceptible at a global level. Second, the issues around global democracy—engagement of different actors, balancing rights with responsibilities, diversity with common human goals—is to be a focus. Third, the colloquium is to bring together leading voices for peace and dialogue in the Islamic world, broadly, and the Middle East, more concretely, to explore new avenues for joining their efforts toward better and more just worlds.

NOTES

1. Information about the Fez Festival can be found on its website: www.fesfestival.com

2. A book about the 2001 and 2002 colloquia, edited by Edgar Morin, Trinh Xuan Thuan, and others, was published in June 2003: *Donner une âme à la mondialisation: Une anthologie des Rencontres de Fès publiée sous la direction de Patrice van Eersel* (Paris: Albin Michel).

3. Works by these participants well illustrate their diversity of views: John Lane (2001), *Timeless Simplicity: Creative Living in a Consumer Society* (Foxhole, Devon, U.K.: Green Books); Sulak Sivaraksa and others (1998), *Loyalty Demands Dissent: Autobiography of an Engaged Buddhist* (Berkeley, Calif.: Parallax Publishers); Thierry de Montbrial (2003), *Ramses 2004: les Grandes Tendances du Monde* (Paris: Dunod).

CHAPTER 5

Attacking Extreme Poverty

Learning from the ATD Fourth World Movement

The late Father Joseph Wresinski, a Catholic priest who grew up in poverty, founded the International Movement of ATD Fourth World in 1957 in a camp for homeless families outside Paris. The group's first name was *Aide à Toute Détresse* (Aid to All Distress); the rest of the name derives from the Fourth Estate of the French Revolution—thus the very poorest people struggling to be represented in the political changes of the time. Today, ATD Fourth World operates in 27 countries on five continents. The movement aims to encourage other people to become involved with low-income families, to enable poor people themselves to do research on poverty, and to mobilize public opinion at local, national, and international levels about the need to ensure basic human rights for the very poor.[1]

ATD Fourth World seeks input from poor families and communities in housing estates, slums, and isolated shantytowns in designing, planning, and implementing its programs. Because the most vulnerable and disadvantaged communities place great importance on the family unit, ATD does, too. ATD also follows the expressed wishes of the very poor in

This chapter draws primarily on Quentin Wodon's work on ATD Fourth World, undertaken as part of the World Bank's Latin America poverty assessment work (see Wodon 2001).

emphasizing education and training. The organization's programs include nursery schools, family centers, training in literacy and basic skills, and artistic and cultural programs with children and young people. Activities vary from providing direct services in the most impoverished and desolate communities to mounting campaigns with local, national, and international official bodies, including a consultative status with several United Nation organizations.

ATD Fourth World relies heavily on its volunteer corps to run its programs. Composed of people of different nationalities, faiths, and professions, these volunteers bear witness to the courage and endurance of the families in poverty and foster links between these families and mainstream society.

ATD'S HUMAN RIGHTS FRAMEWORK

Joseph Wresinski was born to immigrant parents in a poor neighborhood of Angers, France, in 1917. As a child he experienced great poverty and social exclusion. Ordained a priest in 1946, he served in urban and rural parishes, where he related to the country's most deprived families. In 1956 he was assigned to serve as chaplain for 250 families in an emergency housing camp in Noisy-le-Grand. It was among their huts set in a muddy field that he found the inspiration for ATD Fourth World: "The families in that camp have inspired me in everything I have undertaken for their liberation. They took hold of me, they lived within me, they carried me forward, they pushed me to found the movement with them."[2]

In 1957, Father Joseph and the camp families founded the association that later became ATD Fourth World. They replaced soup kitchens and the distribution of old clothes with a library, a kindergarten, and a chapel. Joined by a few volunteers, Father Joseph soon created a research institute on extreme poverty that brought together people from different countries and disciplines. Father Joseph's firm purpose was to unite all sections of society around the very poorest, and he was determined that ATD Fourth World would remain open to people of all faiths, cultures, and races. He believed that every man and woman he met represented a chance for the world's poorest people, and this aim prompted him to meet with leaders of state, churches, and international bodies.

From its conception in a shantytown on the outskirts of Paris in 1957, ATD Fourth World has expanded to work in eight European countries as well as in North and Central America and in Africa and Asia. Its Permanent Forum, Extreme Poverty in the World, provides a network of support, knowledge, and initiative along with a global voice for the poor.

Father Joseph championed the idea that extreme poverty is a violation of human rights, basing this notion on three concepts. First, a lack of basic security may have a cumulative impact and undermine all dimensions of people's lives. Second, the insecurity associated with poverty persists over long periods of time. And third, the extreme poor are unable to exercise their rights or assume their responsibilities. Severe poverty evolves as a way of life, passed on from generation to generation. A child whose parent has never had a job will have little idea of what regular employment entails. A person who has been brought up in foster care will have little experience of what it means to be a parent. People living in poor housing will have little chance to maintain good health.

The ATD Fourth World movement asserts that civil and political rights are effectively nonexistent when people are deprived of the economic, social, and cultural means to exercise them. The normal channels through which individuals can be heard are often inaccessible to those whose lives are characterized by illiteracy and temporary addresses. Granting civil and political liberties without providing the practical means to exercise them may be worse than denying them altogether.

As governments in developing countries and international organizations seek to scale up their programs for reducing poverty, they face particular challenges in reaching the extreme poor. A lack of basic security and assets— including not only financial resources but also education, employment, housing, health care, and empowerment—often traps very poor individuals, families, and communities in a vicious cycle of economic and social isolation. Lacking a solid foundation, such people often find improving their situation nearly impossible despite heroic efforts. These efforts to emerge from poverty may not be visible to outsiders. Indeed, poor people do not really exist: the state does not acknowledge them and the census does not count them, and many children live and die without official recognition.

Father Joseph believed that the poor themselves are the most important allies in the struggle against poverty, as they are the first to resist their exclusion and to understand the conditions under which it can be reversed. Slow progress in facilitating opportunities for choice among the poor may reflect a lack of knowledge of what life is really like for those whose deep poverty forces them to depend on the goodwill of others. If we would only listen to poor people, they would remind us of what we appear to have forgotten: that we should defend human rights not in the name of a principle or law but in the name of the human being.

DOÑA MATILDA AND THE STREET LIBRARY

The story of Doña Matilda illustrates the work of the ATD Fourth World movement to reach the poorest. Full-time Fourth World volunteers arrived in Guatemala in 1979, introduced to the country by Caritas, a small faith-based NGO founded in the United States. By 1988, the volunteers had expanded their reach from their original community in the small village of San Jacinto to the poorest neighborhoods of Guatemala City. In the neighborhood known as Ferrocarril, along the railroad tracks, they met the protagonist of this story.

Doña Matilda lived in one of the shelters at the edge of the railroad track with her five children and Maria, a young Salvadoran woman who had been staying with them for nearly a year. Their home measured just 9 feet by 9 feet; the sound of water leaking through the disjointed boards at the back of the shelter attested to the proximity of a mechanic's workshop. The earthen floor was uneven, and the shelter had neither running water nor electricity. Two beds occupied half the room, one in good condition, the other with two broken legs replaced by a large stone and a tin can turned upside down. A little table and a rusty trough-shaped wood stove covered with a grill occupied part of the wall. During the daytime a curtain fluttering in the entry served as a makeshift door. A clothesline ran between the shelter's facade and a long bamboo pole planted in the middle of the tracks. When the train whistled in the distance, the occupants hurriedly pulled up the pole and brought it into the house to prevent the engine from sweeping away the laundry.

The parents and elder children responsible for the little children lived in constant fear of the trains. A terrible crash in 1991 destroyed the facades of eight homes; the fire department managed to dig 115 people out of the ruins. Doña Matilda said she lost all her belongings, but neither the railroad company nor the police paid any compensation. Instead, the people were blamed for living on land that was not theirs. Days later they began to build new shelters along the other side of the tracks, still haunted by the fears of the powerful and dangerous trains. Doña Matilda observed: "The train makes you nervous and the children are not free to play unsupervised. We need a playground where they would be able to play freely without any danger."

Recognizing this need and the lack of educational resources for the children of Ferrocarril, ATD Fourth World volunteers created a street library and a preschool on an empty plot of land four or five meters from the track. The area was not large enough to house the number of children who attended, at times nearing 100, so some of the children sat on the rails to read and draw. The street library was conceived as a place for children to come to learn, to play, to express their creativity, and to enjoy their childhood. For Doña Matilda's children, the street library provided a place to gather safely with their friends, to read stories, to draw pictures, to laugh, and to learn. Doña Matilda saw the street library as a beacon of hope amid the daily trials of her life: "The only thing that will remain after my death is my children's education. It will enable them to go forward, alone."

LEARNING WITH THE POOREST

While social scientists have forged powerful tools for examining poverty, they reside in a world very different from that of the extreme poor, and thus find it difficult to grasp their life experiences and understand their aspirations. To value the knowledge of the very poor and those who work with them at a grassroots level, ATD Fourth World has developed a "participant observation methodology"—the approach used to tell Doña Matilda's story. This method is characterized by the daily recording of observations and the long-term commitment of staff members to eradicating poverty.

ATD Fourth World volunteers often know some of the families for many years and are able to chronicle—and learn from—their life experience. This long-term commitment gives the volunteers a privileged role with many families, who share feelings and stories they would not express to outsiders.

Thus, volunteers who live through events with families can provide insights far beyond those a social scientist might provide. The best way to learn is to listen to women like Doña Matilda, to observe the experiences of her children, and to discover ways to support them consistent with their understanding of life. The proximity of volunteers to poor people lets them see and understand the requirements of social justice and human rights from the perspective of the poor rather than the nonpoor.

Although this methodology has its weaknesses, including potential bias in reporting and interpreting observations, it complements more traditional scientific methods of inquiry with new sources of knowledge based on the experiences of the poor and those engaged at their side. This consideration of different perspectives enhances the understanding of poverty and programs to alleviate it.

In early 2001, the World Bank's Latin America and Caribbean Program commissioned a regional study of extreme poverty and social exclusion in Latin America. One ensuing report—a collection of essays—focused on the visionary work of ATD Fourth World. These essays describe what it means to live in extreme poverty, how to reach the very poorest through programs and interventions, and how public and private institutions can be more responsive to their needs and aspirations. The essays also analyze the relationship between extreme poverty and human rights by emphasizing Father Joseph's philosophy.

Other reports emanating from the project rely on both quantitative and qualitative perspectives, including case studies, to analyze poverty and social exclusion in Latin America, for example among indigenous populations and youth. Each report provides a unique lens through which to observe the situation of the poorest in Latin America and around the world. Of special interest are the experiences of Father Wresinski in reaching out to these often forgotten people, his firm belief in their value as human beings, and the lessons that ATD Fourth World's work with the world's poorest continues to provide.[3]

NOTES

1. See ATD Quart Monde Web site for more information http://www.atd-quartmonde.org/pj/pj-uk.html.

2. De vos Van Stiwijk 1996.

3. Wodon 2001.

REFERENCES

Anouil, Gilles. 2002. *The Poor Are the Church: A Conversation with Fr. Joseph Wresinski, Founder of the Fourth World Movement*. Mystic, Conn.: Twenty-Third Publications.

De vos Van Stiwijk, Alwine. 1996. *Father Joseph Wresinski.*. Paris: ATD Fourth World Movement.

Wodon, Quentin. ed. 2001. "Attacking Extreme Poverty: Learning from the Lessons of the International Movement ATD Fourth World." World Bank Technical Paper No. 502. Washington, D.C.

CHAPTER 6

The Inter-American Development Bank Initiative on Social Capital, Ethics, and Development

Enrique Iglesias, president of the Inter-American Development Bank (IDB) since 1988, has, throughout his tenure, worked to develop a thoughtful and far-ranging set of relationships with faith communities. This has entailed, among other activities, meetings at the regional level with the major religious groups active in Latin America—Catholic, Protestant, and Jewish—to discuss their perspectives on development issues and perceptions and priorities for the work of the IDB. Faith leaders and institutions are represented in the full range of dialogue processes that IDB sponsors at regional and country levels. And specific support has been extended by the IDB to faith communities in a few instances. One particularly interesting example is the project with the Argentinian Jewish community outlined in the appendix to this chapter.

The engagement with faith groups, in its various dimensions, prompted the IDB to undertake a special initiative to respond to the keen interest and wide range of issues emerging from the dialogue processes.

This chapter draws heavily on discussions with Bernardo Kliksberg in 2002–2004; on publications of the Initiative on Social Capital, Ethics, and Development; and on author engagement in initiative activities.

The IDB launched a program in 1999–2000, termed the Initiative on Social Capital, Ethics, and Development. This is led directly by IDB's president and comes under the jurisdiction of the IDB's secretary. It is supported both by IDB resources and by the government of Norway.[1] The initiative's impressive advisory board comprises leading economists, academics, religious leaders, and former heads of state.

VISION FOR THE INITIATIVE

IDB has found great interest, in Latin America and elsewhere in the world, in the challenge of integrating, or as it terms it, "merging" ethical dimensions into discussions on development and decisions about policies and programs. Because governmental policies alone are insufficient to bring change in the region's development practices, the initiative has offered a vehicle to engage, in a constructive and organized manner, the demands from civil society to examine ethical challenges and dilemmas and to take them into account. The goal is to encourage all social players to assume their responsibilities.

The initiative has given priority to the following issues and questions:

- What values should be kept in mind when designing development strategies and public policies?
- How should regional leaders react to issues that involve serious ethical problems such as poverty, social exclusion, sharp inequalities, discrimination against minorities, and others?
- What codes of ethical conduct should key groups in society, such as political leaders and civil society organizations, adopt?
- How can the ethics of solidarity be promoted today?

The initiative was launched at a time when, throughout the Latin American region, there were the beginnings of an awakening to the vast latent potential of social capital as a factor in development and change. This awakening began as new research was emerging from academic centers, highlighting the ways that social capital enhances economic performance and stimulates democracy. The IDB initiative thus represented an attempt to merge this growing awareness with academic insights into the value of social capital and ethical perspectives in development. The Initiative on Social Capital, Ethics, and Development aims to create propitious conditions for developing the basic components of social capital, such as associative and cooperative capacity, interpersonal trust, and civic conscience.

CONCRETE GOALS

"The new challenges of the contemporary world not only demand that we re-examine old issues (for example the role of the market) in new light, but also that we address new ethical issues that have been brought to prominence by the interactive world in which we live (including the demands of un-segmented global ethics)."

— Amartya Sen[2]

The goals for the initiative are framed by IDB as follows:

1. To promote the analysis and discussion of ethical challenges and dilemmas and ensure that the chief decisionmakers take them into account.
2. To cooperate in areas such as volunteerism, greater social accountability by private enterprise, and the adoption of ethical codes for the development of social capital in the region by the key social players.
3. To promote the inclusion of ethical goals and criteria, and the mobilization of social capital, in development projects prepared and implemented by international organizations and government agencies.
4. To promote the integration of ethics into educational curricula and with people who work for growth of social capital.
5. To establish a network of academic and research centers to carry out systematic long-term actions in areas such as training, research, publications, and contributions to public debate.
6. To promote, through the mass media, an ethical understanding in subjects such as development and social capital.

The initiative aspires to be a catalyst in awakening interest in ethics, development, and social capital in governments, businesses, labor unions, universities, religious communities, NGOs, and organizations of all kinds that work for the collective well-being of societies in the western hemisphere.

Mobilization of joint efforts in these crucial fields is intended to raise the quality of debate on development, enrich policy frameworks, increase the likelihood of broad consensus on actions, and contribute to development leaders' adoption of codes of conduct based on desirable ethical criteria.

> *"It will be collectively contributing to the strengthening and entrenchment of democracy and economic and social development, and to forging a vigorous, participative and just Latin America that is the strong wish of all the community of Latin America."*
>
> —IDB Web site[3]

PROGRAMS AND ACTIONS

The initiative's work falls under three rough headings: seminars and forums, network support, and research and knowledge dissemination. These channels aim to provide the broader development community with ideas and abstracts that allow quick access to the latest scientific and technological findings in the field as well as recent applications.

Seminars and Forums

Perhaps the most important and visible part of the IDB program has been an ambitious series of seminars and public forums. The seminars focus on approaches to and issues around ethics in the broadening framework of the globalization debates. The forums have treated more specific topics within the general framework of the initiative, including poverty reduction, education, health, and the environment.

The May 22–23, 2003, meeting in Chile was the most ambitious forum to date, with over 5,000 participants. Its main focus was "Mobilizing Social Capital and Volunteer Action in Latin America." The forum provided a meeting place at the Diego Portales Convention Centre in Santiago for voluntary workers from all over Chile and neighboring countries. An important forum outcome was that it conveyed to volunteer workers in Latin America a message from high-level politicians that their work forms a vital part of the region's development effort and that it is highly appreciated by the governments. Because volunteerism has had so little focus among Latin American governments in the past, this was not a trivial message.

Another important forum in Tegucigalpa, Honduras, in September 2001 addressed the broad subject of ethics and development. The seminar highlighted what Iglesias described as a "hunger" for ethics in Central America. The seminar aimed both to help frame the issues and to transform these issues into operational practices and reality. Topics mentioned most frequently were corruption, the need to reinstill values in education, the mounting challenges of poverty, and also inequality and unemployment. Through panels and academic networks, knowledge on these topics was shared and disseminated.

Another seminar in Paraguay, in September 2003, addressed the subject of "mobilizing social capital." Paraguay is in a new historical phase in which it faces important economic, social, and political problems. Fully mobilizing its social capital could be a significant step in achieving the mandate that the citizenship has demanded from the new government: to strengthen democracy.

The initiative programs have addressed both broad topics and quite specific operational subjects. A meeting on "Ethics as an Administration Instrument" in Rio de Janeiro, Brazil, in December 2003 addressed effective ways to include ethics in public administration. The central themes were the dramatic growth of "new poverty" in Latin America and its devastating impact on all communities, especially the Jewish ones. The meeting was dominated by an array of groups engaged in direct poverty alleviation work, with a heavy emphasis on Argentina and Brazil, but representatives from other Latin American countries also attended.

Network Support

The success of the seminars and forums is largely due to the large network that supports the initiative's goals and work, from academia to government. The initiative has also formed several important partnerships with specific institutions that cover a range of issues and provide channels and support for information dissemination.

Research and Knowledge Dissemination

The initiative disseminates its knowledge through forums, seminars, and networks, but another important channel is its digital library, which provides online access to all the initiative's ideas, findings, and news (see www.iadb.org).

The large numbers of people attending conferences organized through the initiative and visiting the initiative Web site is worthy of note. The initiative's Web site was, in early 2004, the second most popular homepage on the IDB site. This is demonstrative of the significant interest and curiosity in the ideas it propounds and aims to disseminate and suggests that it has been quite successful so far in drawing attention to these issues.

> "Indeed, a great number of people have been led, by the Initiative, to think about development ethics and consider ways and means of advancing the use of ethical thinking and normative behavior in the cause of economic, social and political progress. Aside from its impact on policy analysis and practical decisions, initiatives like this have done much in recent years to broaden the intellectual horizon of economists and other social scientists some of whom tend to presume that the hard work of development demands only canniness and prudence—not ideals of commitments or morals."
>
> —Amartya Sen[4]

APPENDIX. ECONOMIC CRISIS AND THE "NEW POOR": AIDING THE JEWISH POPULATION IN ARGENTINA

Argentina's economic crisis has had a particularly devastating impact on the country's large Jewish population. Growing poverty has profoundly affected this community's religious, social, and educational institutions, as the old poor have become even poorer, the lower middle class has become the new poor, and some of the middle and upper middle class have become the sudden poor. An imaginative and unusual partnership involving the IDB and Argentine and international Jewish organizations allowed all to move quickly to provide support as the Jewish community suffered an economic, emotional, and institutional meltdown.

Argentina is home to the world's seventh-largest Jewish community, with some 230,000 members, the majority of whom live in Buenos Aires. The community's roots date from the fifteenth-century Spanish Inquisition and its aftermath, which sparked a mass migration of Jews from Spain and Portugal, including to various parts of Latin America, with the largest number settling in Argentina. The Jewish Colonization Association, founded in 1891 by Baron Maurice de Hirsch, also facilitated the mass emigration of Jews from Russia and other Eastern European countries, settling them in agricultural colonies on lands purchased by the committee, particularly in North and South America. Thus, the Jewish population established a strong presence in Argentina, with 80 percent in the middle or upper income brackets.

The Argentine economic crisis, which began in 1999, put 25 percent of the country's Jews—about 58,000 people—below the poverty line. This new poverty affected laid-off professionals and civil servants, small merchants, and industrialists who had to close their businesses, recent university graduates, and older people with meager pensions. Some 1,700 Jewish families lost their homes and came to live in cheap hotels in poor neighborhoods of Buenos Aires, under bridges, in public squares, and in parks.[5] Other members of the new poor with middle-class cultural attitudes, education, and consumer expectations suddenly found themselves with income levels that did not allow them to fulfill those expectations.[6]

The stigma, social exclusion, and shame of living in poverty prompted the Jewish new poor to withdraw from the community, schools, and other institutions, isolating themselves and their families from Jewish life. Some Jews in Buenos Aires preferred to beg for food at a Catholic church to avoid the shame of looking for food at a community institution where people would recognize them.[7] Jewish emigration to Israel increased sharply despite worsening security and economic concerns there.[8] Many saw the Argentinean Jewish community in great danger and possibly disintegrating.

Jewish Institutions Respond

The Argentine Israelite Mutual Aid Association (AMIA), founded in 1894 by immigrants and now the country's central Jewish organization, led a broad group of Argentine institutions in assisting the Jewish community in this crisis. AMIA services include the Central Council for Jewish

Education, which develops and strengthens the schools and youth seminars that form the community scholar network in Argentina.

AMIA also operates Centro Ocupacional de Desarrollo Laboral (CODLA), which provides job placement services and personalized training to both the Jewish and general population of Buenos Aires. This program provides employers with a professional prescreening service to make their search for qualified personnel more efficient while offering potential employees job counseling, training, and other tools to optimize their employability. AMIA has been recognized by the Argentine Labor Ministry as one of the country's leading employment agencies, having placed more than 1,000 people in jobs in 2000. Beneficiaries include underemployed as well as unemployed residents of Buenos Aires, and microenterprises and small companies.

The IDB awarded a US$1.73 million grant to AMIA in October 2001 designed to systematize and strengthen CODLA, and thus to offer more timely and effective employment services to both employers and job seekers. The grant provides CODLA with technical assistance to incorporate information technology, a market and client-service approach, and occupational profiles to bridge the gap between labor supply and demand. The grant also aims to expand the CODLA model by creating a network of job placement services throughout metropolitan Buenos Aires and the country.

The program carries two main risks: It could fail to recruit enough potential employers, and the qualifications of the job seekers it registers may not match the job profiles of potential employers. To tackle the first risk, CODLA will conduct promotional campaigns to recruit companies with job vacancies using specific strategies designed by specialists. To minimize the second risk, the program will develop new training courses to upgrade candidates' skills to meet employers' needs.

AMIA has also created the Tzedaka Foundation to work with Jewish organizations from abroad, including the American Jewish Joint Distribution Committee and the United Jewish Communities, which run social assistance centers throughout Argentina. "This alliance has created a community social welfare system to provide basic services to the most vulnerable, strengthening their capacity to help themselves and prevent their social exclusion."[9] Services include distribution of food packages, medical assistance, social work, small business loans, work opportunities and training, and help in revitalizing community institutions.

NOTES

1. http://www.iadb.org/etica/ingles/index-i.cfm (accessed May 4, 2004)
2. Sen 2003.
3. http://www.iadb.org/etica/ingles/index-i.cfm
4. Sen 2004.
5. Jewish Community Relations Council 2002.
6. Kliksberg 2000.
7. Kliksberg 2001.
8. Kovadloff 2002.
9. MacCulloch 2000.

REFERENCES

Jewish Community Relations Council. 2002. "Special Update on Jewish Community of Argentina." Cherry Hill, N. J. Available at http://www.jcrcsnj.org/actionalerts.asp?intCategoryID=60&intArticleID=20

Kliksberg, Bernardo. 2000. "Fighting a New Kind of Poverty," *IDB America*. September-October.

———. 2001. "A Jewish Community in Danger: Argentinean and Latin-American Judaism Faced by Disquieting Question Marks."

Kovadloff, Jacob. 2002. "Crisis in Argentina." New York: The American Jewish Committee. Available at http://www.ajc.org/InTheMedia/Publications.asp?did=555&pid=1290

MacCulloch, Christina. 2000. "Acts of Faith." *IDB America*. September-October issue. pp. 2-3.

Sen, Amartya. 2003. "Ethical Challenges: Old and New." Paper prepared for the International Congress on the Ethical Dimensions of Development: The New Ethical Challenges of State, Business, and Society. Brazil. July 3-4.

———. 2004. Speech delivered on Ethics and Development Day. IDB. Washington, D.C., January 16.

7

The Significance of Decent Work

Faith Insights into an International Priority

Debates about labor issues as they relate to broader questions of sustainable livelihood, poverty, and social exclusion have until quite recently focused on wages, the quality of the physical workplace, and social protections. This perspective—while valuable—overlooked the spiritual foundations that have, from time immemorial, made work central to human society. In an effort to explore some of these deeper dimensions of debates underlying labor questions, the International Labour Organisation (ILO) and the World Council of Churches (WCC) convened a working group in 2002, to address ILO's central theme, which is reflected in the goal termed "decent work."

ILO's primary goal is to promote opportunities for women and men to obtain decent and productive work under conditions of freedom, equity, and security. The 1998 ILO Declaration of Fundamental Principles of Rights at Work aimed to set a basic foundation defining what constitutes decent work that includes freedom of association and the right to collective bargaining, and the elimination of compulsory labor, child labor, and discrimination.

This chapter draws heavily on an early draft prepared by Dominique Peccoud, S. J., ILO, and on his edited summary of the ILO dialogue (Peccoud 2004).

The Decent Work Agenda, as ILO has shaped it since 1998, goes a step further in highlighting the degree to which human dignity is central to work. By coupling the concepts of work and dignity, the agenda links labor with cultural, ethical, religious, and spiritual values. At the same time, the agenda shifts the way we think about decent work.

THE FOUNDATION: UTILITARIAN AND VALUES-BASED APPROACHES TO REGULATION

Dominique Peccoud, a priest by training and vocation, holds the position, noteworthy within the United Nations system, of special adviser for socioreligious affairs to ILO's director general. He argues that we should shape our thinking about decent work in two realms. The ILO's traditional role has focused on creating legal instruments that shape just and progressive work environments. The history that has produced these legal instruments has been grounded in the view that they serve as tools to force action, rather than a representation of the values or mores of the culture(s) from whence they came. This view is *utilitarian*. The merits of different courses of action can be measured against one another by intrinsic values such as happiness, freedom, generosity, or preference. Two major questions are raised in the development of utilitarian international legal instruments: Who is to assess the impact of one or another course of action? What is envisaged when we seek to optimize the overall good in the world, that is, what constitutes the world—is it our country, race, all human beings, all sentient beings including animals, or even "Mother Earth?"[1]

The second realm—*a values-based approach*—is mirrored in the ILO–WCC dialogue around decent work. Its focus is to promote the values of decent work through the frameworks and legal instruments that support it. Peccoud argues that the basic instruments also embody values-based concepts that promote the norms of decent work through structure and shape as well as measurement of outcome. Legal instruments embody values that, individually and taken together, address the question: What is a meaningful human life? Outcomes take on relatively less importance; one's intent in carrying out one's actions, in complement or counter to fundamental values of justice, freedom and progress, takes on far greater meaning.

Law making at the ILO is a hybrid of these two approaches—utilitarian and values-based—to building legal instruments. Kenneth Arrow's groundbreaking work on preferences treats expressed preferences as an intrinsic value. The ILO has adopted this approach in part, using statistical analyses to evaluate discrete phenomena, or qualitative work to gauge and rank the interests of different ILO stakeholders. Both quantitative and qualitative analyses are used to choose between different policy or legal options.

The development of international regulatory instruments poses questions also in terms of process, because these processes tend to address local cultural circumstances (including faith perspectives) at a relatively late stage. Once a given option is chosen, draft legal texts are written, and documents circulated among stakeholders to feed in another round of preferences. Legal texts, once revised, are presented to the International Labour Conference for approval. After ratification, each member country begins to examine how the legal instrument in question can be translated into law. Only at this stage, long after the development of the initial legal concept around which an instrument will be designed, do states begin to ask questions about culture, to inquire about how this sterile legal instrument will be adapted into laws cognizant of cultural specificities or religious differences.

The argument that emerges from these reflections about approaches to decent work is that it would be far preferable to attempt to reflect more explicitly and carefully the issues around transcendent values in shaping legal instruments, at a much earlier stage. This pragmatic reflection in turn highlights the underlying question of to what extent such international regulatory instruments can and should be based on universal human values. The pending challenge is how far it is possible to design international legal instruments around a set of values that we agree are common to human existence, or are differences of culture so deep, and so intense, that a "clash of civilizations" is inevitable?

ILO–WCC DIALOGUE

Juan Somavia, director-general of the ILO, has affirmed the critical links between international policy initiatives such as the Decent Work Agenda and the spiritual, religious, and secular traditions that reflect the values and aspirations of humankind.

With Somavia's endorsement and blessing, the ILO convened the dialogue with the WCC to begin inquiry into the questions of utilitarian and transcendent values, and of shared or sharply differing mores. Twenty-five representatives of religious and secular traditions gathered in Geneva in February 2002 (and maintained a dialogue after the event itself). Their aim was to shed light on how their ideas, values, and precepts support the principles of the Decent Work Agenda. Experts and scholars in Buddhist, Confucian, Christian, Muslim, Jewish, Reformed Hindu, the *Arya Samaj* movement, the Brahma Kumaris University, and secular traditions offered both written and oral contributions.

The central message emerging from this ILO–WCC interfaith dialogue was that the lack of moral and ethical underpinnings for today's economic realities makes these realities increasingly fragile. Although some workers have attained high levels of welfare, slavery, child labor, forced labor, and other gross violations of human rights still exist. This situation reflects economic imperatives that reduce the value of labor to raw quantitative units and equate it with a cost factor, like capital, measuring a person's worth in units of output and amount of profit generated.

The Decent Work Agenda aims to offer an alternative—a people-centered approach that encompasses humans' material and spiritual aspirations. It reflects the conviction that work is more important than capital and constitutes the source of dignity, family stability, and peace.

REFLECTIONS ON DECENT WORK AND FAITH TRADITIONS

A central theme emerging from the ILO–WCC dialogue, and of the ILO's Decent Work Agenda itself, is the notion that decent work encompasses not only jobs, future employment prospects, and working conditions, but also people's ability to receive a fair share of the wealth they help create. The notion of a decent salary presupposes that an individual has a legal identity as a worker and also freedom of association and collective bargaining. These rights ensure that people can fight for secure income, better health care, and safer working conditions. All these ideas, and the complex social justice issues that underlie them, found expression in the different faith traditions, with both important common themes and some significant differences (for example, around individual versus collective interests and rights).

Decent work finds further expression in workers' feelings of value and satisfaction, and gives them a voice in both the workplace and the community.[2] Decent work affords a balance between work and family life and provides equal recognition and gender equity. Decent work allows people to develop their personality, skills, wisdom, and potential, and thus is one of the most fundamental expressions of human worth and dignity.

Today's world confronts a decent work deficit, as individuals lack dignity in both the material and spiritual arenas. The Decent Work Agenda aims to raise awareness of this deficit at the community and international levels. The ILO report *Reducing the Decent Work Deficit: A Global Challenge* noted that "everywhere and for everybody, Decent Work is about securing human dignity."[3] This idea echoes the ILO 1944 Declaration of Philadelphia, which highlighted the spiritual-growth component of human welfare: "All human beings, irrespective of race, creed or sex, have the right to pursue both their material well-being and their spiritual development in conditions of freedom and dignity, of economic security and equal opportunity."[4]

In the course of the ILO–WCC dialogue, different faith traditions shared their quite varied views of work, revolving around work as a fundamental, noble expression of human dignity.[5] This view is rooted in the idea—explicitly shared by Muslims, Christians, Jews, and Hindus— that God or the Creator is the archetypal worker, and that human work is an extension of that divine activity.[6] As an essential dimension of everyday life, work includes a profound and creative dimension closely tied with the Creator. The Jewish and Christian traditions, for example, invite humans to accomplish God's creation through work, and fulfill their call to live in the image of God.[7] Man and woman as co-creators have a responsibility to work based on the divine command in the book of Genesis.[8] Christian tradition holds that through work people honor the gifts and talents the Creator has bestowed on them, and that man and woman are called to bring these skills and aptitudes to fruition. The *Arya Samaj* movement similarly perceives work as a divine duty through which individuals express their faith in God.

Diverse religious and spiritual traditions also assume that workers are human beings first and laborers second. Thus, labor should never reduce people to their material output, or regard them as a production factor dedicated to a function such as producing capital.

Most faith traditions that were part of the ILO–WCC dialogue defined work as any type of productive activity—whether physical, intellectual, artistic, or spiritual. For example, the Buddhist tradition focuses strongly on the value of work even by monks in meditation. In the words of the dying Buddha, "Strive diligently and conscientiously." The Christian tradition identifies work with the many years Jesus labored as a carpenter. In the Islamic tradition, work—as opposed to usury—is the only legitimate basis for wealth and property. And in the Buddhist tradition, *ashram* is a place where everyone works and lives and enhances the dignity of labor.

All traditions represented in the dialogue tied decent work to the capacity of men and women both to earn a livelihood and live life abundantly. Work must go beyond subsistence wages that meet only material needs and address social, psychological, and spiritual needs. It must be fulfilling and also dignify the world. Work can enable people to become fully human through having a family, educating children, and participating fully in social life.[9]

Only work that enables an individual's growth can be called decent. Decent work allows people's creative potential, and their willingness to contribute to their surroundings, to unfold freely. Reducing human labor to a purely mechanical function inhibits the possibility that work will reveal the authentic person. These themes echo throughout the Confucian tradition, which sees every human's moral task as to "continuously work on his or her own self improvement and let the sprouts of the innate moral potential flourish." Decent work is thus a means for both self-realization and human progress.

Work should allow human dignity to shine without overvaluing labor as the only source of dignity. In the Judeo-Christian tradition the Sabbath exists precisely to limit work. Sabbath prevents work from becoming the final word in a person's life, and demonstrates that production stems from a combination of human effort and divine grace.

Collective Action

Another theme to emerge from the ILO–WCC dialogue was support for the freedom of association and collective bargaining as a fundamental right:

Buddhist, Catholic, and Calvinist traditions alike subscribed to these views. The idea of a social dialogue between workers, employers, and others resonates in the nonhierarchical governance of Reformed Churches, for example, and the literature of Reformed thinkers from the sixteenth century onward highlights the need for a contract between employers and employees. However, the struggle for social justice must serve overall social cohesion, and one group or class should not dominate another.

Some spiritual traditions specify that workers must first receive a legal identity that enables them to exercise their freedom of association and formulate collective claims. Rabbinical texts such as the Ten Commandments clearly establish these basic principles. In the Jewish tradition, the common responsibility of employers and workers to achieve God's creation calls for a joint agreement on work to be completed and its compensation. Similarly, all Muslims are considered equals within the community, or *Umma*, and thus should strive together as a group rather than as individuals. In this way Islam, too, supports collective bargaining and freedom of association.

Compulsory Labor

International laws and norms have long viewed slavery as illegal. However, compulsory labor still exists today owing to persistent economic and social inequality. These conditions exclude entire groups from dignity. Migrants, landless peasants, the unemployed, and the voiceless have no legal status and often work in indecent situations. These include the *Dalits* (untouchables) in India, forced laborers in Myanmar, landless peasants in Brazil, people subjected to the sex trade throughout the world, and illegal migrant farm workers in the United States and Europe.

The ILO regards anything less than a living wage as exploitation, or a contemporary form of slavery; participants in the ILO–WCC dialogue spoke of parallel views within their own faiths. A Reformed Hindu tradition states that work for less than the minimum wage should be considered forced labor, which is dehumanizing. The Calvinist tradition from the first denounced this form of labor as incompatible with God's will. Islam also explicitly condemns compulsory labor; the Koran designates freeing a slave as one of the highest deeds a person can accomplish.

Although India has long been a democratic country and outlawed discrimination based on caste, cultural norms force *Dalits* in many communities, by virtue of their status at birth, to perform low-paid, dangerous work, sometimes in conditions approaching servitude. According to one human rights activist in India, "The caste system is largely responsible for the poor work culture and also explains the lack of the basic attitude of dignity of labor."[10] Buddhists and Reformed Hindu traditions, such as the *Arya Samaj* movement, openly challenge this system. In strongly criticizing the caste system, the Buddha emphasized that people undertake work for their spiritual development and choose it freely and consciously to realize their humanity. In the caste system, work subordinates people. Buddhist teachings counter this by asserting that "work is for people."[11]

Child Labor

In June 1999, ILO member states voted unanimously to adopt Convention 182 on the Worst Forms of Child Labor, thereby designating ending the commercial exploitation of children as a top priority. Some 186 million children under age 15 labor around the world. Of these, 111 million engage in hazardous work that includes extended hours and days, very low pay, and dangerous conditions. Another 8.4 million work in the worst forms of child labor, which include forced and bonded labor, prostitution and pornography, illicit activities, and armed conflict.[12] (Child labor excludes children age 12 and older who are performing only a few hours a week of permitted light work, and those age 15 and above whose work is not considered hazardous.) Since 1999, many governments, organizations, and individuals have stepped forward to address this challenge, and countries have ratified Convention 182 more quickly than any other international treaty.

Within the ILO–WCC dialogue, the participants stressed that child labor denies education as the starting point of the humanization process and short-circuits people's ability to realize their true vocational, moral, and spiritual potential. Many religious and spiritual traditions affirm the necessity of eliminating child labor, especially the worst forms. The Buddhist tradition, for example, sets 19 as the minimum age for full ordination into the monastic life. This suggests that young people should not be fully part of the world of labor before that age.

Free education is the best way to protect children and prepare them to become workers. Education teaches children the values of decency, dignity, love, justice, service, responsibility, and spirituality. Education prepares children to incorporate these values into decent work—labor that is self-realized, dedicated to the community, and directed toward larger spiritual goals. Child labor hampers education and prevents children from taking their place in society as responsible citizens. Various faith traditions stress the importance of education as a primary goal. Calvinist thought, for example, mandates free and compulsory education.

Discrimination in Occupation and Employment

Discrimination on the basis of race, color, gender, or religion fails to respect the intrinsic dignity of each human being, and freedom from discrimination is central to decent work. This idea echoes throughout religious and spiritual traditions, and was clearly articulated within the ILO–WCC dialogue. The Buddha rejects all forms of discrimination in the workplace, and Judeo-Christian tradition also strongly prohibits discrimination, with its various parables about equal treatment of natives and foreigners throughout the Bible. However, the notion of gender equality challenges a number of contemporary faiths. Despite historical texts that may present a more progressive view of women, these traditions often offer a different picture in actual practice, to this day.

THE ETHICAL RESPONSIBILITY OF WORK

Because work always entails labor with and for others, through work the individual becomes responsible for other human beings and the community. This idea resonated with Muslim, Confucian, Hindu, Buddhist, and Christian participants in the ILO–WCC dialogue.[13] In Judaism, for instance, Rabbi Hillel the elder admonished, "Do not inflict on the other what you would not want the other to inflict on you."

The implications of responsibility to those beyond one's self and family are immediate for the individual, family, community, and international economy. According to Catholic social teaching, "If the organization of economic life is such that the human dignity of workers is compromised or their freedom of action is removed, then the Church does not hesitate to judge such an economic order to be unjust, even if it produces a vast amount of goods. It is even right to speak of a struggle against an economic order that upholds the absolute predominance of capital, the possession of the means of production, in contrast to the free and personal nature of human work."[14]

The ILO–WCC interfaith dialogue closed by gently but firmly reminding its audience that to support decent work is to object to an unjust order that marginalizes labor and dehumanizes individuals. Such an order has the potential to destabilize families, communities, and the world.

The ILO–WCC interfaith dialogue underscored that decent work is of paramount importance to all. The depth of the issues at stake can be fully understood only if we challenge ourselves to consider decent work from both pragmatic and transcendental perspectives. With a mind to Peccoud's observations, the gradual rapprochement of organizations of faith and agencies of development—of worlds of shared and differing values—will help decent work to resonate ever more deeply in human lives.

NOTES

1. Peccoud 2004, p. xiii.

2. Schwettmann 2001.

3. ILO 2001, Section 1.2.

4. http://www.ilo.org/public/english/bureau/inf/download/brochure/pdf/page5.pdf

5. However, misread tradition can distort the work paradigm. A Brazilian reform theologian, Professor Wanda Deifelt, holds that Latin America's social and economic disparities are rooted in misconceptions of work. One group, the indigenous people, needed to prove its worth through work. The other, the Christian Europeans, had already inherited their dignity through birth or creed. The result was a negative view of work as punishment—unpleasant and alienating. Work does not dignify but rather dehumanizes. The challenge is to change this deeply rooted cultural misconception.

6. The Muslim tradition does not consider human work a continuation of the divine work of creation. For Muslims, human beings cannot qualify as co-creators because of the radical transcendence of God. In the creation narrative of the Koran, humanity is not invited to give names to the animals nor participate in creation. The animals are named and ordered by God.

7. God created the universe but leaves humans to collaborate in forming a perfect, finished universe.

8. So God created human beings, making them like himself. He created them to be male and female, blessed them, and said, "Have many children, so that your descendents will live all over the world and bring it under your control." Genesis 1: 27–28.

9. In this sense, work is not on the same level as land or capital, for the landowner and the capitalist do not work. Calvin, for instance, condemned people who lived off unearned income, based on St. Paul's letter to the Thessalonians, and in turn praised all forms of work.

10. Swami Agnivesh, quoted in Peccoud 2004.

11. Sikh gurus have also developed a sense of the dignity in labor from which emerged a healthy and energetic attitude toward work. The same is true in the Indian state of Kerala, which acknowledges the dignity of labor in the context of a strong Indian–Christian tradition.

12. ILO 2002.

13. For example, in Islam (Hadith) the prophet says, "Not one of you truly believes until you wish for others what you wish for yourself." According to Confucius, "One word which sums up the basis of all good conduct. Do not do unto others what you would not want done unto yourself." Hinduism holds that "this is the sum of duty: do not to others what would cause pain if done to you." The Buddha taught, "Treat not others in ways that you yourself would find hurtful." And according to Jesus Christ, "In everything, do to others as you would have them do to you; for this is the law of the prophets."

14. Quoted in Peccoud 2004.

REFERENCES

ILO (International Labour Organisation). 2001. "Reducing the Decent Work Deficit: A Global Challenge." Report of the Director-General to the 89th Session of the International Labour Conference. Geneva. June. http://www.ilo.org/public/english/standards/relm/ilc/ilc89/rep-i-a.htm

———. 2002. "Every Child Counts: New Global Estimates on Child Labor." International Program on the Elimination of Child Labor, Statistical Implementation and Monitoring Programme. Geneva.

Peccoud, Dominique. ed. 2004. *Philosophical and Spiritual Perspectives on Decent Work*. Geneva: International Labour Office.

Schwettmann, Jurgen. 2001. *Cooperation and Globalization: An ILO Perspective*. Seoul: ICA General Assembly, October 16.

8

Exploring Country Faith–Development Partnerships

The World Faiths Development Dialogue (WFDD) was founded with the central goal of putting theoretical admonitions about the need for collaboration between faith and development groups into practice through dialogue and joint exploration of specific issues and development challenges. Toward that end, the WFDD has worked in three countries—Guatemala, Ethiopia, and Tanzania—to explore common interests and competing priorities among various faith traditions and development partners, especially the World Bank. These efforts provide invaluable guideposts to the evolving faith–development dialogue.[1]

GUATEMALA

Guatemala faces a legacy of decades—even centuries—of armed conflict, huge and highly visible social inequalities, frayed confidence in public leaders and institutions, and an enormous backlog of basic development challenges. Although the country's dynamic faith scene offers great potential for addressing the raw post-conflict situation and enriching development work, the faith community is also full of tensions and discord.

Working against the backdrop of these barriers, the WFDD supported a joining together of several major faith traditions, beginning in January

2000, in a group known as the Guatemala Interreligious Dialogue on Development (DIRGD). Participants included the Catholic Church, itself far from monolithic, and evangelical churches, which have grown rapidly in Guatemala and are omnipresent throughout the country, as well as other Protestant churches. Participants also included adherents of Mayan spirituality, which is interwoven with other traditions but maintains a separate identity and experience, and the Jewish faith—tiny in members but holding significant economic power and a special convening role intrinsic to its history and minority status.

The basic rationale for launching the dialogue was to build bridges with the World Bank and other development institutions. Faith groups regarded the World Bank as a complex and rather shadowy presence, difficult to decipher, and one that often used obscure language. The challenge for faith groups was to both understand the Bank's purview and find effective ways to work within it.

Guatemala also represents a classic challenge for development institutions, especially the World Bank, with respect to religion. The realm of the Bank and its more traditional development partners appears to be far removed from that of the faith institutions, particularly at the community level. While many Bank staff members are well attuned to the country's faith-based organizations and Guatemalan culture, the Bank's traditional divorce of secular and faith worlds has constrained formal partnerships. The country's extraordinary development challenges accentuate this problem.

Two years of experience there affirmed the potential power of building bridges within the faith community, and between it and the World Bank, but also highlighted the challenges and pitfalls. DIRGD's most significant and tangible output has been "Ethical Values," a document intended to spur national dialogue on development and serve as the basis for development of a new curriculum throughout the education system, promoted by the education ministry. The document focuses especially on corruption and how to combat it in the Guatemalan context.

Work on "Ethical Values" revealed a glaring lack of documentation, understanding, and use of the rich store of knowledge, work, and ideas of faith institutions in development realms. These gaps only magnify the task of building bridges among faith traditions across wide cultural divides—

work that does not lend itself to early "wins," visible "results on the ground," or rapid or steady progress.

Lessons from the Guatemala dialogue include the following:

- *Weakness of interfaith perspectives and institutional support.* The role of religious communities in shaping national directions and mediating crises is long established (especially for the Catholic Church), and the potential to wield strategic influence is substantial. However, interfaith action to address social crises and development challenges has been rare, and finding common voice, common ground, and common leaders is challenging.
- *Important role of churches and relevance of their contact and knowledge for different facets of the development agenda.* Although faith traditions deeply permeate the country's culture, the work of faith groups is not well known or shared, even within the communities themselves.
- *Striking differences in concepts of development among different faith traditions.* Mayan, evangelical, and Catholic perspectives on progress differ sharply (for example, on the value of education, means to a job, reasons for corruption, and potential for agricultural growth), although participants rarely articulate these differences with precision.
- *Unease around inequality.* The vast gulfs in social welfare and economic opportunity within Guatemala's society are a central concern of faith communities. However, some faith groups regard inequality as almost a given—part of the landscape—while for others it is a source of constant if subdued rage. Solutions remain murky.
- *Poverty.* The definition and causes of poverty are far from self-evident. Many members of faith communities regard poverty, inequality, and social justice as interwoven strands. Thus, the idea that a nation should formulate a poverty strategy, as encouraged by the World Bank, was not easy to communicate in many circles. Forging a common approach will require clear definitions and nuanced dialogue.
- *Social violence.* This pervasive threat evokes deep concern across the faith spectrum. Those who engaged in the dialogue saw links at multiple levels among ethics, corruption, and quality of governance, and the violence in Guatemalan society and its associated ills.
- *Disillusionment with the public sector and government services.* The dialogue highlighted the difficulties standing in the way of restoring

confidence in the public sector. Faith participants evinced strong skepticism regarding the role of the public sector and its leaders, and little confidence in the judicial system and the rule of law.

The interfaith dialogue group often characterized as miraculous the group's achievement in sticking to the effort and producing some tangible results, given the difficult Guatemalan environment for such dialogue. They described the potential for real contributions as still largely unrealized.

ETHIOPIA

Civil society, including faith-based organizations, faces a complex transition in Ethiopia. Following severe government repression during the 1970s and 1980s, civil society began to reassert itself during the 1990s. Some 350 NGOs are now at work in the country, although the sector remains small compared with other African countries. Although the climate for NGOs is improving and the government is recognizing their potential to contribute to development, mutual mistrust and a reluctance to share information remain a significant legacy of past repression.

An important backdrop is the overwhelming importance of religion in Ethiopia. Some 95 percent of the population reportedly practices one of the country's major faiths. More than 50 percent of Ethiopians adhere to a Christian faith, with the Ethiopian Orthodox Church accounting for most of these and the Catholic Church and a range of Protestant evangelical faiths the rest. The other major faith is Islam, accounting for 40 to 45 percent (some say more) of the population. As in Guatemala, the Jewish community is small but significant.

Religion is a vital aspect of daily life, immediately visible on the streets of Addis Ababa and more so in the countryside. Faith-based organizations sponsor a multitude of poverty alleviation initiatives that span the entire relief–development spectrum. These groups have an intimate community-level knowledge of the poor and well-developed, on-the-ground networks that constitute a significant social capital asset. The faith-based approach to poverty and development is generally holistic, based on the notion that social and cultural factors are inseparable from economic and financial ones, and thus could spur more sustainable policies and programs.

This suggests enormous potential for faith-based groups to influence development and poverty alleviation policies in Ethiopia, and indeed, many of these groups aim to move from providing relief to pursuing development-related activities. Yet the capacity to do so remains uneven. What is more, interfaith cooperation has been limited at best; competition and lack of confidence have been more common. While Christian groups have come together around specific issues, the WFDD pilot is the first instance in which all religious groups have formally collaborated.

The WFDD launched its initiative in Ethiopia in September 1999 and supported three regional workshops and one national workshop in 2000, hosted jointly by development organizations, the Ethiopian Orthodox Church, and the Kale Hiwot Protestant church. These meetings were designed to allow faith groups to share their experiences in relief, rehabilitation, and development work; discuss food security issues; and explore mechanisms for cooperation. Participants decided to create the Ethiopian Interfaith Forum for Development Dialogue and Action (EIFDDA) representing all the major Ethiopian religions and some 13 faith-based organizations. Trinity Wall Street Foundation provided support to the effort, as did the World Bank.

As its first project, EIFDDA decided to inventory faith-based development activities in Ethiopia. The inventory was to alert government and donors to faith groups' significant contributions, as no reliable data on these activities existed; it was also to serve as a networking vehicle. Although the process of creating the inventory promoted interfaith dialogue, completing it proved extraordinarily difficult because the information in practice was so scattered and kept in quite different formats. Some organizations were less than enthusiastic about sharing detailed information, particularly about finance. The final product was thus a partial inventory, which is to be seen as a first step in a significant information challenge.

The interfaith group initially resolved to focus on food security, but common action again proved challenging, as perspectives on food security differed widely. Whereas the experience of many faith groups was largely around emergency food distribution, for others, and for the development institutions, the problems were far more complex. Some faith groups pressed to feed the hungry directly while others emphasized issues such as land tenure, storage and distribution infrastructure, and crop mix. What is more, while many faith groups have some experience with food relief and distribution, their knowledge of developmentally oriented food security questions is limited. EIFDDA thus moved to expand its agenda to encompass poverty alleviation, with the option of addressing food security, HIV/AIDS, debt forgiveness, peace, and reconciliation.

The Ethiopian experience with HIV/AIDS, in particular, cries out for input from the faith community. Most faith groups maintain HIV/AIDS-related activities—they are a high priority of the Patriarch of the Orthodox Church, for example—but interfaith sharing of information and best practices has been limited. Furthermore, the need to tailor HIV/AIDS-related messages, education, counseling, and care to the tapestry of religious practices is great. Ethiopians continue to associate AIDS with shame, and faith groups need to collaborate in spreading messages based on moral precepts and the importance of embracing rather than ostracizing AIDS victims and their families. The World Bank–supported HIV/AIDS Project in Ethiopia, under way since early 2001, is an important vehicle for advancing faith-based cooperation at both regional and national levels, as are other elements of the national HIV/AIDS strategy and international partnerships.

The Ethiopian interfaith group also hoped to participate in the continuing processes of engagement around the Poverty Reduction Strategy Paper (see chapter 2). However, understanding the economic framework of the PRSP process and finding effective entry points proved daunting. While individual members of faith groups have participated in the process, the potential for collective, in-depth engagement remains to be exploited. Furthermore, while eventually the Ethiopian interfaith group formalized its membership structure, because of capacity constraints among its members coupled with its very broad focus, the group has yet to coalesce around a clear strategic direction.

TANZANIA

Faith institutions are central providers of basic health care in Tanzania, yet they have been strikingly absent from much of the country's dialogue with the World Bank. The reason and the result have been general unease, including animosity, toward the Bank among many faith groups, driven by misinformation as well as the longstanding failure to win meaningful collaboration. Also, as in Ethiopia, there is little experience of joint cooperation or dialogue between and among Tanzania's faith groups.

The WFDD pilot in Tanzania focused on health, with a loose-knit interfaith group guiding the project. Early on, the group commissioned a survey of health services provided by faith-based groups. While the survey confirmed the importance of faith communities as important providers of health services throughout Tanzania, its contributions toward analysis and qualitative aspects of the sector were modest at best. Although the group has defined a promising agenda for faith–development coopera- tion, it has so far scarcely scratched the surface. Two potential avenues for future engagement are work on specific challenges such as HIV/AIDS, and efforts to fill the glaring need for better information and analysis of people's health-related needs. In addition, while the group expressed an early interest in engaging in the PRSP process, this has yet to take material form; it could nonetheless represent another fruitful option for exploration. The early exploratory work highlighted the extent to which government officials need better information on the potential contribu- tion of an effective interfaith dialogue so they can take a next step toward effective alliances.

NOTE

1. More detailed information on the case studies is available on the WFDD Web site at www.wfdd.org.uk; see especially Progress Report www.wfdd.org.uk/ documents/publications/wfdd_1998_2000_progress_report.pdf.

PART II

Millennium
Challenges for
Faith and
Development

Introduction

The following chapters explore a set of inspirational and exemplary experiences between faith and development institutions that bear on specific challenges set by the Millennium Development Goals (see chapter 1 and box 1.1). In each instance, faith institutions have engaged with partners in the development community in a sector targeted for action through the MDGs. Underlying the selection and presentation of the cases here is the prospect of lessons—and inspiration—for future action. The cases also present remarkable examples of creative work and partnerships that are generally not well known and that deserve greater attention from analysts of prospects for development.

HIV/AIDS—TODAY'S MORAL IMPERATIVE FOR DEVELOPMENT

The first cases relate to work to combat the HIV/AIDS pandemic, arguably the single greatest challenge facing the world community today. A myriad of reasons argue that faith and development institutions must work together in creative harmony in the face of the HIV/AIDS challenge. This has often been the case, but by no means always. Troubling instances of discord have arisen among faith institutions and between faith and development actors as they struggle to come to terms with a new and devastating disease that defies traditional solutions and confronts them with a harsh picture of human behavior. The pandemic's very characteristics—long periods of silent, invisible incubation; association with the most intimate of human behaviors; and rapid and silent spread—have rendered this challenge acutely difficult. Only as the disease has reached levels that threaten to devastate communities and nations, and where countless individuals are suffering themselves or through the illness or death of people around them, has the response approached levels commensurate with the challenge.

Today, however, we are witnessing an extraordinary process of dialogue, debate, reflection, and action—church by church, mosque by mosque, and denomination by denomination—at community, national, and international levels. Remarkable stories of dedicated, creative, and caring programs are taking shape—and, increasingly, a new and dynamic mosaic of partnerships is being formed, bringing the skills and assets of different partners together to confront HIV/AIDS.

Uganda's mobilization against HIV/AIDS is well known in bullet points, but the government's extraordinary effort in reaching out to institutions of various stripes as well as the activism of different faiths is less known. Chapter 9, "Conquering Slim: Uganda's War on HIV/AIDS," describes these elements. Chapter 10, "A DREAM? Sant'Egidio Fighting HIV/AIDS in Mozambique," suggests that faith organizations and other NGOs can catalyze government service provision by illustrating that contentious and thorny issues—such as the provision of antiretroviral therapy in Mozambique—are difficult but, fundamentally, manageable with will and organization. Chapter 11, "Creative Partnerships in Fighting HIV/AIDS," tells two stories. The first story, of the Hope for Africa's Children Initiative, recounts the evolution of an HIV-prevention partnership that allows each of six member organizations to build upon community-based initiatives and draw on each other's technical expertise, with bold financing from the Bill and Melinda Gates Foundation. The second story, a Prescription for Hope, explores how one evangelical relief organization, Samaritan's Purse, was able to bring some 1,000 participants from 82 countries together to discuss the role of the Christian church in the fight against HIV/AIDS.

These remarkable stories take the form of dedicated, creative, and caring programs, and, increasingly, of a new and dynamic mosaic of partnerships bringing the skills and assets of different partners together to confront HIV/AIDS. These programs and partnerships can serve as inspiration to the governments, churches, and organizations that continue to resist the deadly realities of this epidemic, that they may act now instead of joining the ranks of the many nations and institutions that have waited until the epidemic is visible and widespread to take serious action against it.

MATERNAL AND CHILD HEALTH

Chapter 12, "Religious Organizations for Reproductive Health: A Ghana-UNFPA Partnership," highlights cases of partnerships involving the broader field of health, where faith institutions historically have played such active and often leadership roles. The chapter looks at the U.N. Population Fund's outreach to faith organizations as part of a program strategy designed to improve adolescents' and young adults' reproductive health by tailoring programming specifically to location, religion, or culture. Chapter 13 describes the complex and sensitive topic of female genital cutting, and the constructive roles that religious and traditional leaders have played in community action to change the practice. The story reminds us that small initiatives, of faith and of local origin, can indeed catalyze regional, national, or international social change. In both of these examples, faith organizations and development agencies have pushed a bit deeper, to see how they might make health services relevant to intransigent problems that are at first blush health related, but are fundamentally linked to culture, faith, and education.

CHILDREN'S EDUCATION

The next set of cases focuses on education and training, offering two contrasting models for enhancing educational quality and access. "Educating Successful Leaders for Successful Latin American Societies," chapter 14, paints the development-centered, life-affirming educational philosophy of the Fe y Alegría educational movement, and the contribution of private sector monies to overhauling Fe y Alegría's organization while remaining loyal to its message and spirit. Chapter 15, "Expanding Early Childhood Education: *Madrasas* in East Africa" describes the Aga Khan Foundation and local Ismaili communities' pilot initiative to reinforce early childhood schooling in *madrasas* throughout East Africa. Though the Madrasa Early Childhood Program was very much a Muslim initiative, it has sought national educational reforms that may create a broader regulatory space for other innovative educational projects. Each of these stories has entailed creative and patient efforts over long periods, but each may spark our imagination.

ENVIRONMENTAL PRESERVATION

This section's final theme is an area with enormous potential for collaboration at every level, from advocacy to education to action on the ground: environmental protection. Chapter 16, " 'Mountains Have Deities and Water a Spirit': The Mongolian Sacred Sites Initiative—A Partnership Linking Faith and Forests" highlights a case of collaboration involving the Buddhist faith in Mongolia, where the effort was designed to help build on traditions long dormant to reinstill a community awareness of, and engagement with, the protection of the natural environment. Chapter 16 includes inspirational stories about environmental initiatives involving faith communities. The chapter presents highlights from sacred texts and traditions reflecting reverence for nature and creation. It should be read in conjunction with the 2003 World Bank publication *Faith in Conservation: New Approaches to Religions and the Environment* by Martin Palmer and Victoria Finlay.

Throughout these pages, faith organizations' depth of commitment to the millennium challenges, where their efforts are engaged, are well illustrated, as is a commitment to development that extends over time and reaches deep into local context and vision. As faith and development partnerships gain a higher profile, however, there will be increased calls for measurement of the material results of such partnerships. Though thin on the ground today, the results of such evaluations can be compelling. One of the first of its kind, an excellent economic analysis of the contribution of faith-based organizations to service delivery, is summarized in the subsequent box: "'Working for God': Cost-Benefit Reflections on Faith-Run Clinics in Uganda."

These are all stories of success, with implications for the challenge of scaling up efforts, for the design of new forms of partnerships, and for specific program content and design. Each of the rich case studies in these chapters highlights the merits of careful reflection on the underlying issues involved and the insights and energies that come from the varying perspectives, notably from faith perspectives and institutions. A summary observation is that, in drawing conclusions about how to interpret these different and often intricate experiences, we would do well to heed Oscar Arias' caution that: "Nothing could be more reckless than oversimplification of the truth."[1]

"WORKING FOR GOD": COST-BENEFIT REFLECTIONS ON FAITH-RUN CLINICS IN UGANDA

Bringing issues of faith and development together is an unwieldy task for the most seasoned of philosophical thinkers. Rather than attempting to unravel these questions, we often shy away from them. Debate is drawn in broad brushstrokes, with points of view on the collaboration between the state and religious institutions falling into one of three camps: religious institutions must not deliver public service at all, as the state is secular; religious institutions must deliver service, but only because the state is unable to; or religion must be involved in public service delivery, as the state mandates that it be so. None of these positions is intellectually satisfying; each draws an ideological line without examining its philosophical underpinnings. The contribution of faith-based organizations is considered in overwhelmingly output-oriented terms, though it would seem that the shape of service delivery by organizations with an otherworldly life vision might differ in significant respects from other models.

In their recent *Working for God? Evaluating Service Delivery of Religious Not-for-Profit Health Care Providers in Uganda*, economists Ritva Reinikka and Jakob Svensson outline the contribution of religious health care providers in offering critical primary health care services in Uganda. A central finding is that religious health care providers appear to deliver service primarily for altruistic reasons. Reinikka and Svensson's work explores the premium of "working for God" through an econometric lens.

Hypotheses

The authors posit that there is not a significant regulatory benefit to not-for-profit (NFP) status in Uganda. There is virtually no regulation of health care facilities, and NFP actors have no tax advantage over for-profit institutions. Other reasons, then, must explain why clinics choose to operate under NFP status. Specifically, the authors set out to

(Box continues on the following page.)

(box continued)

examine two alternative hypotheses about the drivers of nonprofit actors' behavior in the Ugandan health sector: one, that NFP facilities are driven by altruistic concerns; or, two, that they are driven by the regulatory benefits of NFP status.

Methodological Summary

Reinikka and Svensson started from the government of Uganda's register of health care facilities. They culled the register for dispensaries with and without a maternity unit; separated them by region, and then by ownership category (only government and NFP facilities were included in the register); then selected clinics at random from within each of these categories. The private for-profits had to be identified during the field work in the 10 randomly selected districts. The final sample included 155 facilities, of which 81 were government health facilities, 44 were private NFPs (42 of which were religious), and 30 were private for-profit facilities. Data were collected at the district and health-facility level, as well as through exit polls given to 1,617 patients at the 155 facilities.

To determine whether NFP health facilities were indeed "working for God," the authors attempted to distinguish empirically the behavior of these facilities from that of private for-profit facilities, and to compare the behavior of NFP health care facilities that did and did not receive government financial aid. They also compared NFP facilities with government facilities, allowing an additional comparison.

In 1999–2000, the government of Uganda provided grants of about US$1,650 to each dispensary. Facilities seeking to maximize their profit would not have changed their service delivery pattern upon receiving aid. Whether the NFP health care facilities that received government aid chose to appropriate benefits, or to use them to provide higher quality or less expensive care, would be a critical test of the authors' "working for God" thesis.

Findings

Reinikka and Svensson indeed found that managers and staff of religious NFP health care facilities in Uganda appeared to be working for God. Their key findings included the following:

- Religious NFPs hired qualified medical staff at well under the market wage.
- Religious NFPs were more likely to offer pro-poor services and services with a public goods dimension, such as outreach and training of community health workers, than for-profit facilities. Though they offered these services less often than government facilities, they did more of it than government when it did it.
- Both for-profits and NFPs offered care of similar observable quality, and of higher quality than government dispensaries.
- But religious NFPs charged lower prices than the private sector.
- Religious NFPs that received government financial aid increased laboratory testing for malaria and intestinal worms and lowered their prices for out-patient consultations.

Based on these results, religious NFP health facilities in Uganda appear to be "working for God." The NFPs made decisions about the provision of service that could not be explained under a profit-maximization framework, whether ex ante decisions about how to maximize profit or ex post decisions about how to appropriate an NFP's increased resources. Of particular interest for development agencies focusing on aid effectiveness is the last finding: that the quality of service as measured by laboratory testing improved when NFP health facilities received government aid. Not all aid investments yield improvements to quality or reductions in price, and knowing which types of assistance do is an enormous help in the design of effective development projects.

In addition to expanding our stock of knowledge about the quantified value of faith to development, *Working for God* serves a catalytic function: it illustrates that the value of faith can be rigorously analyzed and quantified. A "typical" economic perspective might consider

(Box continues on the following page.)

(box continued)

that faith is too ephemeral a concept to test within a rigorous framework. And, paradoxically, what cannot be measured is considered to have less value within a growth-oriented development framework. *Working for God* provides numerical footholds and rigorous analysis for those who understand development in primarily analytic terms.

What should not be lost from sight, however, is that faith will still be a complex and ultimately unknowable "orienting life force" first, and a value to subject to measure only second.

Source: Reinikka, Ritva, and Jakob Svensson. 2004. "Working for God? *Evaluation Service Delivery of Religious Not-for-Profit Health Care Providers in Uganda.*" Centre for Economic Policy Research (CEPR) Discussion Paper 4214. CEPR, London.

NOTE

1. Speech at "Walking the Talk" Symposium in San Jose, Costa Rica, October 9, 2003.

Conquering Slim: Uganda's War on HIV/AIDS

"It all started as a rumor, then we realized it was a disease. Then we realized it was an epidemic. Now we have accepted it as a tragedy."
—Dr. Sam Okware, First Chair, Uganda National Committee for the Prevention of AIDS[1]

"Since the end of the guerilla war, a mysterious disease which slimmed people to the bones had started killing in big numbers. Judging by the sneaky way it operated—recurrent fevers, rashes, blisters—it looked like witchcraft. Many people went to witchdoctors for consultations. . .The theory was that this witchcraft was punishment meted out by Tanzanian smugglers who had been cheated by their Ugandan counterparts in the seventies and eighties when smuggling was rife in those marshy areas. . . Not long after, the disease had a medical name—AIDS—but remained Slim to us."

—*Abyssinian Chronicles*, Moses Isegawa[2]

From Bwindi Forest and its fabled gorillas, to the Bujagali Falls, to Jinja, the source of the Nile on Lake Victoria, Uganda is a country of exceptional physical beauty, often called the "Pearl of Africa." When it became independent in 1962, its prospects looked bright. For nearly a decade, Uganda witnessed a rapidly expanding economy, comparable to some in Southeast Asia. However, the period of 1971–1986 was marked by constitutional crisis, economic collapse, and civil war. During this time, it is believed that more than 1 million Ugandans were killed. Midway through these difficulties, silently, at least at first, the worst scourge to attack the twentieth century was also quietly assaulting Uganda's population. In 1982, Uganda was the first African nation to identify HIV/AIDS within its borders, and would become one of the worst-hit countries on the African continent.

The first cases of HIV in Uganda were confirmed in Rakai District in the fishing village of Kasensero, on the shores of Lake Victoria, in 1982. The first to be infected were fishermen and traders, many alleged smugglers, who were trafficking goods between Uganda and Tanzania. The disease, popularly known as "Slim" because of its emaciating effect on its victims, was thought to be the result of witchcraft and ancestor revenge. Many of the afflicted were among the more affluent traders, promoting the notion that the disease was a curse from God, retribution for illicit business practices. As the true cause of the disease gradually became known, as in other countries, it was shrouded in a haze of stigma, shame, and discrimination, associated with promiscuous sexual behavior, homosexuality, drug use, and, still, witchcraft.[3]

POLITICAL COMMITMENT AND LEADERSHIP

"If you go into a field and see an anthill full of holes, and you put your hand into a hole and get bitten by a snake, whose fault is it?"
—President Yoweri Museveni[4]

In the mid-to-late 1980s, AIDS was beginning to take hold in many African countries, but it was contained behind a wall of silence and denial. Few public or private leaders, secular or religious, had the courage and commitment to face openly the scourge of AIDS in all its dimensions. Almost from the first moment that HIV/AIDS was recognized in Uganda, however, the government of President Yoweri Museveni's National Resistance Movement recognized the threat the disease posed.

In January 1986, Museveni assumed the presidency over a country emerging from two decades of civil war and state-sponsored terrorism, its economy in tatters, its social services devastated, and the confidence of its people at a low ebb. A new alert sounded when, as early as 1986, President Museveni himself received warning of the threat of HIV/AIDS in his country. He learned that of some 60 soldiers sent to Cuba for training, nearly a third had tested positive for HIV. Given the myriad challenges it faced on many fronts, the new government could easily have ignored or at least postponed addressing HIV/AIDS. Instead, Museveni openly disclosed his anxiety to the people and the press. In the late 1980s, when taboos against public discussion of sex were strong and pervasive throughout Uganda, President Museveni's openness about HIV/AIDS showed considerable political courage.

In 1986, President Museveni established the National Commission for the Prevention of AIDS and, in collaboration with the World Health Organization, launched the AIDS Control Program (ACP) in October that same year. The ACP met weekly under the leadership of the president. The program had seven major objectives: health education, blood screening, rehabilitation of blood transfusion facilities and services, surveillance and data collection, distribution of condoms, research, and patient care. From the start the government sought a critical partnership with religious communities in the struggle against AIDS, sending a special appeal to all church leaders. Uganda's program was quickly recognized internationally as a model for other countries, not only in Africa but as far away as Thailand.

For the next several years President Museveni toured extensively throughout the country, his charisma attracting large attendance at public rallies on a host of political and development issues; some say he visited every district in Uganda. He consistently closed each gathering with HIV/AIDS messages. Frequently alluding to African proverbs or storytelling and making extensive use of colorful images and earthy humor, his messages combined fear and information on preventing the disease with exhortations about morality, national pride, and patriotic duty. Building on the demands of a population now clamoring for a voice in civic affairs, Museveni called for an assault-like public information campaign on HIV/AIDS aimed at building broad consensus on a national response.

The National AIDS Prevention and Control Committee—a precursor to the Uganda AIDS Commission established several years later—was composed of a broad base of government, nongovernmental, and faith leaders and organizations, and was charged with launching the public debate on HIV/AIDS. The government targeted NGOs and faith-based organizations as creative and respected change agents sensitive to local conditions and able to engage a wide range of stakeholders not traditionally involved in health issues, including politicians, community leaders, educators, students, administrators, commercial traders, and sex workers. The government also enlisted the media as an important partner in the fight against HIV/AIDS. When Museveni came to power, the media included a small number of state-controlled newspapers and radio stations. After the government largely liberalized the media in the early 1990s, they became an important vehicle for informing the public on a number of topical issues, key among them HIV/AIDS.

By 1990, the government recognized that HIV/AIDS posed a critical challenge to the country's development prospects, requiring human and financial resources and strategies beyond the scope of the Health Ministry. The government established an interim secretariat, again with a broad cross-section of government, private sector, civil society, and faith-based organizations. This led in 1992 to the formal inauguration of the Uganda AIDS Commission (UAC) within the Office of the President.

Religious leaders from all three major faith traditions—Catholic, Protestant, and Muslim—have actively participated in the commission. Religious leaders have chaired the commission since 1995: Bishop Kauma of the Church of Uganda did so from 1995 to 1998, and retired Bishop Barnabas Halem'Imana of the Catholic Church has headed the commission up to the time of this writing. The participation of faith communities has added credibility to the commission and ensured sensitivity and relevance to local cultural and religious beliefs and practices.

In 2001 the UAC established the Uganda HIV/AIDS Partnership Committee, composed of representatives of parliament, government ministries, U.N. and bilateral donors, national and international NGOs, private sector groups, faith-based organizations, networks of people living with HIV/AIDS, and academia. This forum is meant to extend well beyond classic government–donor partnerships and ensure a voice for less powerful constituencies, as well as to pool efforts to scale up measures to combat the disease.

As further evidence of Uganda's efforts to situate HIV/AIDS in a multisectoral context, the government defined a five-year National Strategic Framework in 2000. This framework included three overarching goals: reducing HIV prevalence by 25 percent; mitigating the effect of the disease; and strengthening the national capacity to coordinate initiatives and monitor HIV/AIDS. A key objective was to integrate these efforts with other national planning strategies, including the five pillars of the country's Poverty Eradication Action Plan: economic management, security and disaster management, governance, production and competitiveness, and human resource development. Following a midterm review, the government revised the framework in early 2004 to ensure greater emphasis on care and treatment in parallel with prevention efforts.

THE ABC STRATEGY

The cornerstone of Uganda's HIV/AIDS program is based on ABC: promote abstinence, be faithful, and use condoms responsibly. In formulating and implementing this approach, policymakers reached out to a wide spectrum of partners, taking great care to avoid pitting the moral precepts of one against another, especially those of the faith communities regarding condoms. This approach encouraged wide-ranging consensus among a broadly inclusive group of constituencies.

Practice abstinence. The abstinence message, mainly geared to younger people, encourages delayed onset of sexual activity, ideally until marriage. The impact of this message, seen in declines in indicators of sexual activity, appeared more pronounced in the early half of the 1990s.

Be faithful. Many experts believe that the single most important factor driving the AIDS epidemic is multiple sexual partners, and that the number of sexual partners matters most in determining whether people contract HIV. Efforts to promote fidelity aim at both married and unmarried couples. Uganda coined the terms "zero grazing" (for monogamous, mainly Christian relationships) and "paddock grazing" (for polygamous, mainly Muslim relationships).

Use condoms. Condom distribution rose dramatically—from 300,000 to over 20 million—between 1991 and 2000, as did knowledge about condoms. However, condom use remains relatively low. Some critics hold that the donor community has overemphasized condom distribution, and that behavioral change—toward abstinence and monogamy—is at least as important yet has received less attention. Although debate over the relative impact of A, B, and C in reducing HIV/AIDS prevalence has not reached a resolution, all three have clearly been important pillars.

It is important to underscore that ABC is only one segment of a broader approach. Uganda has made significant strides—and indeed has been a pioneer—in a number of other interventions: blood screening, prevention of mother-to-child transmission, and voluntary counseling and testing (VCT). ABC does not address the rights of orphans and vulnerable children affected by HIV/AIDS. Nor does it recognize the need to work to change cultural practices that may contribute to HIV/AIDS, such as the custom of allowing male relatives to "inherit" widows, wife sharing, and spontaneous sex during cultural rites and ceremonies. Finally, the ABC strategy is geared exclusively toward prevention, even though the growing availability of better and less costly drugs to combat AIDS and opportunistic infections suggests the need to rebalance care and treatment with prevention.

One of the strengths of the ABC approach is its simplicity. However, because HIV/AIDS involves deep-seated culture and gender sensitivities, the ABC approach does not always fully address the needs of all stakeholders. In fact, some people living with AIDS feel that ABC perversely reinforces stigma, since HIV-positive status suggests nonadherence to abstinence and faithfulness.

ABC may not always fully address women's issues. The approach encourages young women to abstain from sexual activity until marriage. However, a cruel irony is that young, single women have more power to assert themselves in insisting on safe sexual practices. Once married, a woman is more at the mercy of her husband, who is much more likely than she to engage in extramarital sexual relationships, at which point she is less able to influence his high-risk behavior and negotiate safe sexual practices. A noted Ugandan HIV/AIDS activist, Anglican priest Canon Gideon Byamugisha, frequently notes the difference between lawful sex and safe sex. "Unlawful sex," according to most religious teachings, is sex outside marriage, but with a condom, it is safe. In discordant or HIV-positive couples, including married couples, sex can be lawful, but without a condom, it is not safe. Canon Gideon stresses the need to address both sets of circumstances.

Nevertheless, the ABC model has contributed significantly to the Ugandan success in preventing HIV/AIDS. Many younger adults now delay sexual activity, and once in a relationship, make a more marked effort to be faithful. More people now also use condoms, particularly in nonmarital, noncohabiting sexual relationships.

THE ROLE OF RELIGIOUS LEADERS

"Religion is inextricably woven into every aspect of life in Uganda. For most Ugandans, religious beliefs play a major role in their sense of personal identity, their thought patterns, their moral judgments and their perceptions of the disease."

—Kaleeba and others 2000.[5]

In the early days of the epidemic, Slim was a cause for shame and withdrawal from family and community. However, the courage and openness of the government and many religious and community leaders paved the way—albeit gradually—for a candid national response to HIV/AIDS. Openness enabled a multitude of leaders and organizations, including those from faith communities, to launch public information campaigns and establish care and treatment facilities. Public information campaigns gradually shifted from messages of fear and recrimination to hope, comfort, and dignity, motivating and empowering people to seek testing and adopt less risky behaviors.

Religious leaders and faith communities have played a central role in Uganda's efforts to combat Slim. In the epidemic's early days, when the government focused on prevention, faith-based health services recognized that patient care and counseling were woefully neglected. In the intervening years, faith-based groups and a host of volunteers, many trained and administered by religious organizations, have provided counseling, home-based care, care of orphans and vulnerable children, and, increasingly, antiretroviral (ARV) drug therapy. Partnerships with faith-based organizations have permeated virtually every aspect of Uganda's HIV/AIDS program since its inception. UAC estimates that about half of some 2,000 NGOs engaged in HIV/AIDS initiatives—spanning education, prevention, counseling, care, and treatment—are faith based. Moreover, many of Uganda's key HIV/AIDS organizations, while not directly faith based, have long-standing and deeply rooted partnerships with faith-based organizations, both Ugandan and international.

The Response of the Christian Community

A host of Christian organizations—affiliated both directly and indirectly with Christian denominations—have joined the battle against HIV/AIDS.

The Catholic community in Uganda was among the first to commit itself to the battle against HIV/AIDS. In the late 1980s, the Catholic Church was providing basic health services through some 200 local centers and regional hospitals, representing perhaps 25 percent of the country's health infrastructure. As Slim patients quickly overwhelmed these facilities, the Uganda Catholic Medical Bureau responded by formulating a more structured and scaled-up program.

The Uganda Catholic Secretariat created the new post of AIDS program coordinator and a special desk for HIV/AIDS within the Catholic Medical Bureau. These offices began training counselors and distributed a letter from the Catholic Bishops of Uganda in 1989 urging love and compassion for AIDS patients and others affected by the disease, especially orphans. "Let each one of us look into his or her innermost self, in order to find out what this epidemic means for him or her here and now. It challenges us in all aspects of our living."[6]

Catholic churches and hospitals designed special programs for AIDS widows and orphans, while Catholic medical services focused on home-based care and treatment of opportunistic infections. The secretariat also advocated for orphans and vulnerable children and launched educational programs within communities and Catholic-supported schools.

In 2001, the Uganda Catholic Secretariat determined that despite these efforts and successes, Church-based activities had not effectively integrated efforts to combat HIV/AIDS. After consulting with government, civil society, and faith-based representatives, the secretariat formulated a five-year strategic plan designed to mainstream HIV/AIDS prevention and control at national, diocesan, and parish levels, with a view toward ensuring maximum efficiency and cost-effectiveness. Today, each of the 19 Catholic dioceses has hired a focal person for HIV/AIDS who works through schools and other community services, targeting adolescents and young adults. Most parishes also maintain programs, ranging in size from quite small to US$1 million. Nevertheless, the secretariat still sees a need for more coordination to scale up these initiatives and exert greater impact.

As in other African countries, the Anglican Communion has been at the forefront of HIV/AIDS advocacy and care and support services. As early as 1991, the Communion organized a workshop for bishops and other religious leaders, as well as extensive HIV/AIDS education programs in many dioceses. The leadership of Reverend Canon Gideon Byamugisha, and support from his bishop, Samuel Ssekkadde, provided an early and powerful message that transcended the Anglican community. Canon Gideon is among the best known of Uganda's early pioneer champions in the fight against HIV/AIDS. Canon Gideon was ordained in 1992, shortly after the death of his wife in 1991. Once he discovered that his wife had tested positive, posthumously, for HIV, he discovered he too was HIV-positive. Three years later, in 1995, Canon Gideon disclosed his status to his bishop, who was very supportive, encouraging Canon Gideon to continue his advocacy efforts, and Canon Gideon became the first practicing priest in Africa to break the silence and openly declare his HIV-positive status. Since then, Canon Gideon has campaigned tirelessly and courageously against the stigma and discrimination associated with HIV/AIDS. His efforts have mobilized grassroots and community action and increased understanding of the many difficult and multifaceted issues around HIV/AIDS and the acceptance of people living with the virus. His focus is very pointedly on living positively with AIDS and helping HIV-positive people to remain productive, contributing members of society. His articulate and humane passion and his openness and willingness to confront any issue have helped in countless ways to unbundle many of the complex and nuanced issues presented by the ABC strategy.

On the outskirts of Kampala, Namirembe Diocese—in existence for some 100 years and thus regarded as the mother of all Anglican dioceses in Uganda—has been deeply involved in fighting HIV/AIDS. Training and mobilization are its central focus: It trains health workers down to the parish level in a holistic array of services, including personal hygiene and health, reproductive health, nutrition, and HIV prevention, care, and support. The diocese also supports VCT, provides medical supplies for treating opportunistic infections, and conducts home visits. The diocese has developed an entire prayer service around HIV/AIDS designed to raise awareness, combat stigma, and promote solidarity. Anglican Communions around the world have used this liturgy.

Namirembe Diocese maintains four targeted programs:

- The Child to Child Program aims to safeguard children under 13 from HIV/AIDS and other diseases and offers basic training in home care, working through both primary schools and Sunday school. The program provides children with sound information to cope with peer pressure as they enter their teens.
- The Youth to Youth Program relies on peer support groups to enable adolescents to change morals and behavior, safeguard them from HIV infection, and involve them in home care.
- The Positive Parenting Program helps parents improve their ability to communicate with children and each other on gender relations, health and hygiene, and HIV/AIDS.
- The Post-Test Club provides modest material support and emotional and spiritual guidance to people who have tested positive for HIV/AIDS.

The Muslim Community

The Islamic Medical Association of Uganda (IMAU) has played a leading role in educating Uganda's Islamic community, especially religious leaders, about HIV/AIDS, and in mobilizing a community response. The Joint United Nations Programme on HIV/AIDS has cited IMAU's interventions as best practice. The organization joined the fight against HIV/AIDS by the late 1980s, pioneering the first HIV/AIDS prevention program oriented toward the Muslim community. With support from the Ministry of Health and the World Health Organization, IMAU held a national AIDS education workshop in September 1989 aimed at shaping the response of the Muslim community. This conference laid the foundation for the Family AIDS Education and Prevention through Imams Project (FAEPTI), created in 1992. FAEPTI gives imams and teams of community volunteers information about AIDS, linking these messages to the Koran wherever possible.

A first step was to conduct a baseline survey in two districts (Mpigi and Iganga), designed to assess knowledge and practices related to the disease. Some 2,000 people responded. The survey revealed that most people knew that HIV is transmitted through sexual intercourse, but also uncovered a dearth of information about mother-to-child transmission and the risks associated with certain cultural practices associated with the religion, including circumcision and ablution of corpses.

Within five years the project had expanded to 10 more districts. More than 8,000 religious leaders and community volunteers—about half of whom are women—have been trained to provide support and counseling to over 100,000 households. IMAU has ensured the active participation of women at every level of its AIDS education efforts, recognizing that only female volunteers can gain the confidence of women. The group thus requires every imam to have both a female and a male assistant. Female volunteers target teenage girls, a higher risk group than teenage boys to contract the disease. Volunteers also encourage women to establish income-earning micro-enterprises, which empower them to insist that their husbands practice safe sex and refrain from seeking partners outside marriage, and to ensure enough household income for expenses such as school fees. Home visits complement mass media campaigns, and volunteers obtain bicycles and income-earning activities to sustain their motivation.

The issue of condoms initially generated considerable controversy, so IMAU set it aside for more than a year while encouraging religious leaders to voice their concerns openly. Alluding to the basic tenet in the Koran concerning the protection of life, IMAU underscored its intention to promote only responsible condom use, after other defenses against AIDS had failed, adding that parents who ignore condoms leave behind orphans. In response to concerns that condoms would promote promiscuity, IMAU pointed out that Muslims know about alcohol yet do not necessarily consume it. Religious leaders eventually came to consensus, and FAEPTI's curriculum now includes condom education.

FAEPTI gave rise to two follow-on projects. First, the Community Action for AIDS Prevention Project offers training to Muslim and Christian leaders and community volunteers, mainly in Kampala. This program is also reaching beyond faith leaders and engaging *boda boda* drivers (bicycle taxi drivers) and market vendors to pass along AIDS messages during their commerce with clients. Second, the Madrasa AIDS Education and Prevention Project has developed age-appropriate curricula explaining HIV/AIDS transmission, prevention, and control, as well as care of AIDS patients. Relying on *madrasas* (informal schools attached to mosques that provide religious instruction), the curriculum makes frequent reference to music, dance, and drama. The program operated in 350 *madrasas* in Kamuli and Mpigi districts and reached more than 20,000 children from 1995 to 1998.

THE IMPORTANCE OF ORGANIZATION AND NETWORKING

A host of organizations and networks—many of which have significant indirect links with religious groups—support people living with HIV/AIDS and their families. These networks encourage people to seek counseling and testing, and, if positive, provide comfort and support to them and their families, making it easier to live positively. Such networks are generally credited with helping people personalize risk, thereby contributing to behavioral change. Compared with other countries, Ugandans are more likely to receive HIV/AIDS information through friends and personal networks (including many that are faith based) than through the mass media. Many observers consider this type of information a better means of bridging the gap between information and behavior change.[7]

Among the earliest organizations providing care and support to people living with AIDS was TASO, the AIDS Service Organization. The first indigenous AIDS organization in Africa, and considered by many to set the standard, TASO was founded in 1987 by Dr. Noerine Kaleeba and 15 colleagues. Many of TASO's early founders were HIV-positive or had a close family member who was HIV-positive, giving them particular sensitivity to stigma, discrimination, and the need for care, treatment, and quality of life.

From modest beginnings, TASO has expanded to become the largest AIDS service organization in Uganda. Reflecting its slogan "Living Positively with AIDS," TASO aimed to bring the disease into the public domain. TASO called on those with AIDS to live responsibly, and on society to recognize its responsibility to support those infected. Whereas the government's message was effectively, "If you contract HIV/AIDS, you will die," TASO was among the first organizations both to encourage people to determine their status and to offer hope and dignity. The range of services provided by TASO includes counseling (pretest, posttest, prevention, couples, and bereavement); medical care; home care; health and nutrition education; social support, including food distribution and school fees for children; capacity building; and training.

Another important NGO is the AIDS Information Center (AIC). In the late 1980s, when HIV/AIDS was spreading unchecked, the national blood bank was overwhelmed with people offering blood donations as a way to be tested safely and in confidence. Few testing facilities existed then in Uganda, and almost none had affiliated counseling services. Collaboration among the Ministry of Health, a group of national and international NGOs, and the World Health Organization led to the creation of AIC in 1990, and it has become perhaps the most important VCT organization in Uganda.

Counseling was a new job description. Quite apart from the emotional stress of what was, in effect, a death sentence, patients needed to understand the difference between HIV and AIDS. Few doctors within an overwhelmed health system had time to explain that patients had a fatal disease that might not yet be symptomatic. Training an army of a new kind of health care worker was required. Many of these staff were volunteers, many were from faith communities, and many were living with HIV/AIDS.

AIC is careful to ensure confidentiality, and, with today's technology, test results are available in under an hour. With some government support and donor funding, its services are heavily subsidized, charging fees of Uganda Shillings 1,000 for youth (approximately US$0.60) and USh 4,000 (approximately US$2.40) for adults compared with a cost of USh 13,000 (approximately US$7.80). AIC works in close collaboration with TASO and frequently refers its clients who have tested positive to a TASO branch. Posttest clubs, especially among youth, are very active and engage in advocacy in schools and community groups. In the first 11 months after opening, AIC reported more than 9,000 clients, compared with its target of 5,000 for a full year. By 2002, the organization had served more than 700,000 clients.

Many other groups are engaged in one aspect or another of HIV/AIDS intervention. The Uganda Network of AIDS Service Organizations, founded in 1997, serves as a central networking and coordinating body for all local HIV/AIDS initiatives, thereby improving access in underserved areas. Many of these initiatives are associated with community-based, nongovernmental, and faith-based organizations and also function as national advocacy groups.

One noteworthy effort is the National Community of Women Living with HIV/AIDS in Uganda (NACWOLA). This network of HIV-positive women includes many single mothers who provide each other with emotional support and practical assistance. NACWOLA has close ties to local religious congregations, and its members are frequent public speakers at church and community gatherings. NACWOLA members report greater empowerment among themselves and women in general because of the country's more open environment about HIV/AIDS and sexual issues:

> Not so long ago if a woman tried to discuss sex with her partner, he would view her as a prostitute. A woman was expected to be humble and wait for her husband to make advances. In African culture, it was taboo for a woman to show sexual desire, or express dissatisfaction. You could never complain, even if your husband was having "away matches" (extramarital affairs) you couldn't object. . . Now you find that, through a lot of sensitization. . .the old taboos are gradually being broken. Women are starting. . .to persuade their husbands to use condoms.[8]

NACWOLA's top priorities include women's inheritance rights, and the group informs members of their legal rights and helps them prepare wills. Another priority is providing guidance on disclosing one's HIV status to children. As mothers, NACWOLA members are keenly attuned to children's sensitivities and worries. An important effort is the Memory Project. Modeled on Barnardo, a program developed by a London children's charity, Memory Books help prepare children for the impending death of a parent. Traditionally, Ugandan parents do not discuss death with children. HIV/AIDS has rendered that approach inappropriate in many, especially poor, households where children may have to cope, with minimal adult guidance. Memory Books, created by mothers and children, recount family history, important life events, and significant people who have shaped a child's life. They provide children with a sense of identity.

Efforts to reach out to youth have been a special focus in Uganda. Concerned that past gains could be lost without a concerted effort to provide schoolchildren with better information, President Museveni recently launched the Presidential Initiative on AIDS Strategy for Communication to Youth, in collaboration with the Ministries of Education, Health, Gender, Labor and Social Development, and Local Government. Building on the country's policy of universal primary education, the initiative seeks to reach some 7 million schoolchildren. Manuals train teachers to deliver age-appropriate messages across a full range of HIV/AIDS, gender, reproductive health, and sexually transmitted disease issues, shared at least bimonthly in school assemblies. Faith leaders have collaborated extensively on this initiative.

The newspaper *Straight Talk*, aimed at adolescents ages 15 to 19, has become an important forum enabling young people to voice their concerns about emerging sexuality, reproductive health, and HIV/AIDS. More recent developments include *Young Talk* (for ages 10 to 14), *Teacher Talk*, and, in the latter part of 2004, *Parent Talk*. These newspapers all stress age-appropriate messages concerning postponing sexual activity, avoiding early pregnancy, and establishing relationships, and also provide information about HIV/AIDS.

A popular feature of *Straight Talk* is letters from young people asking questions about sexuality, reproductive health, and HIV/AIDS. The candor with which these are written (letters may be anonymous or signed) has provided a wealth of information enabling *Straight Talk*, government, and NGOs to design messages for young people. The March 2004 edition focused on religion. Headlined "Religion Helps to Keep You Safe," the issue includes articles by Christian and Muslim leaders, such as Canon Gideon, and young people supporting the contention that religious beliefs can help them handle emerging sexuality, resist temptation, and avoid risky behavior.

CHALLENGES AHEAD

Despite its widely acknowledged success, Uganda still faces a huge challenge in reducing the prevalence of HIV/AIDS. The estimated prevalence rate is still about 6 percent nationwide and 8 percent in Kampala, and the disease remains the leading cause of death among the country's most productive age group: people ages 15 to 49. A number of critical issues remain to be addressed.

Prevention versus Treatment

Many policymakers and service providers recognize that past efforts have concentrated on prevention, with little focus on treatment issues. Among the more prominent challenges will be ARV drug treatment.[9] Costs have plummeted, generics have become more available, and resources are rising substantially. U.S. monies from the President's Emergency Plan for AIDS Relief are already expanding access to ARVs (although this funding is so far limited to branded drugs).[10] The World Bank–supported Multi-Country AIDS Programs and the Global Fund are also likely to boost funding for ARVs.

The challenge for Uganda's health system—public, private, and supported by nongovernmental and faith organizations—is to build the capacity to deliver treatment, including training staff, ensuring quality control, reinforcing distribution systems, and providing appropriate storage facilities. Some 18,000 people are now receiving ARV treatment, and the target for Uganda under the World Health Organization's "3 by 5" Initiative[11] is 60,000, which many see as feasible. The government is in the final stages of formulating a national policy on ARVs, but the question of whether these will be free or subsidized and to what extent remains outstanding. Many people see faith-based groups as likely key players in expanding ARV treatment, as they can provide sound logistics and accountability and are better able to reach the poor. Some faith groups have already established community adherence teams to monitor patients receiving treatment.

The Challenge of Coordination

With Uganda's success have come a growing number of agents and organizations anxious to become engaged. Several observers point to a need for improved coordination, especially at the district and subdistrict levels, between local government authorities and nongovernmental partners, particularly the multitude of faith-based organizations, to ensure equitable distribution of services and adherence to medical standards and protocols. This will be particularly important with greater access to ARVs.

Stigma

While the degree of openness that Uganda has fostered has been a major factor in its success in combating HIV/AIDS, stigma persists, imposing high economic and social costs on many HIV-positive people. A number of analysts familiar with the Uganda situation point to some faith leaders as a continuing source of stigma, as they link HIV/AIDS to sin and God's punishment. Women are especially vulnerable to stigma, within both the family and the workplace. Women risk being thrown out of the house and separated from their children if they reveal HIV-positive status to their husbands. Faith communities have a special role to play in broadening and deepening their efforts to combat stigma, discrimination, and exclusion. Income-generating projects, especially for women, provide empowerment and independence and exert a significant impact on their ability to protect their health.

Funding

While significant incremental resources from multiple sources are becoming available at the national level, especially for treatment, inadequate funding poses a significant barrier to efforts to scale up grassroots, community-based activities. This barrier appears to reflect poor procedures for moving funding to the local level. Ironically, a number of projects report that decentralization is compounding this situation, as accountability among central, district, and subdistrict levels is particularly weak.

In conclusion, Uganda's success in combating HIV/AIDS—which far exceeds that of other African countries—is the result of the cascading effect of multiple interventions. These activities, appropriately sequenced and gradually scaled up, have been built on a foundation of strong political commitment, openness to civil society, outreach to faith communities, and complementary measures beyond ABC. The latter include prevention of mother-to-child transmission, support groups for people living with AIDS, blood screening, voluntary counseling (at least in urban areas), and training. What sets Uganda apart is a clear if silent understanding among a wide range of stakeholders that success requires that all work in tandem in a spirit of cooperation rather than confrontation.

The role of faith leaders and faith-based organizations merits special credit. Faith-based organizations have been intimately involved in all aspects of HIV/AIDS intervention. And while most faith communities opposed condom use in principle, few openly opposed the government's distribution programs, and churches and mosques did not allow their initial reticence with respect to condoms to hinder their active contribution. The government, in turn, was sensitive to the concerns of the faiths regarding condoms and avoided overly aggressive promotion. Thus, the religious communities emphasized abstinence and faithfulness while the government (and other nongovernmental groups) promoted the use of condoms. Each and every element has been vital to Uganda's success in reversing HIV/AIDS trends.

NOTES

1. Eckholm 1990.
2. Isegawa 2000, p. 396.
3. One observer has noted HIV/AIDS was termed the 4H disease in its early days: that of homosexuals, heroin users, hemophiliacs, and Haitians (with reference to witchcraft). East Africa in general and Uganda in particular spearheaded much of the early international research on HIV/AIDS. At a time when the disease was associated primarily with homosexuals and drug users, early longitudinal studies in East Africa examined incubation periods, epidemiological progression, and social behavior that influences risk. After considerable political debate, the chief risk to infection was revealed to be multiple heterosexual partners, and this risk was highest along transport routes.
4. Kaleeba and others 2000, p. 10.
5. Kaleeba and others 2000, p. 58.
6. *The AIDS Epidemic: Message of the Catholic Bishops of Uganda* 1989, p. 19.
7. USAID 2002.
8. Kaleeba and others 2000, p. 69.

9. Along with Côte d'Ivoire, Uganda was the first country to pilot test ARVs in Africa.

10. Critics maintain that far more people could receive treatment if U.S. funds would support generic drugs. On the other hand, some providers are grateful that any additional monies are available for lifesaving drugs. The differential between generic and branded drugs ranges from 1:2 to 1:5.

11. The 3 by 5 initiative was launched by the World Health Organization as a response to the urgent need for increased access to ARV drug treatment by people living with AIDS in developing countries. The target is to distribute ARV treatment to 3 million people in 50 developing countries by the end of 2005.

REFERENCES

The AIDS Epidemic: Message of the Catholic Bishops of Uganda. 1989. Kampala. September.

Eckholm, Eric. 1990. "Confronting the Cruel Reality of Africa's AIDS Epidemic." *New York Times.* September 19.

Green, Edward C. 2001. "The Impact of Religious Organizations on Promoting HIV/AIDS Prevention." Harvard School of Public Health, Cambridge, Mass. Processed.

———. 2003. *Rethinking AIDS Prevention: Learning from Successes in Developing Countries.* New York: Praeger.

Isegawa, Moses. 2000. *Abyssinian Chronicles.* New York: Alfred A. Knopf.

Kaleeba, Noerine, Joyce Kadowe, Daniel Kalinaki, and Glen Williams. 2000. *Open Secret, People Facing Up to HIV and AIDS in Uganda.* Strategies for Hope Series. London: ActionAid.

USAID (United States Agency for International Development). 2002. "What Happened in Uganda." Washington, D.C.

10

A DREAM? Sant'Egidio Fighting HIV/AIDS in Mozambique

Mozambique today faces both dreams and hopes for a great future, and some tragic ironies and enormous challenges. It exemplifies in many respects the notion that it lives in both the "best of times" and yet also the "worst of times." Mozambique emerged from one of the world's most devastating civil wars with its population scattered and numb from decades of bloody internecine strife, yet has succeeded in resettlement and reconciliation with a speed and harmony that have defied even optimistic pundits.[1] Mozambique remains one of the very poorest countries in the world (ranked 170 in the 2003 Human Development Index),[2] yet its economic growth performance puts it near the top of most lists of strongly performing developing countries. And Mozambique began to rebuild a nation after decades of physical war, only to find itself enmeshed in a different war—one that takes still more lives—against HIV/AIDS.

The emerging effort to provide treatment to people affected by HIV/AIDS, involving Mozambique's government, the Community of Sant'Egidio (one of Mozambique's principal partners in the earlier peace negotiations and the subsequent early start in nation-building), and the development community, including the World Bank, is an inspirational story of a complex and creative partnership that seeks to respond to the

---

This chapter, prepared by Katherine Marshall, draws on Community of Sant'-Egidio presentations and publications and an early draft by Olivia Donnelly.

country's changing circumstances and demands. It brings home how the perspectives, energies, and dedication of a community motivated in large measure by its faith and its commitment to friendship with poor people has pioneered new approaches to caring for people with HIV/AIDS in places where many, until very recently, argued that care was impossible to provide at reasonable cost. The Community of Sant'Egidio is now proceeding relentlessly to highlight both the real, tangible hope that its experience holds out and the moral challenge it presents for the global community in extending its hands to work with African countries in the fight against HIV/AIDS.

MOZAMBIQUE AND THE CHALLENGE OF HIV/AIDS

Mozambique is today one of nine African countries hit hardest by the HIV/AIDS epidemic, and the disease stands as the single greatest threat confronting Mozambique's development. An estimated 13 percent of the adult population are HIV-positive—that is, 1.2 million people, of whom 630,000 are adult women. The numbers increase by an estimated 600 cases per day. The highest concentrations are found in the country's central zones, with the most rapid increase of new cases occurring in the southern region. Infection rates are highest along transportation and commerce routes, disproportionately affecting mobile populations such as migrant workers and traders.

During the long war years, the social and economic isolation that resulted from the civil war ironically protected Mozambique to some extent from the HIV epidemic that was raging in neighboring countries, mainly because the war impeded movement. However, with the war's end in 1992, vulnerability to HIV/AIDS increased dramatically, above all with the return of refugees from Malawi, Zimbabwe, and Tanzania, where HIV/AIDS rates were extraordinarily high. Peacekeeping forces from high-prevalence countries and a marked increase in cross-border trade also contributed. Mozambique's deep poverty, low levels of literacy (adult literacy in 2001 was estimated at only 45 percent), and both rural-urban and cross-border movements, have fueled the rapid spread of the epidemic.

The classic burdens of the HIV/AIDS pandemic are all present in Mozambique, accentuated by the country's poverty and the many development challenges it faces. HIV/AIDS is increasingly sapping the country's productive capacity, as it affects a high proportion of economically active people, especially young workers. Projections suggest that life expectancy could drop to 27 years by 2010. In 2000, life expectancy was estimated to be 39 years; without AIDS, it would have been 50 years.[3] HIV/AIDS imposes a crippling burden on the country's fragile health care system, with HIV/AIDS patients occupying well over half of all hospital beds. Health care workers, already far too few in number, are ill prepared to care for those with HIV/AIDS, and many themselves are living with HIV/AIDS.

The Mozambican government has given steadily increasing priority to the fight against HIV/AIDS. The Ministry of Health approved a National Strategic Plan in 2000 to combat sexually transmitted diseases and HIV/AIDS for 2000–2002.[4] As was common to most African countries at the time, it highlighted the central challenges of prevention as the heart of the strategy. The plan emphasized a wide range of interventions to make information about the disease widely available, to develop VCT programs, to highlight programs addressed to youth, and to make the HIV/AIDS fight a national priority. The United States Agency for International Development (USAID) was, in the early period, the lead donor in HIV/AIDS in Mozambique, providing some US$6.6 million in 2001.[5] The World Bank in 2003 approved substantial grant financing for the HIV/AIDS program through the Multi-Country AIDS Program. Many other programs, prominent among them the Global AIDS Fund, the Clinton Foundation, and the new U.S. government HIV/AIDS program, are all active in Mozambique.

In 2003–2004, the issues of the balance between prevention and care and treatment of people living with HIV/AIDS came increasingly to the fore in Mozambique as in other countries. The issues of affordability and of capacity to deliver demanding programs gave special poignancy to the debate. It was in this context, and primarily as a result of a protracted dialogue among the Mozambique government, the World Bank, and the Community of Sant'Egidio, that the World Bank undertook to consider a special program in three countries (Burkina Faso, Ghana, and Mozambique): the Treatment Acceleration Project, with Sant'Egidio as a leading partner. This program is to focus on the specific challenges of scaling up the implementation of treatment programs in poor communities. Its primary focus is learning by doing, with sharing of experiences among the different kinds of programs that are now delivering treatment in different settings at its core. The United Nations AIDS Program and the World Health Organization are key partners in the venture.[6]

As in other African countries, the HIV/AIDS pandemic in Mozambique presents profoundly difficult challenges and issues. Among the most intractable are the phenomenon of stigma and discrimination, including within the medical profession and the media; the lack of or poor state of health infrastructure; and weak legal and social protections for people living with HIV/AIDS. Other more specific, pragmatic issues include inadequate and unreliable supplies of drugs to treat opportunistic infections, low condom availability, and Mozambique's chronic shortage of doctors and nurses. Although costs of ARV drugs have dropped dramatically within the past few years, they are still well beyond the means of most Mozambicans. As an illustration of the gap, the national health budget can presently make available less than US$10 per person per year, compared with costs for ARV therapy now in the US$300 a year range.[7] Mozambique's extremely low literacy rate presents special challenges for the design and implementation of effective HIV/AIDS education and behavior change campaigns. Women face huge social and economic disadvantages. Poverty makes young women and girls particularly vulnerable, because of the pattern of intergenerational sexual relationships. Finally, there is relatively limited capacity within community-based organizations to establish and manage HIV/AIDS programs. It is here that the Community of Sant'Egidio has had a remarkable and unique impact.

THE COMMUNITY OF SANT'EGIDIO

The Community of Sant'Egidio, a Christian lay association that often describes itself as a movement, began its work in Rome in 1968.[8] Its subsequent development has been marked by a fervent commitment to the service of the poor and dispossessed on a local level. It now operates in more than 70 countries, with approximately 40,000 member volunteers who work at the community level on a wide array of interventions designed to alleviate poverty, provide social services, and foster peace and reconciliation. The Community's work touches many categories of the poor, the vulnerable, and the marginalized, including children, elderly, handicapped, refugees, immigrants and particularly the Roma people, people living with HIV/AIDS, prisoners, and the homeless. Its activities span the gamut from humanitarian programs to development projects and to peace and reconciliation interventions.

SANT'EGIDIO AND MOZAMBIQUE

Among the activities for which the Community is best known is its engagement, and indeed, its steering of the peace process in Mozambique. This stands out as one of the most remarkable episodes in Sant'Egidio's 26-year history (see chapter 22). There, as in other instances, Sant'Egidio has, through friendship, dialogue, patience, determined advocacy, and commitment, been able to bring together government, nongovernmental groups, and private partners in finding solutions.

The Community of Sant'Egidio first became involved in Mozambique in 1976 through its work with very poor communities. In 1984, the Catholic Archbishop of Beira appealed to the Community to become more deeply engaged in drought relief efforts and the consequences of war. Sant'Edigio sent and distributed humanitarian relief aid, coordinated and monitored by volunteers from the Community, together with missionaries and Caritas, Mozambique (a Catholic relief organization). As it became increasingly obvious that the problems of poverty could not be separated from the ongoing, brutal civil war that began with independence, the Community began to focus on the problem of peace. It embarked on a persistent and creative effort to promote dialogue between the government and different factions in the context of "two track" diplomacy (an approach combining official negotiations and informal processes led by unofficial actors). Negotiations began in July 1990, in Rome, and lasted some 27 months. On October 4, 1992, the Peace Agreement was signed in Rome, putting an end to 16 years of war. Remarkably, this agreement has not been violated since.

The Community of Sant'Egidio was there at the start of the war, and continued its presence and work after the peace settlement. It focused initially on projects to support democracy and the country's social and economic development The movement now operates through some 38 communities in different parts of the country, forming a strong network of local Mozambican volunteers.

HIV/AIDS—THE DREAM PROJECT

> *"We turn to you, leaders of Africa who are gathered in Maputo. We are young Africans. An heir of this continent, Martin Luther King Jr, forty years ago has said: 'I have a dream.' We too have dreams. Often only those. But dreams can become reality. . .Our dream is that soon medical care may be accessible to all the children of Africa, that AIDS may no more be a death sentence but an illness that can be treated and prevented."*
> —Youth Leaders Declaration presented at the African Union Conference, Maputo, Mozambique, July 10–12, 2003.

Sant'Edigio, through its work in many African countries, but particularly in Mozambique where it has such strong roots, has come to view the HIV/AIDS pandemic as the most serious threat to Africa's future, perhaps an even greater challenge than war. It has pressed hard first, to demonstrate through a practical program on the ground that a program of care can be implemented with the appropriate will, and second, to advocate for the rapid acceleration of such programs. At a meeting in Rome on May 12, 2004, involving many leaders including 13 African ministers of health, the right to treatment and care for people with HIV/AIDS was presented as a fundamental human right. This was reflected in a joint declaration signed on May 13 by the Community of Sant'Egidio and the African ministers.

Sant'Egidio launched its broadly based HIV/AIDS treatment program in August 2001 and called it Drug Resource Enhancement against AIDS and Malnutrition in Mozambique (DREAM). The term DREAM echoes back to the appeal of young people of Africa (whom Sant'Egidio helped to mobilize) and to the underlying philosophy of hope reflected in the program.

Initially located in Maputo Province, southern Mozambique, the program is now working in two other areas: Sofala in the central region and Nampula in the North. The program provides broad-based support for people affected by HIV/AIDS, with a focus on providing drug therapy for prevention of mother-to-child transmission as well as ARV therapy, both in the context of a comprehensive treatment approach. More specifically, the DREAM program provides the following:

- VCT for HIV status
- Training of local staff (doctors, nurses, laboratory technicians, health workers, and training staff)
- Health education, especially for at-risk populations
- Drug therapy for preventing mother-to-child transmission of HIV infection during pregnancy, birth, and breastfeeding
- ARV drug therapy for people living with AIDS
- Expanded laboratory facilities to monitor patients receiving ARV drug therapy
- Monitoring of blood donations
- Prevention and care of the diseases linked to AIDS (opportunistic infections, sexually transmitted diseases)
- Nutritional education and supplements for people living with AIDS
- Home care for the seriously ill.

Under a 10-year agreement with the government of Mozambique, the DREAM project provides health care training (a top priority), personnel, laboratory equipment and supplies, and will import, store, and deliver ARVs for patients under its program. ARV therapy is provided at no cost to the patient, and it is a central premise of the entire Sant'Egidio approach and program that all services are fully in line with western-level quality and standards. Sant'Egidio works in a complex partnership, with, in addition to the government of Mozambique (the central partner), universities in Italy and Mozambique, pharmaceutical companies, communities, other NGOs, and international development agencies. The principle of Sant'Egidio of volunteerism is fully carried through in this program: the Sant'Egidio team is composed of volunteers who maintain a relay of people coming to Mozambique as well as members of the Mozambique communities. The core program staff are qualified Mozambicans and are, of course, paid.

The Community of Sant'Egidio reported, at the May 2004 meeting on the DREAM program, that it had to date provided VCT to close to 8,000 people. The number of HIV/AIDS-positive people in care is 4,315, a significant increase (58 percent) from the level of 2,731 reported in September. Most are on the generic three-drug therapy. The number of babies born to HIV/AIDS-positive mothers is 413. Sant'Egidio describes its approach as holistic. Particular focus is given to nutrition, for example, as well as treatment for tuberculosis, malaria, and sexually transmitted diseases. The DREAM project is housed within existing public hospitals and maternity wards, reflecting its partnership with government. The staff focuses on people whose viral loads are extremely high and are in need of immediate intervention. Once they go on the full treatment, they never come off. Other people who seek help from the centers, and whose viral load is lower, receive assistance ranging from home care and medication for opportunistic infections to food parcels to meet nutritional needs. Finally, Sant'Egidio gives special focus to the issue of women, initially through its mother-to-child transmission programs, but more broadly in its work with households.

Sant'Egidio puts considerable emphasis on cost efficiency. The Community estimates the annual cost of caring for an HIV/AIDS patient in 2003 as averaging Euros 399 (US$330), including all costs for personnel; construction and depreciation of facilities; and drugs, diagnostic work, and nutritional supplements. To lower costs, Sant'Egidio is engaging with large pharmaceutical companies such as GlaxoSmithKline, Merck, and Boehringer Ingelheim, seeking better deals on drugs and test kits.

The Community of Sant'Egidio reports outstanding results from its program. These results have been widely reported and supported at leading medical conferences and in a wide range of peer reviews. They are working closely with the World Health Organization, a collaboration that will be a focus of the Treatment Acceleration Project to be supported by the World Bank. The program is led by Dr. Leonardo Palombi, professor of epidemiology. Sant'Egidio estimates that 97 percent of children born of HIV-positive women in the program have tested negative for the virus. The ARV therapy results are also outstanding, with 95 percent adherence to treatment programs and the remarkable "Lazarus" effect of people recovering from near death to happy and productive lives when on the ARV therapy.

Sant'Egidio sees its program as part of the broad international strategies to fight HIV/AIDS, with its focus on integrated approaches and different partners bringing different assets and emphases to the battle. However, it sees the inclusion of a major program that provides care for HIV/AIDS-positive people, including ARV therapy, as a critical factor in developing more effective overall strategies for fighting the HIV/AIDS pandemic. The arguments are first, that no disease in history has been fought successfully with prevention alone; second, the fact that drug therapy is successfully used in richer countries makes it morally imperative to apply similar standards of care in poorer countries; and third, the pragmatic set of arguments that contend that prevention will not succeed if there is no hope held out for HIV/AIDS-positive people. This applies above all for testing, where they have found that people will not volunteer for testing in large numbers until they have the prospect of care if they find they are HIV-positive.

Sant'Egidio describes its greatest challenge now as mobilizing sustainable sources of funding to scale up the present scope of the project while ensuring that those receiving ARVs have the assurance of a reliable and continuing source of care and drugs.

Sant'Egidio aims to provide the support it can for similar DREAM programs in other parts of Africa. It recently opened a facility in Malawi and has plans to expand into Angola, Guinea, Guinea-Bissau, South Africa, and Swaziland over the next five years.

NOTES

1. The resettlement process is described in many texts, including Marshall 1998.
2. http://www.undp.org/hdr2003/indicator/cty_f_MOZ.html.
3. Community of Sant'Egidio Web site description of DREAM project (http://www.santegidio.org/en/index.html)
4. USAID 2002.
5. USAID 2002.
6. Treatment Acceleration Project, under appraisal by the World Bank in May 2004, approval planned June 2004.
7. Médécins Sans Frontières 2003.
8. Chapter 22 of this book presents more background information on the Community of Sant'Egidio.

REFERENCES

Community of Sant'Egidio. 2003. "AIDS Care and Prevention in Mozambique." Rome, Italy. Available at http://www.santegidio.org/en/amicimondo/aids/mozambico.htm

———. 2003. *Treating AIDS in Africa: A Model for Introducing Antiretoviral Treatment of HIV into Health Care Systems in Limited Resource Countries.* Rome: Leonardo International.

———. 2004. "Drug Resources Enhancement against AIDS and Malnutrition: Report No. 2." Rome, Italy. March.

Marshall, Katherine. 1998. *From War and Resettlement to Peace and Development: Some Lessons from Mozambique and UNHCR and World Bank Collaboration.* Cambridge, Mass.: Harvard Institute for International Development.

Médécins Sans Frontières. 2003. "Mozambique and AIDS: The Silent Atomic Bomb." Paris. June. Available at http://www.msf.org/countries/page.cfm?articleid=1C3A8933-16B6-4CA6-B551EAE6AF5E562B

USAID (United States Agency for International Development). 2002. "HIV/AIDS in Mozambique." USAID Brief. Washington, D.C. July.

11

Creative Partnerships in Fighting HIV/AIDS

The challenges of fighting the HIV/AIDS pandemic go far beyond the specific issues of health and medical care. HIV/AIDS involves every facet of the development agenda, and thus needs to engage the widest possible variety of partners—private businesses, NGOs, community organizations, government, and, perhaps most directly, faith communities. This chapter describes two initiatives that entail creative partnerships in combating HIV/AIDS, both engaging faith organizations. One is directed specifically to the smallest victims of HIV/AIDS—the millions of children living with, affected by, or orphaned by the disease; the second describes the "prescription for hope" endeavor, an ongoing effort to mobilize, across continents, the energies of a diverse group of faith communities working on HIV/AIDS issues, spanning care and action at the grassroots level through international and national advocacy.

ANOTHER CHANCE: HOPE FOR AFRICAN CHILDREN INITIATIVE

No infectious disease of the modern era has had such a devastating impact on the world's youngest and most vulnerable citizens as HIV/AIDS. It has created a terrible crisis, an explosion of orphans. The deep-rooted kinship system that exists in Africa—the extended family networks of aunts and uncles, cousins, and grandparents—is an age-old social safety net for

---

This chapter draws on the authors' discussions with HACI and the organizers of the Prescription for Hope meeting, as well as published materials.

vulnerable children that has long proved resilient even in circumstances of major social change. This safety net is unraveling rapidly in many places under the strain of the stigma and discrimination associated with HIV/AIDS and the crushing weight of economic reality facing aging grandparents, relatives, and communities as they attempt to care for an ever-increasing number of children. This most important coping mechanism of the African social fabric is clearly at risk as the number of children in need increases while the number of caregivers declines.

The numbers are staggering: By 2002, an estimated 4 percent of African children under age 15 had been orphaned as their parents died of HIV/AIDS. Worldwide, more than 13 million children under age 15, most of them in Sub-Saharan Africa, have lost one or both parents to AIDS. The numbers are projected to rise rapidly, with estimates suggesting that by 2010, an estimated 25 million children will have lost one or both parents to HIV/AIDS, with some 80 percent of these orphaned children in Sub-Saharan Africa.[1] In a dozen African countries, orphans, the majority due to HIV/AIDS, will make up 15 to 20 percent of all children under age 15 by 2010. As an illustration, just over 15 percent of children are orphaned in Burundi, the Central African Republic, and South Africa, and more than 25 percent of children in Lesotho.[2] While Africa has and will continue to have the highest proportion of children orphaned by AIDS, obstacles are daunting throughout the world.[3]

The impact of HIV/AIDS on children is complex and multifaceted, with the social and economic costs both high and long term, including malnutrition, migration, homelessness, vulnerability to violence and exploitation, and sharply reduced access to education and health care. HIV/AIDS has serious psychological repercussions as well, including depression, guilt, and possible long-term mental health issues. The stigma that continues to be associated with HIV/AIDS is most devastating for its youngest victims. Turning the tide of this emergency requires immediate and sustained action at all levels.

The challenge of helping these orphans has galvanized faith leaders in many parts of the world, both individually and working through faith and interfaith organizations and with other partners. One such example is the Hope for African Children Initiative (HACI).[4] Launched in the summer of 2000, HACI is a pan-African, community-based effort to address the enormous challenges faced by children orphaned by the AIDS pandemic in Africa and the millions more whose parents are sick or dying of AIDS-related illnesses. With the purpose of increasing the capacity of African communities to provide care, other services, and assistance to children affected by HIV/AIDS, HACI is a partnership of six international NGOs— CARE, Plan, Save the Children, Society of Women and AIDS in Africa, World Vision, and the World Conference on Religions for Peace (WCRP), the latter two being among the largest and most influential international NGOs with direct faith connections.

The rationale underlying the partnership is that each of the core partners has a particular expertise and country experience on which HACI-supported efforts can draw. Each partner brings to HACI its unique strengths, technical expertise, and important constituencies on the ground in Africa. By working in concert, the HACI partnership can provide intellectual, technical, and financial resources (in the form of small grants) to local religious and sectarian organizations, charities, hospitals, and faith-based and other caregivers. Resources channeled to these programs enable them to expand and coordinate their efforts to provide much-needed services such as family support, HIV counseling and testing, legal assistance, and educational support. HACI also views local partnerships as essential, and one of its key objectives is local capacity building. It thus works in collaboration with hundreds of national NGO partners in each of the countries where it is engaged.

English-speaking eastern and southern Africa has served as the organization's testing ground, and HACI has been active in Kenya, Malawi, and Uganda for nearly two years. Since early 2003, it has also launched basic operations in six more countries: Cameroon, Ethiopia, Ghana, Mozambique, Senegal, and Zambia. Future plans call for expansion into four additional countries: Democratic Republic of the Congo, Mali, Namibia, and Tanzania. HACI's programs are focused squarely on community-based initiatives, and thus, community participation lies at the core of each individual program. HACI's secretariat works closely with the country representatives of each of the six partner organizations to set up Country Program Councils, national broadly based representative bodies of community-based organizations and other major actors in the fight against HIV/AIDS. The secretariat's role is to provide technical assistance to country teams and ensure that program development is in accordance with HACI's technical framework.

HACI received a US$10 million planning grant from the Bill and Melinda Gates Foundation in 2001, enabling its partner organizations to identify and build on a variety of existing community-based programs that offer proven and cost-effective services to children and families affected by HIV/AIDS.

Creating awareness and reducing stigma associated with HIV/AIDS is among HACI's central goals. The organization feels strongly that faith leaders and communities have a particularly important role to play, and therefore has turned to WCRP, one of its core partners, to spearhead initiatives to attack stigma, particularly as its relates to children. WCRP, with its broad-ranging, pan-African network of religious leaders, is well situated to undertake this effort. With this in mind, and to help develop HACI's work program, WCRP organized an unusual gathering of pan-African religious leaders in Nairobi in June 2002, focusing on the response of religious organizations to the impact of HIV/AIDS on children. With 30 countries represented, the meeting assembled some 150 of Africa's senior religious leaders, reflecting all of the major religious traditions on the continent— Christian, Muslim, Hindu, Jewish, Ba'hai, and traditional religions. The specific focus was on issues of stigma and discrimination and the need to expand care for children living with or orphaned by HIV/AIDS. The event was an opportunity for participants to endorse, together, principles and common action around HIV/AIDS. The African Religious Leaders' Assembly also gave WCRP an excellent platform to spotlight HACI and the issues it seeks to address.

HACI's programs were launched first in Kenya, Malawi, and Uganda. In Kenya, in the initial year of operation HACI provided about US$1.6 million in small grants in 20 districts in all eight provinces of the country. These grants aim to provide direct support for basic needs (food, clothing, school uniforms and fees, medical treatment, and shelter) to some 7,000 orphans and vulnerable children. Indirect support is provided through grants for health and education programs in areas hardest hit by HIV/AIDS, support for people living with AIDS and their families, and capacity building for community and faith-based organizations. Although it is not its preferred approach, as a last resort, HACI is supporting three orphanages for abandoned HIV-positive children in Kenya. In Kenya's Isiolo region, in the troubled northern part of the country close to the Somali border, a HACI grant to the local association, Pepo La Tumaini Jangwani (which means "winds of hope in the desert"), allows community health workers to track the health and well-being of orphans and other children at risk through three main activities: training of volunteer "mother carers," training and support to care for opportunistic infections associated with HIV/AIDS, and education and skills training to rehabilitate child sex workers. Among its many benefits, the project has provided the community, and especially the children, with religiously and socially neutral space where Christians and Muslims come together. By integrating HIV-positive children with others from the community, the project is helping to reduce stigma.

In Malawi, HACI's efforts are geared toward significant scaling up of existing activities. With program support of some US$1.6 million, its work is focused on supporting the efforts of district, community, and village AIDS committees, youth clubs, credit associations, and faith-based and community groups. In response to the famine that has plagued Malawi, HACI supports relief food distribution to thousands of orphans and vulnerable children, especially those in child-headed households. About 47,500 orphans have received direct support for basic needs from HACI while another 76,000 have benefited indirectly from HACI's efforts to improve health and education infrastructure and capacity building for groups from district to community to village levels.

In Uganda, HACI builds on the already broad-ranging and well-developed HIV/AIDS initiatives, and thus sought out areas where it could bring additional value. HACI adopted several strategic niches: stigma reduction through prevention strategies and life skills development aimed at children and youth; various measures to enhance relations between parents and children in HIV-positive households through promotion of integrated community-based care, including for ARV programs; home-based care and psychosocial support and succession planning for households affected by HIV/AIDS; and finally, measures aimed at enhancing the future prospects of children orphaned or affected by HIV/AIDS through support for health and education and income-earning initiatives. HACI grants totaled US$1.5 million as of early 2004, providing direct support to about 1,400 children and indirect support to 3,000 more. Three well-established faith-based programs receive HACI support: the Villa Maria Hospital in Masaka, the St. Francis Hospital in Kisoro, and the Reach Out Mbuya Parish project in Kampala.

Three basic principles underpin HACI's approach. It is child focused; it is community focused; and it encourages integrated interventions, as the needs of orphans and vulnerable children do not exist in isolation. HACI remains a nascent initiative, one that shows considerable promise, but has yet to have a fully proven track record. Though definitive assessments are clearly premature, HACI's cross-country reach and broad support across religions and sectarian organizations offers a compelling partnership model in an environment where resources are stretched thin, and imaginations often harried. In all HACI countries—present and future—partner organizations are committed to identify and replicate proven interventions in a broad range of child-focused activities and to promote the sharing of technical expertise among countries in the region that confront extraordinary new challenges that are similar in so many respects.

PRESCRIPTION FOR HOPE: AN EVANGELICAL MOVEMENT'S OUTREACH ON HIV/AIDS

Samaritan's Purse, a nondenominational Christian relief and evangelism organization that works in more than 100 countries, has been moved deeply by the HIV/AIDS crisis, reflecting the direct witness of many church members working in affected countries. The organization has become an active part of the emerging alliance to support work on HIV/AIDS in the United States and to ensure that work in affected countries receives both the backing and recognition it needs. Among the challenges and lessons that this alliance highlights, particularly with respect to its U.S. constituency, are those around communicating clearly about the scope and impact of the HIV/AIDS pandemic. It aims to mobilize support among communities inclined to see the problem as one that is distant and foreign, and that poses uncomfortable values and ethics questions to which there are no easy answers.

The focus of Samaritan's Purse on HIV/AIDS is well illustrated in the major conference in Washington, D.C., that it organized in February 2002 called, appropriately, Prescription for Hope. The meeting assembled about 1,000 participants from 82 countries, including church leaders, direct care providers, physicians, government officials, and foundation representatives. The event itself focused on Christian church roles and HIV/AIDS, and it represented a powerful call to church action on HIV/AIDS at a global level. The organizers described the participants as the very finest people and programs working "on the ground." A feature of the event and the partnerships it represents was the diversity of messages that emerged, about the causes of the pandemic, its prospects, and solutions. The messages reflected the reach of different churches in different parts of the world, and thus the voice of their experience. Against an excellent scientific backdrop and poignant stories of individuals working on HIV/AIDS programs for orphans, the dying, and youth, their views on such topics as condoms, awareness programs, and stigma covered a wide range—some accepting, some strongly against.

The event was well funded and professionally organized. Plenary sessions, with a generally formidable list of speakers from the religious, foundation, and government communities, were followed by workshops led mostly by direct care providers and program implementers. The rhetoric was remarkable for its passion and detailed links to realities in communities all over the world; the communication of messages was outstanding. The timing of plenary speakers was carefully controlled—no one exceeded the time allotment. Time between speeches was punctuated with music and specially made videos showing "saint candidates" working with HIV/AIDS from around the world. Attention to detail was obvious throughout—for example, jackets to protect against winter weather in Washington were provided to participants from warm climates. In sum, it was a spectacularly choreographed event.

Keynote remarks by Dr. Robert Redfield set the scene and tone of the event in many respects, lending recurring metaphors and topics. He traced explicit analogies between HIV/AIDS and the terrorist attacks of September 11, 2001, noting that terrorism killed 3,000 people whereas HIV/AIDS had already resulted in more than 3 million deaths. His biblical references resounded throughout the meeting—the Sermon on the Mount, the parable of the good Samaritan. Calling on his experience as a medical doctor, Dr. Redfield questioned the world's performance in stewarding scientific knowledge and resources, pointing to likely shifts in patterns and scope of HIV infections in the years ahead. Will medical advances and technological progress be available to the whole world or just the rich in the West? He set out a six-point agenda:

- The urgent need for Church leadership, which has thus far been lacking.
- The need to remedy the stigma that has stood in the way of HIV/AIDS treatment, in all countries, both in the developed and developing worlds.
- The role of education, not only on how HIV is spread, but about fidelity, and the need to change behavior. In this he referred to God's law and the "boundaries of what God intended."
- The need for additional resources. He questioned how much of new spending proposed by President Bush would be devoted to HIV/AIDS research.
- Training, both medical and social, as a vital element in anti-AIDS programs.
- Notwithstanding the many negative messages, he stressed the importance of compassion and hope.

The conference focused on three dimensions of the HIV/AIDS challenge: development and economic messages, social messages, and religious messages.

Development Messages

Speakers and audience were well versed in the development impact of HIV/AIDS—its economic growth drag, reduction of overall productivity, repercussions for agricultural cropping patterns and yields, life expectancy, labor force trends, and so forth. One speaker highlighted that disease and death resulting from AIDS inescapably reduce savings and investments. While an impressive array of statistics were presented (and re-presented, since the source of much of the data was the same, namely the Joint United Nations Programme on HIV/AIDS [UNAIDS]), some numbers echoed often: the high share of AIDS-related deaths in Africa, the comparison of AIDS and war deaths (AIDS has killed 10 times as many people as died in twentieth-century wars), and the crucial impact on younger people (with rising HIV infection rates, the highest of any age group, AIDS accounts for 80 percent of deaths among 18 to 40 year olds). Anecdotes described companies that were starting to hire three people for the same job because one or two were likely to die of AIDS. Andrew Natsios, USAID administrator, stressed that in Zambia the number of deaths among teachers is larger than the number who graduate from teachers' colleges.

The links between HIV/AIDS, poverty, and political and economic instability, possibly accentuating many forms of conflict, was mentioned often. The impact on children—an epidemic of orphans—and malnutrition was an equally common topic, with many speakers noting that the ultimate impact of AIDS will be on the next generation. One presenter challenged the group to "Turn this titanic tide around." Expanded access to drugs to reduce mother-to-child transmission was repeatedly called for, although it was noted that, when breastfeeding, these drugs lost their effectiveness after two years. Some sounded a warning beyond Africa: While the worst of the epidemic is in Africa, the places where the fight against HIV/AIDS is most critical in the immediate future are India, Russia, and Eastern Europe.

Social Messages

The social impact of HIV/AIDS was focused squarely on the family. The disease is tearing apart the central fiber of humanity—the family—said one speaker. There was some (but not central) discussion of the gender aspects of HIV/AIDS and the difficulty faced by women in countries where women are expected to remain subservient to their husbands in taking precautions against HIV/AIDS. There were many clarion calls for programs that would accord HIV/AIDS victims dignity and respect; the role of the church in helping to reduce the stigma of HIV/AIDS was underscored time and time again.

Religious Messages

The main religious message was the call for the Christian Church to assume a high-profile leadership role in combating HIV/AIDS, a "plague which is destroying God's creations." Dr. Helen Gayle, head of HIV at the Bill and

Melinda Gates Foundation (previously with the Centers for Disease Control and Prevention [CDC]), quoted an African proverb: "The best time to plant a tree was yesterday. The next best time is now." Thus far, leadership has been taken by non-Christian organizations and because they (namely governments and donors) have tried and failed, now it is up to the church. Senator William Frist (U.S.; R-TN) highlighted what he called "teachable moments" when people were most open to change and pointed to the church's historical ability to "change the course of human events."

The issue of condoms and their role in an overall HIV/AIDS program came up often, with veiled references and not always in a consistent way. One speaker, referring to condom use, noted that children especially were receiving "too many conflicting moral messages," suggesting even that too much education could "weaken human power of self discipline and stimulate sexual experimentation, and promote lust." The same speaker suggested that negative test results could have the perverse effect of stimulating "concubine shopping"; and that, because tests do not register results of sexual activity for three to six months, they could result in spreading AIDS. (Senator Frist, however, noted that negative test results are a powerful incentive to stay healthy.) The now famous call from Kenya's former president, Daniel Arap Moi, for Kenyans to abstain from sex for two years so that AIDS would cease to be a problem, was cited, often with favor. While this particular speaker was an outlier among plenary speakers, his messages resonated strongly with a good part of the audience. There were many who returned in blunt terms to the issue of morality and HIV/AIDS: a strong call against sin.

With respect to program issues, a significant group at the meeting linked prevention and treatment and underlined their view that it was essential to balance the two. Great emphasis was put on local-level delivery vehicles, especially in the many short video presentations that described successes at the grassroots. Many speakers, however, suggested that there has thus far been too much discussion and debate—just get on with it! Andrew Natsios, from USAID, outlined the priorities for the USAID CORE (Communities Responding to the HIV/AIDS Epidemic) initiative: prevention, abstinence, delay of sexual activity; mother-to-child transmission with ARV; increase in immediate test results; support for people living with AIDS; and pursuit of more coordination among donors and multilaterals.

The issue of ARV drugs was highlighted, with several speakers noting that the wider availability of ARVs now presented a moral imperative. Without action to make ARV therapy more widely available, a wider gulf between rich and poor countries would be an inevitability, with likely dire consequences for national and international instability. Speakers with medical backgrounds noted the need for better health infrastructure for ARVs as well as the need for pharmacological treatments for opportunistic infections. While this issue did not appear to be among the hot button items for many participants, especially those from North America, it should be noted that this meeting predated the precipitous declines in the cost of ARV drugs that began to occur later that same year; this underscores the dynamic nature of the dialogue on these issues.

In a plenary session, Dr. Mary Wangai and Dr. Paul Wangai presented moving personal stories of how HIV/AIDS affects its victims and their families in Kenya; its physical, economic, and social aspects; and many of the mythical taboos that continue to be associated with it. Beginning each tale with "I don't know if you were there to see . . . " and closing with " . . . but I was," Dr. Paul Wangai roused his audience. "HIV/AIDS is not a by-the-way interruption in our lives. It is the ministry Christ would use to teach the parable of the good Samaritan." In calling for more coordination among the various actors, Dr. Wangai suggested, "If we fail to plan, we will plan to fail" in our efforts to combat HIV and AIDS.

Senator Jesse Helms (U.S.; R-NC) and Janet Museveni, First Lady of Uganda, were featured at the closing session. Senator Helms recounted his long association with Franklin Graham and Billy Graham (Franklin Graham's father). He confessed that he was a latecomer in appreciating the scourge of AIDS but vowed to correct that in his remaining time in the U.S. Senate. Mrs. Museveni recounted the elements of Uganda's success in combating AIDS. In Uganda, the greatest successes in remote areas of the country in HIV/AIDS interventions have been those by churches. She noted their particular focus on orphans and the firm basis of their programs in Christian faith and compassion. With respect to condoms, she agreed that they have a place in an overall program, but suggested that this could not be the entire foundation of an anti-AIDS campaign, quoting her husband in suggesting it was not realistic to think that "only a thin piece of rubber stands between us and the death of a continent."

The meeting was remarkable for the breadth and depth of its participants and their perspectives across a wide range of issues confronting efforts to combat HIV/AIDS.

NOTES

1. UNAIDS, UNICEF, and USAID 2002, p. 3; UNICEF 2003, p. 3.
2. UNAID, UNICEF, and USAID 2002, p. 8.
3. UNAID, UNICEF, and USAID 2002, p. 6.
4. Information about the program is available at www.hopeforafricanchildren .org

REFERENCES

UNAIDS (Joint United Nations Programme on HIV/AIDS), UNICEF (United Nations Children's Fund), and USAID (United States Agency for International Development). 2002. *Children on the Brink.* New York: UNICEF.

UNICEF (United Nations Children's Fund). 2003. *Africa's Orphaned Generations.* New York.

CHAPTER 12

Religious Organizations for Reproductive Health
A Ghana–UNFPA Partnership

Ghanaian teens and young adults grapple with varying information and advice on reproductive health issues, some correct and
some misleading. Their perceptions both conform to and defy common
perceptions of adolescent sexual behavior in Sub-Saharan Africa. Young
people consistently interact with health care providers who may withhold
sexual health services that providers consider to be inappropriate for adolescents and young adults. In short, Ghanaian teens do not have the clear,
accurate, and readily accessible information they need to make informed
sexual health choices. Sexual health policymakers and care providers, in
turn, rarely have the accurate and nuanced information that they need to
structure information and health services for adolescents and young
adults. This chapter describes the role of a unique partnership, involving
religious organizations and a United Nations executing agency, that sets
out to provide Ghanaian adolescents and young people the clear, correct,
and locally tailored information that is a prerequisite to making strong
sexual health decisions.

As in many countries, there are few easy means to provide teens and
young adults in Ghana with quality information on sexual health or a
complete range of reproductive health services. Clear-headed discussion

---

Hope Neighbor drafted this chapter based on UNFPA case study materials.

of young people's sexual health is often muddied by judgment of how young people *should* act, and considerable worry about how various sexual health strategies may encourage young people to behave differently. Sexual health programs for young people are heavily influenced by the level of social and political acceptance for sexual health strategies, as well as by the orientation of these strategies. Religious organizations are often thought of as complicating this mix, discouraging reproductive health programs, especially those that address sensitive issues such as condom use and the broadening of sexual choices.

In the mid-1990s, the United Nations Population Fund (UNFPA) of Ghana sought to delve into some of these areas, and the limits to collaboration with religious groups in particular. With the support of the government of Ghana, the UNFPA and the Planned Parenthood Association (PPA) of Ghana approached religious organizations in the north of the country about developing a joint reproductive health program. This partnership suggests that concerted effort—a combination of soul and shoe leather—can bear fruit in reducing tensions between family planning agencies and religious groups, and help materially in increasing awareness about sexual health among opinion leaders and young people.

NATIONAL REPRODUCTIVE HEALTH SITUATION

The partnership developed against the backdrop of Ghana's somewhat unusual situation in Africa. Ghanaians' reproductive health status is notably better than the average for the countries that surround it, but absolute numbers remain poor. Ghana is a destination country for immigrants from other African countries, as well. The health of its people is closely linked to that of nearby African nations, true for the transmission of HIV and other sexually transmitted diseases in particular.

Ghana's total fertility rate, or the number of children an average woman will bear in her lifetime, declined from 5.5 children in 1993 to 4.4 children in 1998. By comparison, the fertility rate in countries surrounding Ghana fluctuated between 5.2 and 6.4 births in 1998. Keeping in mind that marriage is more fluidly defined than surveys may reflect, it is apparent that married women used modern contraceptives more often in 1998 than in 1993. The rates in real terms were rather low, however, with

10.1 percent of married women using modern contraceptive methods in 1993 and 13.3 percent in 1998. Over 20 percent of women use some contraceptive method, modern methods included. Again, rates of contraceptive use are higher in Ghana than in neighboring Burkina Faso, Côte d'Ivoire, or Togo.[1]

Similarly, infant mortality is lower in Ghana than elsewhere in the region. Its rate of infant mortality is 57 per 1,000 live births, compared with 105 per 1,000 live births for Sub-Saharan Africa as a whole.[2] Three in 100 Ghanaians carried HIV in 2001.[3] Though a climb in infection is anticipated, Ghana still has lower rates of HIV prevalence than its neighbors. In 2001, 3.5 percent of Burkinabé were HIV-positive; 6 percent of Togolese carried the virus; and 9.7 percent of Ivoiriens were infected with HIV.[4]

Overall, these relatively positive health indicators can be attributed to the government's focus on primary health care and the presence of a network of health facilities across the country. Low absolute levels of health, however, serve as a reminder that fresh thinking combined with steady effort continues to be needed to address Ghana's public health challenges. There is an urgent need for special efforts focused on adolescents and young adults. Spare national-level indicators provide little insight into teen sexual health choices or circumstances.

BEYOND AND BETWEEN THE NUMBERS

While national reproductive health figures are relatively positive, targeted research has revealed significant gaps between perception and reality in regard to reproductive health and sexual activity among Ghanaian youth. There is still relatively little information on how sexual behavior varies by age group, young people's access to sexual health services, or why young women choose to end their pregnancies at remarkably high rates.

Current adolescent and youth sexual health care, as well as advice proffered by mentors, faith leaders, and public servants, may not take what *is* known into account.[5] The frequency of teen partner change is one example. While reproductive health programs are often targeted at individuals in their late teens or early twenties, national survey data suggest that it is the youngest teens, from age 12 to 14, who change their partners most frequently.[6] Current reproductive health programs may target older teens because they believe that this age group has the greatest number of partners, or simply because they believe that younger adolescents should not be sexually active. Either way, the failure to educate and provide services to younger teens is a serious gap in the provision of resources for reproductive health.

Other critical areas for attention include the barriers to contraceptive access for young women in particular, and the high rates of abortion. Girls (on average) first become sexually active at about age 17, but do not marry until age 18 or 19.[7] Resistance to offering contraceptives to unmarried women and girls is persistent, as is reluctance to offer long-term contraceptives to women with lower numbers of children.[8] Though the withholding of service may be well intended, its effectiveness is questionable. In a country where abortion is illegal in most circumstances, pregnancy loss to girls age 15 to 19 is twice as high as in other age groups,[9] and more than 60 percent of the women electing to have an abortion are under the age of 30.[10] Withholding of reproductive health service or counsel might be aimed toward discouraging sexual activity; it may instead leave a significant number of young women feeling as if they have little choice but to terminate their pregnancies.

In considering faith-based organizations' potential contribution to improving reproductive health among young people in Ghana, considerations of perception, judgment, and fact must be central to the discussion. Diving under relatively positive national indicators, youth sexual health appears more precarious—and coping strategies less clear—than what we may have expected. Young Ghanaian men and women struggle to cope with sexual health issues in an environment where reproductive health programs may not take youth behavior or priorities into account; where the role of family and community in sexual health choices is poorly understood, and may not be addressed; and where access to information and contraceptives is poor, with potentially inaccurate information and information or contraceptives withheld. Reproductive health and family planning agencies have an important opportunity to draw faith organizations into the provision of service and counseling on reproductive health in Ghana. In bringing these organizations into reproductive health activities, it is critical that programs and education be designed based on the often uncomfortable realities of youth sexual health in Ghana rather than on the mythical way we wish them to be.

FIRST INITIATIVES IN REPRODUCTIVE HEALTH PROGRAMMING WITH FAITH ORGANIZATIONS

Christianity has the largest following in Ghana, with about 70 percent of the population considering themselves to be Christian. Islam and indigenous religions have significant followings as well. More pertinent than the distribution of faith is the frequency of participation: almost 8 in 10 Ghanaians participate in a religious program at least once a week.[11] Ghana's network of religious organizations is large and well structured, from the capital city down to the grassroots. Churches, mosques, and missions are scattered throughout Ghana, along with religiously affiliated schools, hospitals, and community centers.

In developing its 1996–2001 country strategy, the UNFPA saw an opportunity for building upon the broad influence of faith organizations in reaching out to young people beset by inadequate support for reproductive health. Based upon its deep knowledge of communities, as well as a long history of social service delivery, UNFPA was confident that faith organizations would be able to translate broad-brush national strategies into approaches that were specific to the needs of adolescents and young people in different areas and of different social classes, while fitting the religious doctrines of each organization.

There was hesitancy about creating a place at the decisionmaking table for religious institutions, though. Would their influence be positive, and could it be managed? Although there was no organized religious opposition to family planning in Ghana at the time, there were pockets of resistance and enduring misconceptions about the use of modern family planning methods, which were considered to be at odds with religious beliefs. There was also a lack of knowledge among religious organizations on issues concerning population, health, and development.

To test the potential for collaboration and dialogue, the UNFPA held awareness and advocacy training in the early 1990s for 3,840 religious leaders from eight religious organizations on reproductive health, including adolescent reproductive health and gender issues. Instead of hostility or mistrust, UNFPA and PPA officials found curiosity and enthusiasm for debate. Not whither reproductive health, but how.

Moving forward from this first, positive experience, UNFPA and PPA of Ghana approached four faith-based organizations—the Christian Council of Ghana, the Seventh Day Adventists, the Muslim Family Counseling Services, and the Salvation Army—about collaborating on a joint program to incorporate sexual and reproductive health, population, and family life education into their activities. These groups accepted and signed on to working toward three related reproductive health objectives: bringing the fertility rate down to 3 percent; increasing contraceptive prevalence to 50 percent; and reaching a population growth rate of 1.5 percent by 2020. As the program expanded, other faith-based organizations approached UNFPA and PPA, seeking to be included in the program.

PPA's recognition that religious organizations would need to work in ways that were consistent with the doctrines of their respective faiths was critical to the creation of this partnership. The religious organizations would work toward the three agreed-upon objectives, but would need the freedom to modify their outreach and service delivery as appropriate to their faith. With these caveats, the UNFPA, PPA, and their faith-based partner organizations developed a set of strategies that all were comfortable with.

Several strategies were of particular importance in developing the faith-based partnership. In a first instance, PPA elicited faith leaders' feedback on program principles and, once reviewed, elicited their commitment to them. Feedback played a material role in reorienting program principles, and a common sense role marked the approach to bringing future partners into the decisionmaking process rather than presenting them a preconceived project to implement. After program principles were established, PPA held a series of workshops for pastors, imams, peer educators, and staff of faith-based organizations to raise awareness about sexual health programs. Workshops were divided into those for opinion leaders, focusing on general awareness about reproductive health; and those for implementing organizations and peer educators, which did deeper training on reproductive health, service delivery, and informal education. The opportunity to extend programmatic reach through existing religious networks was superb; neglecting to provide the basic education necessary to promote and deliver the program would have been a wasted opportunity.

Once the program's building blocks of education and awareness raising were in place, the participating faith-based organizations provided two types of services: counseling, referrals, and distribution of nonprescription contraceptives to youth; and peer education across different youth categories. In several instances, existing youth centers were strengthened to provide reproductive health services more effectively. Unique in this partnership was the character of the peer education component. With nuanced knowledge of community and youth networks, faith-based organizations chose to train porters, truck pushers, youth groups, and pastors' wives in peer education. More typical peer education strategies, of choosing a given number of youth to train in a town or village, took a backseat to creative thinking about the youth least likely to access information through traditional channels and how to address those gaps.

Throughout the program, implementing organizations used monitoring and evaluation systems to catch bottlenecks in program implementation or to identify particularly effective services. Restrategizing was essential to making these programs attractive to youth, and ideas drawn from deep local knowledge were as relevant as those developed through rigorous testing and methodological approaches.

STEPS FORWARD FOR FAITH-BASED COLLABORATIONS

While there are limited data so far on program impact, the experience both suggests significant conclusions and raises important questions that have broader applicability for agencies seeking to draw faith-based groups into program activities.

The partnership has illustrated that "taking the plunge" is often the most difficult part of partnering between secular and nonsecular organizations. There were certainly areas in which the UNFPA, PPA, and faith organizations did not agree. Most of the disagreement, however, was due to faith organizations' lower level of knowledge of reproductive health issues and the lack of prior thinking about how and whether different religious doctrines were compatible with modern reproductive health teachings. Initially, there was considerable apprehension about what faith leaders' reactions to sexual health training might be: how to discuss sexual activity subtly, but discuss youth sexual behavior accurately nevertheless.

Would different religious doctrines be compatible with modern reproductive health teachings? The apprehension was healthy, but proved to be unwarranted. After the project was launched, PPA's strong work with the first four faith organizations sparked the interest of other religious groups; 11 more groups joined the program through 2002. Training for faith leaders now covers reproductive health topics as a matter of course. As a result, faith leaders' general knowledge about reproductive health increased. Leaders best positioned to shift public opinion about sex are now armed with a better understanding of, and more information on, the importance of reproductive health.

This project allowed the UNFPA and PPA to tap into a mightily influential set of institutions in Ghana, enabling these agencies to promote sexual health messages more effectively. Faith organizations, for their part, enjoyed significant benefits from the program. Organizations are continuing to improve their formal management and budgeting skills by dint of project participation, thanks to specific training workshops on project preparation and financial management. They have expanded the scope of activities that they undertake to include service delivery, peer education, educational materials development, livelihood skills training programs, outreach, research, monitoring, and evaluation. Complemented by affiliation with the UNFPA–PPA program, this capacity building has enabled several of these organizations to attract funding for other initiatives.

The program allowed religious organizations to attract greater numbers of congregants as well. By extending their work into reproductive health, faith institutions were able to broaden their appeal. They illustrated that they were willing to address issues important to many people, but with which many faith institutions are not comfortable.

This program—and the broader collaboration with faith organizations that came before it—gave UNFPA and PPA of Ghana the opportunity to test collaboration with faith organizations. The program's success has brought benefits for all partners: for UNFPA and PPA, to promote reproductive health messages within resistant faith communities; and more so, for faith organizations, who were able to improve their skills and broaden the reach of their work through their action within this project.

LOOKING AHEAD

The UNFPA and PPA's first foray into collaboration with faith-based organizations has been soundly positive. New areas of common ground were established (or discovered), and awareness heightened about the negative effect of misperceptions in guiding young people's sexual health choices and services offered.

In future iterations of this project, as well as those of other countries or agencies, continued focus on quality sexual health programming will be critical. Programs might focus more closely on different dimensions of youth reproductive health programming—is sexual health programming still targeting older teens when younger teens have the greatest number of sexual partners and protect themselves the least? Is reproductive health programming developing activities based on how we *wish* teens would act, or acknowledging their behavior and responding to it? Should focus on formal health providers be increased, or should we provide more information to the parents, teachers, and other mentors who appear to provide teens the bulk of their information about reproductive health? Can or should we create differentiated sexual health strategies for teens with more sexual partners and for those beginning to create a long-lasting union?

Outreach efforts could be deepened as well, with a particular focus on gender awareness, outreach to charismatic churches, and outreach to traditional leaders. The structure and teachings of religious organizations tend to be male-oriented and hierarchical: greater gender-sensitive training can help faith-based organizations to offer more appropriate services, or services of a more appropriate style, to young women and girls. Both genders need to be sensitized to bearing responsibility for negotiating safer sexual relations.

A second area of focus is outreach to charismatic churches. Charismatic churches are using lively, spirited methods to reach out to youth, but often encourage young people to rely on prayer instead of medical consultation to cure what ails them. Those with HIV are particularly likely to gravitate toward the charismatics, often turning to treatment or palliative care too late. Effectively engaging charismatic churches around reproductive health issues, and HIV/AIDS in particular, will be extremely important.

Finally, greater outreach to traditional leaders could deepen the reach of reproductive health programs. Ghana has a strong, recognized traditional hierarchy, with both a chief and a queen mother (supporter of women's issues) at the village level. These figures can effectively influence the population and provide additional information on reproductive health. This is particularly true in regions where traditional leaders already support initiatives to improve the economic and social life of the region. The Mano Krobo Queen Mothers Association in eastern Ghana, for example, works on HIV/AIDS projects, provides training on income-generating activities to young women, and offers assistance to children orphaned by AIDS. Tapping into indigenous networks may be enormously helpful in rooting programs in local context, increasing their longevity and effect.

The crux of the relationship between the UNFPA, the PPA of Ghana, and the participating faith organizations has been basic trust between partners, and a willingness to work together on an even footing. Though not as frequent as it could be, this type of collaboration seems fairly logical in reproductive health. Religious organizations may have defined positions on, or preconceptions about, reproductive health. Engaging these organizations can dispel misunderstanding on both sides; identifying the areas of common ground for moving forward makes good sense.

NOTES

1. Macro International n.d.
2. World Bank 2003.
3. UNAIDS 2002.
4. UNAIDS 2002, pp. 190–201.
5. See, for example, Ahiadeke 2001; Henry and Fayorsey 2002; or Stanback and Twum-Baah 2001.
6. Karim and others 2003.
7. Macro International n.d.
8. Stanback and Twum-Baah 2001.
9. Macro International n.d.

10. Ahiadeke 2001.

11. PPA of Ghana 2001 survey.

REFERENCES

Ahiadeke, Clement. 2001. "Incidence of Induced Abortion in Southern Ghana." *International Family Planning Perspectives* (27)2:96–101, 108.

Henry, Rebecca, and Clare Fayorsey. 2002. "Coping with Pregnancy Experiences of Adolescents in Ga Mashi Accra." Macro: Processed.

Karim, Ali Mehryar, Robert J. Magnani, Gwendolyn T. Morgan, and Katherine C. Bond. 2003. "Reproductive Health Risk and Protective Factors Among Unmarried Youth in Ghana." *International Family Planning Perspectives* (29)1:14–24.

Macro International. n.d. "Ghana Demographic and Health Surveys." Available at www.measuredhs.com

PPA (Planned Parenthood Association of Ghana). 2001. 2001 Survey. Accra, Ghana.

Stanback, John, and K. A. Twum-Baah. 2001. "Why Do Family Planning Providers Restrict Access to Services? An Examination in Ghana." *International Family Planning Perspectives* (27)1:37–41.

UNAIDS (Joint United Nations Programme on HIV/AIDS). 2002. "Report on the Global HIV-AIDS Epidemic." Geneva.

World Bank. 2003. "Country at a Glance Tables." Washington, D.C.

World Health Organization. 2004. "Epidemiological Fact Sheet on HIV/AIDS and Sexually Transmitted Infections." http://www.who.int/globalatlas/pdffactory/HIV/report. Accessed May 14, 2004.

13

Fighting Female Genital Cutting

Religious and Traditional Leaders' Roles in Combating Genital Cutting in Senegal and Uganda

Sometimes called *kene-kene* or *khitan*, female genital cutting (FGC) has been practiced on an estimated 130 million women and girls living today, with an additional 2 million at risk of undergoing the procedure each year.[1] FGC is practiced almost exclusively in Africa and the Middle East. Mediation between the active international campaign aiming to eliminate the practice, and the far more traditional individuals and communities who can decide to cease the cutting of girls, has been critical to successful eradication efforts.

The rationale for eliminating FGC is clear—the UNFPA qualifies the practice as "unnecessary bodily mutilation"—and its practice is condemned by numerous international conventions. The theoretical argument for its elimination is also quite solid. In what is considered the primary piece of scholarship on FGC, sociologist Gerry Mackie compared FGC today to foot binding in nineteenth-century China. Mackie traced the origin of both practices to the desire of elite men to control the fidelity of women in polygynous societies (where men may have several spouses or mates). The practices soon spread to lower-class men, and eventually became a prerequisite for all women of marriageable age. In the case of foot binding, however, the practice was eliminated long ago, within a generation. Eradication efforts centered on publicity about its harmful physical effects, international campaigning against the practice, and, most critically, parental refusal to submit their daughters to the practice or to allow their sons to marry women with bound feet. Given the similarities between the factors driving foot binding in China and FGC today, Mackie argued that FGC could be quickly eradicated, as well.[2]

Eliminating FGC may appear simple in logic, but the depth and historic reach of the practice have led to a common view that it represents an important and fundamental part of a culture. Many have argued that the practice is tied to religious dictates, though enlightened faith leaders and scholars have consistently disassociated the practice from religious roots or precepts (an illustration of the complexities of perception versus realities). Initial campaigns aimed at stopping FGC through international advocacy resulted in frustration and resentment, with traditional leaders and practitioners decrying western judgment of a fundamentally nonwestern phenomenon. A portion of practitioners and traditional leaders have cited the centrality of FGC to their cultures, which in their minds are often under threat. Other opinion leaders have acknowledged the practice's physical harm, but expressed concern that working to eradicate this traditional practice would lead to ever more clamor to change other culture-based practices and an eventual weakening of the culture in which they are performed. Embedded in work to abolish FGC, then, is an enormous tension between the elimination of a practice harmful to women, and the perception that the primary means of eradication— campaigns led by international groups or national elites—is a proxy for external assault upon strong, valuable, but threatened, cultures.

Two initiatives, in Senegal and in Uganda, have successfully mediated this tense landscape, through subtle and modest support of local efforts to eliminate FGC. Critical to both examples of success was that they followed or accompanied, rather than led, campaigns for eradication of FGC. Though external support was essential in providing information, organizational support, and a degree of financial resources, the eradication campaigns were uniquely locally grown. Education and discussion among equals fostered a consensus for elimination of FGC, all the stronger for having been contested, that arose organically from within communities and regions.

LEADERSHIP OF THE WOMEN OF MALICOUNDA BAMBARA, SENEGAL

In Senegal's Thiès region, the NGO Tostan had run adult nonformal education programs since the early 1900s. The terrain was familiar to Tostan. Tostan's head, Molly Melching, had begun testing different adult nonformal education approaches in the area in the early 1980s, building a strong education approach and materials, and a rich understanding of this part of Senegal.

In July 1996, Tostan introduced an adult nonformal education curriculum on women's health, and included several modules on FGC. In the first appearance of religion in this story, the American Jewish Women's Committee had supported the development of these modules. By September 1996, women of the village of Malicounda Bambara had decided that they wanted to end FGC. From October 1996 to May 1997, the women led a campaign to end the practice, beginning with their husbands and extending to religious leaders, other women, and the village chief. In June 1997, Tostan staff discovered that there had been no cutting in the village that year. On July 31, 1997, 20 Senegalese journalists came to Malicounda Bambara to hear women there make a public declaration for the end of FGC in their village.

A critical leap, from the eradication of FGC in Malicounda Bambara to its eradication in other Senegalese villages and regions, came with the involvement of Imam Demba Diawara. Diawara was invited to hear women's testimony about the harmful effects of cutting in Malicounda Bambara, discussion of which had been virtually taboo. For the first time, FGC became very real, and Diawara was shaken not only by the women's accounting of the practice but also by their steadfast and reasoned determination to end it. In a first step, he walked to 10 neighboring villages to discuss with religious and traditional leaders putting an end to cutting. In February 1998, eight months after the Malicounda Bambara declaration, leaders of 13 villages in the Thiès region issued the

Diabougou Declaration, publicly committing to abandonment of FGC. Diawara continued his advocacy with traditional and religious leaders throughout the region, and then in other Senegalese regions. By late 1998, religious leaders throughout Senegal had begun to support elimination of FGC, and the Senegalese parliament passed a law officially abolishing FGC in 1999. In early 2004 an estimated 1,140 communities have publicly abandoned FGC in Senegal and Burkina Faso after participating in Tostan education programs or community organizing thereafter.[3]

THE SABINY ELDERS AND PROJECT REACH IN UGANDA

While the Tostan example has enjoyed an extremely high profile, with visits by then-President Clinton and his wife, Hillary Rodham Clinton, the example is not unique. The work of Uganda's Sabiny Elders Association, supported by the United Nations Population Fund (UNFPA), offers another thought-provoking model. In Uganda, about 1 in 20 women and girls have undergone FGC.[4] Through the early 1990s, the Sabiny people of eastern Uganda felt so strongly about FGC that it was to all intents and purposes mandatory for all girls who came from the area. The Ugandan government had discouraged the practice, but early efforts to eradicate FGC had met with considerable local resistance.

In 1992, the Sabiny people formed an Elders Association to review the Sabiny traditions systematically and assess what could be adapted or abandoned, given the gradual, increasing awareness of the social and economic price of maintaining various traditions. Sabiny elders decided that FGC, though a practice of many years' standing, should be discarded. The Elders Association led the Sabiny people in changing position, from forcefully endorsing the practice to staunchly advocating for its elimination.

This dramatic shift was supported, and in many respects inspired, by a partnership between the Sabiny Elders Association and a national NGO, Reproductive, Educative and Community Health Program (REACH), which received support from the UNFPA. Project REACH began its work in 1996, helping the Sabiny Elders Association to address the negative effects of FGC without laying blame for the practice, which would only have further entrenched practitioners' and populations' support for it. By 1998, the chairman of the Elders Association, G.W. Cheborian, reported that the Sabiny leadership's strong support for elimination of the practice, combined with Project REACH's diligent and culturally sensitive outreach program, had resulted in a 36 percent reduction of the practice.

Critical in this outreach effort was the Elder Association's desire to review their people's traditional practices, and UNFPA's ability to build upon that first initiative. In recognition of the work of Mr. Cheborian and the Sabiny Elders Association, the UNFPA granted the Elders Association a Population Award in 1998.

CONCLUDING THOUGHTS

Several themes were central to both the Senegalese and Ugandan campaigns for eradication of FGC. The first was the importance of approaches born of communities' own initiative. With massive international publicity against FGC, lines of resistance had been drawn, and loyalty to rich culture and centuries-old tradition shored up. Only locally born efforts could diffuse the frustration at, and perceived threat presented by, externally driven change. The second was the ability to allow the campaigns to grow naturally, without the onslaught of heavy external funding or quick efforts to grow campaigns in size and reach. Supplanting fragile but determined local structures with crippling external support would have weakened local organizations' and peoples' roles as agents of change. Campaigns would be turned into externally driven efforts once again, rather than those identified with local values and commitment, and resentment might have deepened still further. The third theme was making the source of FGC—religious and traditional structures—the source of its elimination. Great respect and authority is reserved for religious and traditional leaders in many societies, including those presented in this case. They, like many people throughout the world with relative power and discretion, are reluctant to change their minds unless they have reasoned through the problem themselves. Once they were able to do this, in Uganda during review of the Sabiny people's traditions and in Senegal after commitment from local women and persuasion by, initially, just one religious leader, religious and traditional figures were extremely effective in mobilizing support for eradication of FGC. They brought their intimate knowledge of the arguments for FGC, a deep understanding of the contours of their culture, and the reverence of their people to bear in campaigning to eradicate FGC.

NOTES

1. www.unfpa.org/gender/faq_fgc.htm
2. Mackie 1996.
3. www.tostan.org
4. www.unfpa.org/gender/faq_app01.htm.

REFERENCE

Mackie, Gerry. 1996. "Ending Foot-binding and Infibulation: A Conventional Account." *The American Sociological Review* (61)6:999–1004.

CHAPTER 14

Educating Successful Leaders for Successful Latin American Societies

Jesuit Education and the Centro Magis

L ittle generates greater frustration than the all-too-common phe-nomenon of a hard-gained graduation from school followed by successive failures to land a decent job or energies dissipated in unproductive work. Just as frustrating, many employers find graduates poorly prepared to cope with the challenges of the "real" world. In common social organization, educational institutions stand at a remove from business, social entrepreneurship, and political leadership, with large disconnects among them. This chapter recounts and explores the lessons from a creative partnership involving business principles, a catalytic philanthropic venture built on a belief that entrepreneurial talents are critical for social domains, and the Jesuit educational networks working in Latin America. This partnership has set out to forge stronger links between education systems and the societies that their graduates will enter. It is a young venture, but it presents important challenges and offers an exciting potential to trace new paths to address central issues for our times.

The case study of Fe y Alegría was undertaken in close partnership with the AVINA Foundation and Centro Magis, by Katherine Marshall. Chris Dragasiic, World Bank intern, prepared an early draft on Fe y Alegría.

This chapter tells three stories, with an onion-like quality of overlap and progression. It begins with the history of the Fe y Alegría movement, an extraordinary educational system that has grown from a single classroom started in a Caracas slum 50 years ago by a Jesuit priest. Today a Federation of Fe y Alegría movements promises and demands high-quality education in many of Latin America's poorest communities, working in 14 countries. Fe y Alegría offers a remarkable example of durable, creative, and focused partnerships in its long-standing relationships with the communities it serves and a wide range of public sector institutions throughout Latin America.

The second layer of the story is the initiative of the AVINA Foundation (founded in 1995 by Swiss entrepreneur Stephan Schmidheiny) to breach its policy of supporting only secular institutions and to enter into dialogue with the Jesuit Order about the links between educational and social challenges facing Latin America. This has led to a strong alliance and continuing program of action.

The resulting third layer is the Centro Magis, a small entity based at the Universidad Católica Andrés Bello in Venezuela, which works as a joint venture between the AVINA Foundation and the Jesuit education system. Its aim is to bring the "best of business" to work together with the historical commitment and inspiration reflected in Jesuit education and social work, all in the interests of progressing toward a more just and prosperous society. Returning to the starting point, one of its central objectives is to build on and extend the lessons of Fe y Alegría as a positive force for social entrepreneurship and leadership in Latin America.

WHERE THE ASPHALT ENDS, FE Y ALEGRÍA BEGINS

The Jesuit Fe y Alegría (Faith and Joy) movement provides basic education to nearly 1 million children in poor communities in 15 Latin American countries. Its motto highlights its purpose and philosophy: "Where the asphalt road ends, where there is no water or electricity, Fe y Alegría begins."

Although Fe y Alegría's thousands of centers teach many of the region's most vulnerable children, the organization reaches beyond basic education to encompass all facets of the communities in which it works. Local schools become neighborhood centers, offering services from preschool to carpentry training to bilingual adult literacy lessons by radio. The schools are open to all, regardless of religious affiliation. Fe y Alegría estimates that its programs reach more than 6 million people directly or indirectly. In each country, Fe y Alegría has established a partnership with government authorities, who normally pay teacher salaries, so that the system operates as a part of the national education system, with a special focus on reaching those areas that are in most need of attention.

Fe y Alegría is decentralized, with local centers and regional and national affiliates functioning independently. The movement employed about 31,000 people in 2002, of whom about 97 percent were lay; religiously affiliated employees represented a variety of religious orders. What holds the movement together is a set of shared principles, concerns, objectives, and projects.

History

> *"Although it makes me blush to say it, the deepest roots of Fe y Alegría lie in my capacity to dream while awake."*
>
> —José María Vélaz[1]

Fe y Alegría is the fruit of the inspiration and hard work of Father José María Vélaz, a Spaniard born in Chile in 1910 and educated largely in Jesuit schools in Spain. In 1936, after he completed his first round of university studies (just on the eve of the Spanish Civil War), Vélaz returned to South America to a teaching post at the Colegio San Ignacio de Caracas in Venezuela. After theological studies in Spain, Father Vélaz returned to the Colegio San Ignacio in what had become his adopted homeland. Here, his interest in the issues of poverty crystallized, and the new Father Vélaz set out to orient the congregation's activities toward the marginalized suburbs of the Venezuelan capital.

As rector of the Colegio San José in the Andean city of Mérida, Father Vélaz started a night school for workers and their children in 1948. The program had 104 students by the end of the first year and grew to 400 by the time Father Vélaz left in 1954. He took with him a deep conviction that the unmet demand for education among the working class was great.

In Caracas, Father Vélaz taught at the Universidad Andrés Bello, and he and a group of students began regular weekend visits to the poor Gato

Negro neighborhood to celebrate mass and first communions and give catechism lessons. The group's members soon won over the residents of this shantytown with their contagious energy and lack of a political message. The university students, meanwhile, became convinced that a "terrible ignorance" lay at the core of the neighborhood's grinding poverty.

Fe y Alegría began simply when a bricklayer, Abrahán Reyes, offered his home to Father Vélaz as a school. The first day after the announcement "School. Male children admitted" went up, 100 boys filled the floor of their first classroom. A few days later 75 girls began classes in a separate room. The children soon carried their own cement blocks to the school for seats—the school's first improvement project. The first three teachers, Diana, Carmen, and Isabel, were 15-year-old neighborhood girls who had completed sixth grade. School was held six days a week to allow frequent contact between the teachers and university students. The new school received its initial income when a student donated a set of earrings for auction—the first of Fe y Alegría's traditional annual raffles.

The movement expanded rapidly, responding to active demand, though there was no blueprint, certainly no notion at the time of the movement Fe y Alegría would become. In 1955 Father Vélaz, with help from his students, founded a vocational school near the university, the Instituto Técnico Laboral, thereby completing Fe y Alegría's "trilogy of ambitions": schools for children; medical, moral, and recreational assistance for youngsters; and efficient help for workers.[2] The school taught a two-year course in each of nine trades and soon enrolled 200 students. The organizers began to plan a program to create schools in popular neighborhoods around Caracas.

As Fe y Alegría expanded, it hired a core professional staff that could dedicate its energy full time to the movement, while volunteers and university students continued to provide support. A board of directors was formed to help guide the movement, freeing Vélaz—whose deep investment in Fe y Alegría and lack of consultation with his Jesuit superiors had angered some at the university—to work full time on what was termed popular education.

Within a few years, the Jesuit Order formally recognized Fe y Alegría and registered it as a nonprofit organization, which eventually became Fe y Alegría del Oriente de Venezuela, authorized to open centers in nine states and two territories. By 1963 the movement encompassed enough schools to celebrate a first national Fe y Alegría convention, with representatives from more than 20 neighborhood schools. An estimated 3 of every 2,000 Venezuelan students were already enrolled in Fe y Alegría schools.

Not everything went smoothly. Mere mention of Fe y Alegría's work was enough to set off a tumultuous session in the Venezuelan Senate because of fears that it was linked with leftist ideologies. Such controversy foreshadowed the complicated relationship the movement would have with Latin American governments over the ensuing decades. The relationship between Fe y Alegría and the Society of Jesus (Jesuits) was also complex and often tense; it was not until 1968 that Jesuit support for its affiliated movement became unambiguous.

The Fe y Alegría educational movement, in large part inspired by Father Vélaz's reputation, soon expanded beyond Venezuela. The first discussions trace back to 1964, when both the Archbishop of El Salvador and the head of the Jesuit Province of Bolivia sought Fe y Alegría schools in their countries. The first school outside Venezuela opened in Barrio Luluncoto, Quito, Ecuador, in October 1964, soon followed by a second in Panama in April 1965, and then five schools in Lima, Peru, in 1967. Father Vélaz had preliminary meetings in Colombia in 1967 and Paraguay in 1968. The Jesuits decided to start Fe y Alegría programs in El Salvador and Nicaragua in 1968, and by 1969 had opened three schools in El Salvador, while Colombia formally established its branch of the movement in 1971. The Third Fe y Alegría Congress and International Assembly, held in Lima in 1972, hosted delegates from seven countries and observers from Mexico. Guatemala joined the movement in 1975, Brazil in 1980, the Dominican Republic in 1990, and Paraguay in 1992.

With Fe y Alegría's rapid expansion outside Venezuela and the explosion of schools within the country, the movement inevitably became less tied to a single individual. Father Vélaz welcomed this shift: "If I have been able to inspire the creative utopia in many… it is logical that it moves away from me following its own will and its own inspiration."[3] The first international convention in Quito agreed on new directions for the movement, renewed leadership, and a fundamental decentralization of executive positions. Vélaz did not attend, and in 1975, when the new head of the Jesuit Order in the Province of Venezuela recommended a change in leadership, he retired from the general directorship, although he remained very active in the organization until the end of his life.

During Vélaz's semi-retirement, progress on one of his pet projects—radio education—continued apace. Modeled on successful programs in Palmas de Gran Canarian, Spain, and La Vega, Dominican Republic, the Instituto Radiofónico Fe y Alegría started broadcasts from Maracaibo in August 1975, and began transmitting lessons from Caracas by October. Similar distance-learning programs quickly spread throughout the movement's member countries.

Another important and pioneering direction that Fe y Alegría took in the 1970s was the development of integrated education, and many of its schools served as models for programs elsewhere. A first example was the Colegio Timoteo Aguirre Pe in Venezuela, which included, in addition to the school, an adjacent handicraft school, a training and recreational center, a school for popular tourism, a recreational forested park, an agro-livestock-forestry school, and a program to train people to teach trade skills.

In 1984, Father Vélaz launched a next great adventure in agricultural technical education. What was termed an "experiment in action education with the plains population in Barinas"[4] was embodied in the Agro-Livestock-Forestry Institute of San Ignacio del Masparro, conceived as a residential school for 500 students. Produce and animals raised at the school would help feed students and professors. Vélaz believed that it would "train a new generation of modern plains peasants"[5] and serve as the first in a chain of rural schools. Fe y Alegría's founder, however, did not live to see his last project fulfilled. José María Vélaz died on July 18, 1985, just as first-phase plans were complete and students had begun to enroll in the new institute. Eight years after Father Vélaz's death a diverse group of missionaries, lay professors, and foreign volunteers completed the San Ignacio del Masparro Institute, and by 1994 more than 200 children lived and learned at the school.

Other agricultural technical schools followed the same model, while the P. Roman Agro-Livestock Indigenous Center offered a new variation. Similar schools were created, inspiring a first National Meeting of Indigenous Teachers in Venezuela in 1992. The Fe y Alegría Latin American Radiophonic Institute was created in 1989 to unite the movement's distance-learning programs; these have educated hundreds of thousands of adults throughout Latin America.

Teacher training became an increasingly central activity. Reflecting the philosophy that Fe y Alegría's training responsibility includes public school-teachers, the Father Joaquín Training Centers, founded in three cities in Venezuela between 1991 and 1996, train teachers who are to be "capable of thinking about the country and education from a popular perspective."[6] In Venezuela, meanwhile, Fe y Alegría opened the Instituto Universitario Jesús Obrero, the only institute of higher learning in a region of more than 800,000 people. The university initially offered courses of study in computer science, accounting, and preschool education, among other subjects.

Over the last 5 to 10 years, the organization has shifted from relying on staff with a primary interest in social action to a greater reliance on leaders and staff trained in education, sociology, and psychology, and with experience in NGO management. This shift has meant greater dependence on lay people throughout the organization. In 2000, to celebrate the 45th anniversary of its founding and to reflect on its mission in a changing context, Fe y Alegría published a global plan that incorporates five objectives, including improving and expanding Fe y Alegría programs and helping formulate and influence national, regional, and international public policy.

As Father Vélaz had hoped, his movement swelled from a spark to a fire. After Vélaz's death, the International Fe y Alegría Federation—formally registered in Cochabamba, Bolivia, in 1986—emerged as a formal link among the programs in each country. Today, the movement, which has been based in the Dominican Republic since 2003, holds regular international congresses and helps to formalize and centralize the flow of people and funds among Fe y Alegría programs throughout Latin America.

The appendix to this chapter provides a more detailed description of Fe y Alegría's operations today.

AVINA FOUNDATION PARTNERSHIP WITH THE JESUIT ORDER

"There can be no successful companies in failed societies."
—Stephan Schmidheiny 2003[7]

The Fe y Alegría movement represents an important if not widely sung part of education systems in the 14 Latin American countries where it operates. It has stood the test of time, survived many difficult episodes in national history, and educated many millions of citizens. The question, though, is whether it could do more, whether it could do it better, and whether others could learn and benefit from the Fe y Alegría experience. Even within the educational system led by the Jesuit Order, there are questions as to whether there is real synergy, for example, between primary schools of Fe y Alegría and Jesuit-run universities and secondary schools, as the Fe y Alegría movement emerged from quite distinct historical roots than other Jesuit educational institutions.

These questions about the potential for wider and deeper impact prompted an unusual dialogue beginning in the late 1990s that engaged the AVINA Foundation and the Jesuit Order, in Latin America and worldwide.

Stephan Schmidheiny, a highly successful Swiss business leader, came to focus on the Jesuit education system through his interest in social entrepreneurship. He created a philanthropic institution in 1995, the AVINA Foundation, whose goal is to establish partnerships in Latin America with individuals "imbued with the pioneering spirit." He was "especially interested in initiatives committed to equal opportunities, democratic processes, education, training programs, nature preservation, and eco-efficiency".[8] As he describes the challenge, "I... tried to work simultaneously in two activities that are usually done by different kinds of people" (business leaders and agents of social change).[9] He was setting out to pioneer a new model of philanthropy, inspired by an entrepreneurial spirit, using tools that had been successful in his business life.

Today, one of AVINA's major strategic initiatives is its partnership with the Jesuit Order to build and strengthen the Jesuit education system as a vehicle for developing leadership and promoting social change. This called from the outset for a fresh look at starting assumptions, as the AVINA Foundation's mission statement indicated that it would not be involved with either political or religious organizations. But the work of the Jesuit Order—in technical universities, in the Fe y Alegría system, and in its philosophy and approach to the challenges for social change in Latin America—so impressed Schmidheiny that he altered course. The concept of the partnership with the Jesuit Order (in common with AVINA's operating philosophy) is that of investing in leaders, and investing as a stakeholder with a long time horizon, thus a commitment to a set of common goals. The AVINA Foundation program in Latin America, and specifically in its partnership with the Jesuit Order, focuses on project support for various types of modernization, technological improvement, knowledge management, and management development. The underlying objective, though, is to engage in a mutual learning and development process that has in its sights the social welfare of Latin America and the powerful links that exist between education, social change, and leadership.

CENTRO MAGIS: INVESTING IN PARTNERSHIPS

In developing AVINA's strategic program of support with the Jesuit Order, the partners agreed to create a joint entity. This is the Centro Magis (Magis, the Latin word for excellence, suggests a striving for continuous improvement and quality), which is based at the Universidad Católica Andrés Bello in Caracas, Venezuela, led and inspired by Father Luis Ugalde, rector of the university. An important, and all too rare, feature of the partnership is AVINA's commitment of long-term financial support to the Centro Magis, with a tentative envelope of some $US 10 million a year over at least 10 years. A steering group including leaders from both the AVINA Foundation and the Jesuit education system provide guidance. Their practice is to meet regularly for in-depth strategic reflections both on the specifics of program content and progress, and on overall social and business challenges in the region.

Centro Magis is developing a set of partnerships with the Jesuit education institutions, starting from the Federation of Fe y Alegría, and extending to all parts of the education system reached by the Jesuit Order. It works through the broader Jesuit education system that includes AUSJAL (Asociación de Universidades Confiades a la Comparia de Jesús en America Latina; the network of 29 Jesuit-linked universities across Latin America), the renowned Jesuit secondary school system, and a range of country-specific social works engaging the Jesuit Order.

Centro Magis is looking to cutting-edge technology ("the best of business") to develop an information base that will allow analysis of Fe y Alegría's strengths and weaknesses and financial management, and facilitate exchange of best practices. A first stage has been the development of information technology systems, which were particularly lacking in the Fe y Alegría system. Another major initial thrust has been a series of strategic planning exercises, including rigorous financial management reviews.

Lessons from the Centro Magis experience include the following:

- Fundamental departures from traditional arrangements, including formal policies, in crafting new types of partnerships: AVINA changed policies to engage directly with a faith institution and has in many different ways brought unconventional partners from business and social realms together in working and creative relationships.
- Long-term vision of change, with the partnership explicitly envisaging a long-term and sustained investment that entails mutual responsibilities and long-term financial and personal engagement.
- Building on the strengths of the Fe y Alegría education movement and the centuries-long Jesuit experience in education in seeking to bring quality and relevant education within the reach of all citizens.
- New concepts of what constitutes the lessons of business and entrepreneurial experience.
- Highlighting the vital role of faith institutions in critical areas for poverty alleviation and attainment of the Millennium Development Goals, insofar as the Jesuit education movement is a leading force in extending education in the poorest areas of Latin America and sustaining quality education under the most demanding educational challenges.

Challenges include bringing the Centro Magis and Fe y Alegría experience more directly to bear in sector and national poverty strategic reflection and action.

APPENDIX. FE Y ALEGRÍA OPERATIONS

The first step to creation of a Fe y Alegría school is a request by the community to Fe y Alegría to open a new center in their neighborhood. If Fe y Alegría agrees, classes begin immediately, even if no appropriate facilities are available. The community donates the land where the center will be built, labor for construction, and often basic materials like bricks. Fe y Alegría, in turn, submits a proposal for donor funding to finance the remaining construction costs.

After the school is built, the community remains actively involved in its operation. Where possible, teachers are chosen from the surrounding area, and members of the religious order that manages the school live in the community. Depending on the type of center built, the community may be responsible for supplying meals to the enrolled students. Lessons are centered on the history and reality of the community, while skills that are applicable in the neighborhood are taught in school. Community members participate in school celebrations, and the students become part of community festivals. The school functions as a community center serving all residents of the neighborhood.

Governance and Organization

At the heart of Fe y Alegría's way of working lies a highly decentralized mode of organization. Individual Fe y Alegría centers have considerable autonomy. Neighborhood religious congregations manage local schools, and a school's director is usually responsible for developing a budget and managing finances in cooperation with the school's parents. Directors hire personnel and coordinate volunteers and design programs that engage parents. Each director is also responsible for the center's pedagogical vision and for designing programs and encouraging innovations that reflect this vision and the neighborhoods served.

An independent national Fe y Alegría office operates as a private nonprofit entity in each country. The national offices train teachers and administrators, develop new projects, manage systemwide finances, obtain accreditation, and represent Fe y Alegría in negotiations with central governments. A project department in each national office works closely with regional offices and individual centers to profile needs, design projects, identify national and international agencies that can provide economic support, monitor project implementation, and prepare reports for financiers. National offices also develop much of the material for teacher training, which the movement regards as extremely important, but employees also sometimes attend outside training sessions. One study of four countries found that annual training days per teacher ranged from an average of 3.4 in Peru to 42.8 in Guatemala.[10]

An office in Spain focuses on fund-raising and coordinates Spanish volunteers who seek to work at Latin American Fe y Alegría centers. Many of these volunteers are young professionals, while others arrive through the conscientious objectors program, which allows youth to perform social work rather than military service.

The Fe y Alegría International Federation oversees joint projects among member countries, shares information and experiences, and expands the movement into new countries. A general assembly composed of the national directors, the federation's general coordinator, members of the board of directors, a representative from each country, and the president of the Provincial Conference of the Latin American Society of Jesus holds ultimate authority for the movement.

Finances

National governments normally pay salaries of Fe y Alegría teachers; the movement finances all other costs, including administrative salaries, materials, and infrastructure, by other means. Most national offices raise funds for operating expenses through annual raffles. Communities also often provide direct support, including food and supplies, to local Fe y Alegría schools. In many cases, small student fees like those commonly in force in many public schools help cover the cost of educational materials.

The national program offices encourage staff at all levels to submit project proposals, which they elaborate before forwarding them to Madrid, which in turn submits them to donors for approval and funding. The Spain office has branches in several large cities across Spain and works closely with national agencies as well as provincial and local governments in Spain to obtain funding. Fe y Alegría is eligible for funding from the Spanish government under a new law limiting state financing to organizations with several years of experience in financing and managing projects.

Fe y Alegría receives aid from the European Union as well as Canada, the Netherlands, and Sweden. Supporters include foreign national, provincial, and local governments, and numerous NGOs. In El Salvador, for example, some 40 percent of the national movement's funding comes from Spanish sources, another 40 percent from other countries, and 20 percent from the El Salvador government.

Fe y Alegría programs are very cost-effective for national governments. Guatemala, for example, invested an average of US$136 per public school student in 1995, but contributed only US$95 for each Fe y Alegría student, while outside funding brought the total expenditures on each Fe y Alegría student to US$171. In Paraguay, per student investment in public schools averaged US$133, but the government spent only US$119 on each Fe y Alegría student while the investment per Fe y Alegría child totaled US$168. Thus, annual government savings were expected to be more than US$4.9 million in Guatemala and US$1.5 million in Paraguay in 2004.[11]

Relationships with Governments and the Jesuit Order

Relations between Fe y Alegría and national governments are generally quite good. Some Fe y Alegría training programs admit public school teachers, reflecting the movement's commitment to strengthening each country's educational system. In Venezuela, the National Library has sought a strategic alliance with Fe y Alegría, and the Ministry of Education considered transferring some state schools to be managed by the movement under a 20-year contract, though this plan provoked protests because of what was seen as privatization and a lack of community consultation. Still, such alliances could presage greater integration between the public sector and Fe y Alegría.

Relations between the national offices and Latin American governments were not always so strong. Throughout the 1960s, 1970s, and 1980s, as military governments and dictators assumed power in most Latin American states and human rights abuses were all too common, Jesuits often found themselves opposing these governments. Even when a government was favorable, state financing often did not cover the full cost of teachers' salaries. With the change in political climate and growing reputation of Fe y Alegría, these problems have faded. However, Fe y Alegría's role in influencing national education policy is a source of debate and tension in some countries, with some arguing that, as a faith-driven organization, the movement should maintain its distinction from the government, while others see benefits in greater engagement in dialogue and common action.

The relationship between the Jesuit Order and Fe y Alegría appears to be entering a new era. Early in its history, the movement's autonomy provoked tension within the order, and attempts by the head of the Jesuits in Venezuela province to expand control over Fe y Alegría may have prompted the semi-retirement of Father Vélaz. Since the mid-1980s, though, relations between Fe y Alegría and the leadership of the order have been much more harmonious. A 1998 speech in Venezuela by Father Peter-Hans Kolvenbach, general superior of the Society of Jesus, affirmed that "in this great apostolic business it is the responsibility of the Society of Jesus to guarantee the continuity and cohesion of the spirit in which Fe y Alegría was born."[12]

Educational Programs

Most Fe y Alegría students enroll at the primary level; schools also teach some secondary students and serve a handful of children in preschools and daycare.[13] A key feature of Fe y Alegría programs is that they are designed to reflect the needs of each student and each community. Thus, vocational training emphasizes agriculture, livestock, and commercial and industrial trades, while centers in some countries offer bilingual, intercultural education for indigenous groups. The radio-based, distance-learning programs are important: Institutos Radiofónicos transmit classes in literacy, basic education for adults, secondary schooling, and trades, while news and opinion programs promote "citizenship and humano-Christian" training.

Specialized education includes Spanish literacy, programs for disabled children (some in special schools, others as part of regular classes), and initial and continuing teacher training. Programs also include job training for youths and adults and a wide range of alternative programs such as tutoring, special attention for street children, residences for children, prevention and treatment of drug addiction, cultural and sports groups, human rights education, and leadership training. A number of Fe y Alegría centers also provide basic health and nutrition services, act as community centers, house cooperatives and micro-enterprises, and promote the development of marginalized communities.

Fe y Alegría focuses on providing practical skills and an education for life. Each center's materials draw from the community in which it works: neighborhood heroes may be the subject of one lesson, popular resistance movements that overcame oppression another. Fe y Alegría also stresses values and ethics in all its programs. In El Salvador, where decades of civil war have created a culture of violence and mistrust as well as dysfunctional families, Fe y Alegría programs focus on nonviolence, friendships, and the primacy of the family.

The problem of student retention and grade repetition is enormous throughout Latin America. The United Nationals Educational, Scientific, and Cultural Organization (UNESCO) estimated in 1988 that 20.8 million Latin American students repeat a grade each year, at a cost of US$2.5 billion. These students are much more likely to drop out of school and experience low self-esteem and social exclusion. Fe y Alegría promotes several strategies to increase student retention, including food programs, health care, and tutoring. One innovative program in Guatemala provides early visual testing with intensive follow-up to ensure that parents do not remove children from school. In Paraguay, children who repeat a grade tutor younger students, thereby recouping some of their self-esteem and improving their academic performance. In one marginalized neighborhood north of Lima, students learn material in a prescribed sequence but at their own pace.[14]

Educational programs highlight the importance of the individual, and care is taken to identify the needs of each student and tailor teaching to that child. This approach has taken various forms in different schools— supplemental training for children lacking visual skills, self-paced modular learning, and an opportunity to repeat advancement exams before the start of a new school year.

Results and Impact

Measuring the output of an educational system—especially one like Fe y Alegría that focuses on ethical, personal, and community development as well as academic achievement—is difficult. One study, *Comunidades Educativas Donde Termina el Asfalto*, examined Fe y Alegría programs throughout Latin America and compared their results with those of public school counterparts. While varying policies and systems makes comparing grades across schools problematic, and while statistics varied from country to country and center to center, the results nevertheless suggested that the Fe y Alegría model is highly successful at keeping poor children in school and promoting them on schedule.

Other results are harder still to measure, especially in quantitative terms. For example, building a Fe y Alegría school may have important ramifications for community unity and organization. Parenting classes may increase child health and well-being, while adult literacy lessons may help community members find more secure, well-paying jobs. Few public school systems have such a strong focus on serving the community.

Perhaps the most difficult outcome to capture is Fe y Alegría's training in values and ethics. In some countries, such as El Salvador, educating children in the importance of nonviolent interactions and healthy family relationships is credited with exerting an enormous impact on communities and the society as a whole.

Fe y Alegría has, overall, met remarkable success over its half-century of life. Some of the movement's strengths include the following:

- An educational system focused on students' lives, while its emphasis on values benefits both students and the community.
- Solid support for Fe y Alegría from the strong Jesuit network of universities, private schools, and youth centers throughout Latin America. Collaboration with other Jesuit institutions includes teacher exchanges and student social work at Fe y Alegría centers.
- The strength of regional associations and the international federation that provide direct support and encourage sharing of experience and information.
- The constructive "symbiosis" with state systems that has ensured basic financing of core education costs and collaboration in school system management; the flexibility of these approaches and relations is another success factor.
- Diversity of funding sources has helped Fe y Alegría to weather periods of political tension and turbulence and to gain from diverse ideas and experience.
- The fund-raising role of the Spain office eases some of the burdens of administrative processes, facilitating financial and project management and enabling each national office to relate to relatively few aid agencies.

There are also important weaknesses, some, as an evaluation team suggested, nigh inevitable, given the "original sin" of Fe y Alegría's roots as "a work which emerged from mysticism, audacity and generosity more than calculated and accurate planning."[15] They include:

- Frequently precarious finances including uncertainties and fluctuations in financing. This is a source of considerable anxiety, especially among administrative staff.
- Center of gravity tending toward basic education programs or training for trades such as carpentry, electrical work, and textiles, with less success in education that opens opportunities for social and economic advancement.
- Ambiguous and sometimes tense relations with some national governments on Fe y Alegría's role in shaping educational policy, with the result that Fe y Alegría's contributions are somewhat haphazard and suboptimal. Fe y Alegría itself contends that the movement must influence public education to improve its deficiencies.[16]

NOTES

1. "Aunque me da rubor decirlo, la raíz más profunda de Fe y Alegría está en mi capacidad de soñar despierto." Quoted in Fe y Alegría 1999.
2. Fe y Alegría 1999, p. 33.
3. Fe y Alegría 1999, p. 47.
4. Fe y Alegría 1999, p. 62.
5. Fe y Alegría 1999.
6. Fe y Alegría 1999, p. 75.
7. Schmidheiny 2003, p. 19.
8. Schmidheiny 2003, p. 15.
9. Schmidheiny 2003, p. 15.
10. Fe y Alegría 2000, p. 157.
11. Fe y Alegría 2000, p. 171.
12. Fe y Alegría 1999, p. 74.
13. Reimers 1993, p. 12.
14. Fe y Alegría 2000, pp. 113–115.
15. Fe y Alegría 2000.
16. Fe y Alegría 1999, p. 75.

REFERENCES

Fe y Alegría. 1999. *De la Chispa al Incendio:la historia y las historias de Fe y Alegría.* Caracas: Ex Libris.

Fe y Alegría. 2000. *Comunidades Educativas Donde Termina el Asfalto.* Caracas: Federación de Fe y Alegría.

Reimers, F. 1993. *Education and Consolidation of Democracy in Latin America: Innovations to Provide Quality Basic Education with Equity.* Cambridge, Mass.: Harvard Institute for International Development.

Schmidheiny, Stephan. 2003. *My Path, My Perspective.* San Juan, Costa Rica: VIVA.

15

Expanding Early Childhood Education

Madrasas in East Africa

P utting communities in charge, insisting on quality, and providing action-based learning are the hallmarks of the Madrasa Early Childhood Program in East Africa, supported by the Aga Khan Foundation (AKF) in Kenya, Tanzania, and Uganda.[1] The program's objective is to marry best practices, community preferences, and local values and customs to exert a significant influence on children's ability to perform well in school, career, and life.

The Madrasa Early Childhood Program provides parents and community leaders with the knowledge, management skills, and mechanisms to facilitate long-term financing to enable them to sustain their efforts. The program is a dynamic and constructive effort to build on local organizations—in this case traditional Islamic educational institutions known as *madrasas*—while bringing to bear international and national technical expertise. The focus on education of girls and engagement of women as teachers, mothers, and administrators is an important aspect of the program.

The Madrasa Early Childhood Program originated as a small pilot initiative in Kenya in the mid-1980s and was designed to address

This chapter, written by Lucy Keough, draws extensively from "The Madrasa Early Childhood Programme in East Africa," written in 2003 by Kathy Bartlett, AKF. We have used it here with the permission of the AKF and Ms. Bartlett.

communities' concerns that their children understand their local culture and religion while also improving their chances for access to and success in formal education. The program emerged from a desire expressed by Muslim community leaders to His Highness the Aga Khan that more of their children should enroll in and succeed at university-level education.

In response, program staff from the AKF, with leaders from the local Ismaili community (followers of the Aga Khan), commissioned studies of the participation of Muslim children and young people across the educational system. The resulting recommendations—fully accepted by the community—suggested that the most effective way to ensure children's educational success would be to establish high-quality preschools. The AKF decided to rely on *madrasas* as sites for the preschools, reflecting the nascent program's basic rationale: the need to build on local culture and religious values. Moreover, in East Africa, *madrasas* went largely unused in the mornings because they held most classes in the afternoons and evenings.

Finding a leader for the pilot initiative who parents, religious teachers, and communities would accept was a high priority. Swafiya Said, a respected Muslim woman trained as a primary teacher, was hired as the first director. (The program also engaged a trainer, a curriculum developer, and a community organizer.) Said began working with a handful of communities that expressed early interest in the program to select local women to train as preschool teachers. Said also developed the program's curriculum and overall approach jointly with communities and religious teachers, with technical support from the AKF. The resulting "integrated" preschool curriculum combined local Swahili culture (language, songs, and stories), key values and teachings from Islam, and contemporary methodology and content.

As enthusiasm for the approach grew, the AKF helped establish the first Madrasa Resource Center (MRC) in Mombasa, Kenya, in 1986.[2] This center began institutionalizing the program and, with additional staff, expanded it to other communities. By 1990, Said and her small team were working with 10 to 12 communities in and around Mombasa.

When community and religious leaders in nearby Zanzibar (part of Tanzania) heard about this integrated approach to preschool education in 1989, they expressed interest in visiting the program and replicating it in

Zanzibar, whose population is more than 95 percent Muslim. The Zanzibar MRC was established in 1990 on a pilot basis.

The third MRC emerged in 1993 in Kampala, Uganda, like the other MRCs, from discussions between community leaders, the Aga Khan, senior staff from the Aga Khan Development Network, and senior Ismaili leaders. As the program expanded, each participating country established a volunteer national board composed of respected Muslim leaders (including one or two from the Ismaili community), local teachers, and business people to oversee the MRCs.

By early 2002, the MRCs were working with some 185 communities across East Africa, each with its own preschool. Local Muslim women, often trained as primary schoolteachers, direct the MRCs and train preschool teachers. Said and her staff in Mombasa initially trained new MRC staff and provided on-the-job instruction and mentoring, ensuring adherence to a similar philosophy during early expansion. The combination of training sessions within the MRCs, significant follow-up on the job, and extended mentoring has continued to be a hallmark of the MRC system.

The preschools accept non-Muslim children on a limited basis, usually in rough proportion to the number of non-Muslim families in the neighborhood. When asked why they have enrolled their children in these faith-based preschools, non-Muslim parents often attest that they are the best and most affordable preschools in the community. Some parents also comment that their children learn to better appreciate their own faith because of their attendance at the preschools.

The reasons behind the success of the MRC are highlighted in box 15.1.

THE MRCS' APPROACH TO COMMUNITY-BASED PRESCHOOL

Building trust and encouraging dialogue: As an initial step, MRC community development officers, often in conjunction with MRC trainers, spend 6 to 12 months in communities that have expressed interest, as well as in areas that may not be aware of the program. The officers hold discussions with community leaders and residents—individually and in groups—on the program's key components, including the roles and responsibilities of each partner. The officers assess the local commitment to developing and maintaining the school and create a

BOX 15.1
KEYS TO SUCCESS

One evaluation team cited five integrated elements composing the MRC system. First is the community development and mobilization process, catalyzed by the community development officer. The resulting community ownership lies at the heart of the MRC system and represents "the critical difference between MRC preschools and other preschool initiatives."

Second, the school management committee process has enabled communities to exhibit high levels of self-help. Training of school management committees by community development officers helps build institutional capacity. The development of school management committees also helps build skills in the wider community. Women are well represented on the committees, as mandated under the MRC contract.

Third, funding is the most challenging aspect of the MRC system. The endowment fund concept, although viable, poses administrative and capacity challenges for many communities. Other concerns are preschool fee collections, payment of teachers' salaries, and the complexities of computing the cost-effectiveness of the system's components.

Fourth, the *madrasa* program is implemented flexibly, relying on local feedback to spur modification and enhancement. Overextending the program could jeopardize quality.

Finally, the administrative process—the glue that holds the system together—has been an important element in the program's success, attracting effective, committed, and dynamic managers at both the regional and country level. The regional office has also made important contributions by facilitating planning and innovation, guiding expansion, and mobilizing resources. The national boards have committed, hard-working chairs, linked through membership in a regional advisory committee.

Source: Bartlett 2003.

management committee composed of both women and men. Community development officers train and support these committees for two years and provide less intensive support thereafter.

Eventually, the MRC signs a contract with the community, usually for two to three years, outlining the responsibilities of all parties. This occurs in the presence of the broader community to ensure transparency and awareness. At the time of contract signing, each community receives the equivalent of US$1,000 as a seed grant for purchasing classroom materials and basic equipment. The grant also serves as a mechanism for assessing the community's ability to plan, budget, and implement preschool-related activities.

Communities open bank accounts for their preschools and find suitable premises, using an existing *madrasa* when possible or building their own schools if necessary. Communities also identify local women whom the MRC will train as teachers and principals. The MRCs work with communities to determine the fees parents will pay to enroll their children, which help cover teachers' salaries and basic supplies. Finally, MRCs help communities register their preschools with local authorities.

Providing training, mentoring, and support: Once a preschool has been established, the MRC provides a month-long orientation that introduces the basic concepts of active learning and shows teachers how to create an appropriate learning environment and develop low-cost classroom materials.[3] Teachers then receive in-school support once a week for 78 weeks, and two or three times a month for another 6 to 10 months, or until the school becomes self-sustaining. For two years or longer, small groups of teachers also meet each week with mentors at the MRC for joint planning and problem solving. *Madrasa* school committees receive training in community mobilization, fund-raising, basic accounting skills, management, and planning.

Building accountability through monitoring and assessment: MRC staff evaluate preschools every six months on the quality of their teaching, interactions between adults and children and among children, the extent of parent and community participation, the efficacy of preschool management, and the presentation of local cultural and religious values. The MRC staff share the results with preschool management committees, which use them to plan the next six-month period. The evaluations establish expected performance levels and are a core component of the eventual school "graduation" process.

PROGRAM DEVELOPMENT, 1995–2001

Favorable initial results led to demand to scale up the program in all three countries. The second phase, from 1995 to 2000, had three primary objectives. These included strengthening MRCs' capacity to develop, implement, and monitor the *madrasa* preschool program on a larger scale; addressing preschools' financial sustainability while also ensuring that they are community-owned and provide high-quality learning; and working toward overall sustainability. The program set targets for the number of additional schools in each country by 2000. A key outcome was the development of monitoring and support systems that the MRCs could use to assess quality across the expanding number of preschools.

The MRCs wanted communities to sustain their own preschools and require less intensive input from MRC staff. The MRCs therefore developed a transparent assessment process with communities that would lead to their graduation. Criteria for graduation included high-quality teaching and learning environments, effective and transparent management and financing, and community participation.

During this expansion phase, the three relatively independent MRCs joined together under a regional structure to facilitate a more coordinated approach to community-based *madrasa* preschools. This change entailed holding joint training sessions for MRC trainers, requiring community development officers to take the lead in mobilizing communities, and strengthening preschool management committees. The regional office now holds regular meetings for program officers and organizes joint sessions for trainers and community development officers two or three times a year, to review emerging lessons and issues and plan and develop new components. MRC staff also provide training manuals to community development officers and trainers. All these components help create a reflective culture within the program.

ADDRESSING LONG-TERM SUSTAINABILITY

AKF early childhood development and education experts provide considerable technical assistance and advice to the MRCs, while the AKF advises them on organizational development. Building the MRCs' capacities and skills to ensure that they become effective institutions remains a priority for the AKF.

The MRCs have received funding from a number of external donors as well as the AKF, but long-term funding remains a challenge. At the community level, the MRCs, with assistance from the AKF, have tested a pilot mini-endowment scheme across a selected number of graduated preschools. This scheme begins at the end of the two- to three-year period of capacity building and after a preschool achieves the graduation goals. After graduation, each participating school receives a grant of US$2,500. Communities may also raise additional funds, which the program will match up to US$2,500. Thus, a community's endowment could total as much as US$7,500.

In 2000–2001, an initial group of 38 graduated schools from the three countries participated in this pilot scheme. Each country pooled its mini-endowment monies, and the communities chose how to invest the funds from a list of options. Today these communities receive a dividend of 5 percent annually on their investment, distributed each quarter, which has helped them meet their preschools' operating costs. However, helping communities and MRC staff understand sustainability and this new form of investment continues to be challenging. The MRCs and regional offices continue to wrestle with choosing investments in accordance with Islamic principles, the interpretation of which can differ among communities; improving communication regarding communities' investments; and determining an appropriate management structure.

EVALUATING THE PROGRAM

By the end of 2002, the Madrasa Early Childhood Program had scaled up well beyond its original scope. Table 15.1 illustrates some key performance indicators in each country:

Table 15.1 Beneficiaries of the Madrasa Early Childhood Education Program

Category	Kenya	Tanzania	Uganda
Year established	1986	1989	1993
Communities contracted	66	69	50
Graduated *madrasa* preschools	51	64	38
Madrasa preschool teachers trained	431	531	133
School management committee members trained	555	571	307
Children enrolled, 2002	2,432	4,336	1,952
Percent girls	51	52	50
Total children enrolled over time	11,917	21,958	8,632
Percent non-Muslim	3.0	0.8	22.0
Non-*madrasa* preschool teachers and trainers trained	500	604	571

Source: Madrasa Regional Program Statistics.

To evaluate the expanding program, AKF recently conducted a tracking study that focused on first-grade performance among more than 720 children, divided among *madrasa* and non-*madrasa* preschools and including some who stayed home. Preliminary results show that average scores are higher for *madrasa* preschools on 9 of 11 dimensions (using an adapted version of Harm and Clifford's early childhood environmental rating scale, which assesses the quality of the learning environment; the difference is statistically significant in 8 of the dimensions). Both *madrasa* and non-*madrasa* preschools appear to fall short in teaching early science concepts. While children are learning such concepts through play, they do not receive enough teacher support to extend this learning. Further monitoring of children after they complete first grade is envisioned for 2004.

An in-depth evaluation of the MRC program in 1999 centered on the content and delivery of the active learning curriculum and on the processes that compose the MRC system.[4] Observation of children in 19 preschools in the three MRCs found positive attitudes and spontaneous behavior among the children as well as supportive relationships between teachers and children. Also evident were the importance of a supply of materials in the hands of each child and teachers' understanding and practice of how to integrate Islamic learning into the overall curriculum.

Evaluators were also impressed with the continuous self-assessment of the preschool learning environment and parental participation.

Trainees acclaimed a two-year teacher training program for both its technical and personal development, as it enabled people of limited educational achievement to become effective teachers. The MRCs have developed instruments for grading the performance of the teachers they train, and trainers are regarded as highly competent, effective, and motivated. The training-of-trainers model has brought regional consistency and quality.

Myriad factors underlie the success of the MRC program. High-quality interactive learning based on local materials, and community ownership and self-sufficient operation of *madrasa* preschools no matter how poor, are key. Preschool teachers and principals are accountable to school management committees, and community support is directly linked to residents' perceptions of teachers' performance and benefits to the children.

Flexibility has been an important feature at the MRC level, with investment in the leadership capacities of MRC staff critical and the program's infrastructure, personnel, and management allowed to develop over time. Perhaps most important, an ethos centered on high-quality education has promoted enthusiasm and commitment and encouraged MRC staff to perceive their accountability to students, parents, and communities.

CHALLENGES AHEAD

The MRC programs in Kenya, Tanzania, and Uganda have provided tens of thousands of children with a head start on formal education and spurred development of public policy in early childhood development. Some communities that have graduated from the program have asked the MRCs and AKF for help in extending their preschools to include primary education.

The AKF and the MRCs have been debating plans for the next phase since 2001. They intend to move from working largely within preschools to also working with families and children in the home and community, and parental support and education will become new components of the MRC approach. The foundation and the MRCs also plan to address the impact of HIV/AIDS in the communities they serve and strengthen the health and nutrition aspects of their curriculum.

The AKF and the MRCs have increasingly viewed sustainability as a long-term undertaking. Providing support for only two or three years, they realize, is insufficient to help communities establish preschools, train the requisite numbers of teachers and committee members, and raise funds. Partly to address this problem, the MRCs have also developed short training courses for non-*madrasa* preschool teachers on a cost-recovery basis. These courses have thus far been well received, and demand for them seems to be growing. This has given the MRCs a better sense of how others view—and value—their work. While the funds generated by these courses are limited, the MRCs hope such training will help diversify their income.

The MRCs will continue to share lessons and disseminate their work more broadly within their respective countries, across the region, and internationally. Each MRC has already begun interacting with the national government, including helping it develop curriculum frameworks and revise requirements for registering community preschools. Early on, the MRCs did not try to exert an impact on government policy, but this changed markedly as they began to scale up and recognized that the same problems were recurring in all three countries. Today the MRCs actively advocate for expansion of their program.

Indeed, governments in all three countries have begun to give greater consideration to early childhood development and preschools, evaluating curriculum, community involvement, and teacher training standards. In Uganda, the director of the MRC sits on the national committee examining government policies for preschools, teacher training, and supervision. She has provided considerable input into policy development, including transmitting MRC curricula and other documentation. In Zanzibar, where *madrasa* preschools comprise about half of all preschools, the government has acknowledged the important role of the MRC.

The MRCs continue to develop strategies to sustain quality. Across the three countries, communities that successfully complete the MRC program have developed independent preschool associations to provide basic support and interaction among schools. The MRCs are also training lead teachers and community mobilizers to assume mentoring and leadership development previously provided by the MRCs. Meanwhile, the regional office provides technical inputs and professional development for the MRCs and will continue its research to gain a deeper understanding of the program's impact, effectiveness, and cost.

On a broader front, AKF and MRC staff receive numerous visitors and requests for information from both African and non-African countries. A common thread in these inquiries is the desire by governments and donors to link with traditional and nonformal educational systems such as *madrasas* to achieve their goal of universal access.

NOTES

1. A private nondenominational development agency created under Swiss law in 1967, the Aga Khan Foundation operates in 14 countries and emphasizes four main areas: rural development, health, education, and NGO enhancement and related concerns, including community participation, women, and the environment. Some 25 percent of the foundation's projects and programs relate to education. They focus on raising the quality of formal and nonformal educational settings and early childhood care and development, as well as boosting educational access, completion, and achievement rates among disadvantaged groups, especially girls, isolated rural children, and the urban poor.

2. AKF worked with the Aga Khan Education Services Company in Kenya (an Aga Khan Development Network institution).

3. The active learning approach is modeled on High/Scope, which encourages children to make choices throughout their school day, to explore, ask questions, solve problems, and interact fully with adults and classmates. Originally designed for low-income, at-risk children, the approach has been widely adopted around the world in urban and rural settings in both developed and developing countries.

4. Brown, Brown, and Sumra 1999. The analysis in this section represents an edited version of the evaluators' executive summary and is used with permission.

REFERENCES

The word *processed* describes informally reproduced works that may not be commonly available through libraries.

Bartlett, Kathy. 2003. "The Madrasa Early Childhood Programme in East Africa. " Aga Khan Foundation. Processed.

Brown, Geof, Janet Brown, and Suleman Sumra. 1999. "The East African Madrasa Programme: The Madrasa Resource Centers and Their Community Based Preschool Program Evaluation Report." Aga Khan Foundation. Processed.

16

"Mountains Have Deities and Water a Spirit"

The Mongolian Sacred Sites Initiative—A Partnership Linking Faith and Forests

U ntil recently, the world's major religions have been relatively voiceless in the environmental debate and marginalized in the decisionmaking process concerning the impacts of development on the environment. However, faith groups can represent a powerful voice for environmental stewardship, given that veneration of nature and the earth are woven throughout scriptures. The moral concerns central to faiths, and the extensive networks of constituents within their reach, also provide a unique vehicle for conveying the importance of protecting forests and other aspects of biodiversity, and their links to alleviating poverty. Faith leaders have a singular opportunity to encourage people to support conservation actively as an expression of their faith.

Recognizing this important and underused resource, the World Bank,[1] in partnership with the Alliance of Religions and Conservation (ARC) and the World Wide Fund for Nature (WWF), agreed in 1999 to support the Religions in Biodiversity project—formally titled Incorporation of Faiths

---

This case study is based on inputs from Anthony Whitten and was drafted by Kelli Mullen.

in Forest/Biodiversity Conservation in East Asia. A grant of US$200,000 underwrote this unusual initiative, designed to raise the profile of religious arguments for stewarding forests and biodiversity among East Asian countries. The grant fell under the purview of the World Bank–Netherlands Partnership Program (BNPP), which supports innovative national, regional, and global projects.[2]

The longer-term aim of the Religions in Biodiversity project is to heighten understanding of the links between religious values and sustainable development. The project reflects a growing conviction among development institutions that religions can exert a material impact on the environmental debate at the grassroots level, not only by teaching facts about the natural world but also by providing leadership and taking direct action on conservation projects.

Initiatives supported by the Religions in Biodiversity project include forest conservation led by Buddhist monks in Thailand, construction of a Christian environmental education and retreat center in Papua New Guinea, and protection of national parks and surrounding areas through the Islamic tradition of *harim* (protected lands). Other proposed initiatives include a handbook on land management for *pesantrans* (Muslim schools) in Indonesia as a model of Islamic environmental management, and work with faith-based NGOs and the Catholic Church to enhance food security and ecological conservation in East Timor villages through sustainable agriculture and resource management. In each case, the World Bank and ARC have combined their own assets and the resources of faith groups to mobilize people to incorporate conservation and ecology into development projects and programs.

In the Mongolia Sacred Sites Initiative, which entails cooperation with WWF, the intersection between religious and cultural values and environmental protection produced practical outcomes within an unusually short time.

THE MONGOLIAN SACRED SITES INITIATIVE

Reverence for nature is central to the identity of Mongolia's people. Originating in the beliefs and rituals of shamanism, these values sustained their power even after people converted to Buddhism in the twelfth century. The Mongolian belief that the fate of humanity and nature are inextricably interwoven complemented Buddhist support for compassion for all life.

Religious beliefs and cultural traditions proved a powerful force in maintaining a tenuous ecological balance in Mongolia's fragile landscape. Across the country, oral traditions enabled people to recount legends of the natural world, including tales of the origin of mountains, the significance of forests, and the sacred value of waters. Through these teachings, people learned the values of conservation and environmental protection. In a country with extreme climatic variations, where a majority of the population depends on agriculture and livestock production for survival, these beliefs have been central to a way of life. Traditional herders carefully observed rules for conserving scarce water and guarding against overgrazing. Hunters respected the animals they hunted, killing only what they needed to survive.

However, Communist rule in Mongolia dramatically altered the country's physical and cultural landscapes. In 1937, Communist dictator Choibalsan destroyed all but one of the 746 Buddhist monasteries and executed more than 17,000 of 110,000 monks.[3] The remaining religious leaders were forced into hiding, and the teachings and practices of Buddhism lay dormant for over 50 years. As people forgot many traditional prayers, the Mongolian Buddhist emphasis on respect for nature faded from view. The carefully guarded ecosystem suffered, leaving a legacy of degraded land, polluted water, and decimated animal populations. The result was growing scarcity of natural resources and a weakening of traditional land-based economies.

Today, Mongolia's landscape is once again changing. Communism's overthrow in 1990 heralded the beginning of a cultural and religious renaissance fully supported by Mongolia's democratic government. Prime Minister Nambar Enkhbayar strongly advocates a critical role for Buddhism and traditional cultural values in the development process. However, Mongolia's initial transition to a market economy has been marked by high unemployment, and, in the absence of alternative livelihoods, many Mongolians have turned to the land for survival. The number of herding households more than doubled, from 75,000 in 1990 to 192,000 in 2000.[4] With only limited understanding of grassland management and cultural appreciation of resource scarcity, herders often linger closer to markets, causing overgrazing in many areas and straining water supplies. The extreme weather conditions typical of Mongolia exacerbate these circumstances. Thus, people lost over 7 million animals—nearly 22 percent of the livestock population—during the winters of 1999–2000 and 2000–2001, leaving thousands of households with little or no income.[5]

Recognizing the close links between environmental degradation and Mongolia's growing poverty, the government, in partnership with development institutions, has sought to include environmental protection as a central tenet in its poverty reduction strategy. The government has also embraced partnerships with NGOs and development institutions in projects such as the Sacred Sites Initiative. The revival of religion and reassertion of cultural values is seen as an opportunity to restore and protect the environment in tandem with growth and development.

Exploring the wealth of religious and cultural traditions of Mongolia also provides a unique avenue for communicating development goals. For example, the profound relationship with nature that is a hallmark of Buddhist Mongolian civilization is evident in the more than 600 venerated mountains and other natural sites identified and recounted in the oral traditions of the Mongolian people. Nearly 280 of these legends were codified in historic holy Buddhist texts known as sutras. Today these sutras provide a connection to the culture, history, language, and religion of pre-Communist Mongolia.

Mongolia aims to preserve the beliefs captured within the sutras by reaffirming their place in Mongolian identity and, concurrently, fostering greater respect for the environment and traditions of ecological conservation. Toward that end, the Sacred Sites Initiative—aided by Mongolian Buddhist leaders such as the Gandan monasteries in Ulaanbaatar—has supported the collection of hundreds of parchments describing the cultural significance of natural wonders throughout Mongolia. One example, documented with project support, is Bogd Khan Sacred Mountain. Among the most treasured and storied sites in Mongolia, Mt. Bogd Khan is represented by a deity who rides 33 gray horses and chants the mantra *"um ma hum."* This image reflects the evolution from shamanic style to Buddhist sacred rituals: the 33 horses originate from shamanism, but the mantra is distinctly Buddhist in tone and spiritual significance.

Outputs of the Sacred Sites Initiative have also included two books. The first explored Mongolian legends of the land and their significance in ensuring ecological health. The second—a more ambitious publication— describes the cultural and religious traditions behind many of the sacred sites. The authors collected several of the sutras and translated their text from Tibetan to Mongolian to better convey their meaning.

Project leaders applied this work and made it visible by concurrently launching conservation projects at five sacred sites representing a diversity of natural zones and regions. Special ceremonies based on the active involvement of local monasteries and communities, complete with stone tablets, have been used to rededicate these sites. For example, monks prepared for a rededication ceremony at the Mt. Bogd Khan Nature Reserve, between the Gobi Desert and Ulaanbaatar, by climbing to the mountaintop and presenting sacrificial offerings, including milk, bread, and sweets. The head lama mounted an *ovoo*, a 15-foot pile of stones draped in prayer flags, while the monks sat cross-legged, chanting and keeping rhythm with small drums. Later, locals witnessed the erection of a memorial stone and the performance of traditional sacred songs.[6] Sessions conducted in local monasteries have also addressed critical environmental issues and identified efficient and effective ways of dealing with local challenges.

Gandan monasteries have been essential to this work, as monks have provided valuable information on Mongolian Buddhist teachings and links to traditional cultural norms, mobilized a network of monasteries in each of the five chosen areas, and helped communicate the purposes of the Sacred Sites Initiative. Local monasteries, in turn, have provided a direct connection with the people. Communities at every sacred site have expressed gratitude for efforts to combine conservation and tradition. These experiences suggest that the Mongolian Buddhist community is an important partner in Mongolia's development.

Mongolian officials are now seeking to build on the values identified through this work and disseminate the ideas more broadly.[7] For example, project partners are considering opportunities for spirituality-based ecotourism in remote mountain monasteries. The challenge will be to maintain the integrity of these sacred areas while sharing their unique cultural and spiritual gifts.

The Sacred Sites Initiative is part of a broader, holistic development strategy embraced by the Mongolian government, religious leaders, and development officials. Examples of this strategy include the creation of nature preserves, bans on large-scale hunting (with exceptions for subsistence hunting), protection of pasturelands, limits on logging, and rehabilitation and upgrading of the water supply infrastructure.

Experience with the Sacred Sites Initiative suggests some important lessons. Most obvious is the need for specific and detailed information on project areas and local customs. For example, in Selenge province, a project team observed that one of the most serious environmental problems related to managing solid waste, especially plastic bottles. While the local monastery had begun to urge people to collect discarded bottles, they were not sure how to dispose of them properly. Time was lost before the partners worked out an eventual arrangement with a local bottling company.

Ultimately, the most important lesson of the Mongolian Sacred Sites Initiative lies in its remarkable success in highlighting the importance of the religious and cultural approach to development. The rededication of Buddhist sacred sites and the introduction of environmental education into monasteries and communities throughout Mongolia will help foster strong moral and religious support for protecting natural resources and the environment. As Dr. Sukhbaatar, author of *Sacred Sites of Mongolia*, notes, "In Mongolia, venerating, fearing and obeying the deities of the mountains, waters, and land was a very important form of environmental protection. The religious ritual both protected nature and instilled overall respect into the people. As such, these stories and the traditions behind the names may yet turn out to be one of the greatest gifts of Mongolia's past to her present."[8]

NOTES

1. Through the Environment and Social Development Department of the East Asia and Pacific Region.
2. For further information on this partnership, which reflects an agreement between the Netherlands Ministry of Foreign Affairs and the World Bank, see www.worldbank.org/publicsector/civilservice.

3. Chandra 1996.

4. World Bank 2003, p. 17.

5. World Bank 2003, p. 20.

6. August 2001.

7. Discussion with Saha Dhevan Meyanathan, World Bank resident representative in Ulaanbaatar, Mongolia, August 2002.

8. Sukhbaatar 2001, p. 34.

REFERENCES

August, Oliver. 2001. "Mongolia's Holy Activists." *The Times* (London), July 21.

Chandra, Rajiv. 1996. "Buddhism Thrives on Communism's Demise." Inter Press Service. August 5.

Palmer, Martin, with Victoria Finlay. 2003. *Faith in Conservation: New Approaches to Religions and the Environment.* Washington, D.C.: World Bank.

Sukhbaatar, O. 2001. *Sacred Sites of Mongolia.* Ulaanbaatar: World Bank.

World Bank. 2003. *Mongolia Environment Monitor.* Washington, D.C.

PART III

Peace for God

Introduction

The role of faith organizations in development is well defined and widely commented on in the area of peace building and conflict resolution. Few people are more strongly associated with India's independence movement than Mahatma Gandhi; with the end to South African apartheid than Archbishop Desmond Tutu, though Nelson Mandela clearly played an amazing role in that country's struggle; with the American civil rights movement than Rev. Martin Luther King Jr.; or with today's struggles for peace in Honduras and other Central American nations than Cardinal Oscar Rodriguez. Few arguments seem as persuasive, or so full of wisdom and insight, as those offered by faith organizations and individuals struggling for social change. They work, or certainly strive to, from perspectives of deep conviction and clarity of vision, bringing a meaning and a moral vision to work that others can view in largely technical or organizational terms.

This series of chapters explores faith organizations' place in holding or strengthening peace in a number of countries. The stories introduce faith institutions' involvement in conflict in a number of dimensions: as a victim of conflict; as a source of strife, and then of resolution; or as an institution capable of mediating thorny issues of reconciliation and reestablishment of trust. Chapter 17, "Faith Dimensions of Peace and Development in Colombia," describes how the Jesuits and others, in Colombia's conflict-ridden Magdalena Medio region, promoted a community-based program to address the growing violence in the region in the mid-1990s. Though Jesuit involvement was not the only element of the success of the Magdalena Medio project, the strength of faith seems to have overcome the threshold of terror and played a critical stabilizing role.

Chapter 18, "Sri Lanka: Delivering Aid and Building Partnerships amid Armed Conflict," explores how faith institutions strengthened two World Bank–supported projects in northeastern Sri Lanka, one seeking broad perspective on relief, rehabilitation, and reconciliation efforts and a second assisting communities affected by conflict in agriculture and small-scale reconstruction activities. "'*Kacel pi Kuc*': Together for Peace in Uganda," chapter 19, links the involvement of faith institutions as mediators with their role as participants in a World Bank–supported community development project in northern Uganda.

While faith organizations as independent agents of change is a fascinating story, their role within Bank-funded projects can also play an essential role. Equal representation of Muslim, Christian, and Lumad representatives formed a basic element of the Bank-funded peace-building and development efforts in the southern Philippines, described in chapter 20, "Social Funds for Peace and Development in Conflict Regions of the Philippines." Chapter 21, "Building Peace in Cambodia: Faith Initiatives 1992–2001," offers a poignant glimpse of the assault upon Buddhism in Cambodia's modern history, a description of Buddhist peace struggles, and examples of the sensitive efforts of international "peace churches" to assist with post-conflict reconstruction and to support the Buddhist struggles. Chapter 22 describes examples of the peace and reconciliation work of the Community of Sant'Egidio, with a focus on its role in Mozambique and in Albania, and its partnership with a wide range of organizations.

In these chapters two types of activity emerge. The first is religious groups' participation in World Bank projects. These chapters highlight religious institutions' involvement in World Bank–supported "social fund" projects—projects that provide communities with funds to undertake small infrastructure endeavors of their choosing, to replace or rehabilitate infrastructure destroyed during war. As in chapter 2 on the Poverty Reduction Strategy Paper consultations, faith institutions' involvement comes within a distinct activity with its own goals and framework; faith institutions are sought out to add strength to the project rather than to propose activities independent of it. The second type of activity is that led by faith organizations, with the Bank involved only peripherally. These initiatives may mark regions or countries with their message or approach, but be hampered in extending or deepening their reach due to funding shortages, vulnerability, or other causes. An outstanding question, then, is whether a middle ground can be found: whether the Bank or other official development organizations can find effective ways to support such faith initiatives so that they can strengthen or broaden their work, without eroding or diluting the facets that make faith initiatives strong.

CHAPTER 17

Faith Dimensions of Peace and Development in Colombia

I n Magdalena Medio, one of Colombia's most turbulent regions, a community-led development program, building on the long-standing Catholic Church engagement in the area and involving a creative partnership with Church, private sector, and government, shows great promise for reducing violence and moving toward the socioeconomic development that must be the foundation for lasting peace. The World Bank, through a flexible new type of lending arrangement, has supported the program and is currently working to extend similar partnerships and development schemes in other parts of Colombia.

Situated in the heart of Colombia, the Magdalena Medio region boasts great natural and productive wealth in the forms of oil, gas, gold, water, and livestock. Indeed, the region is the birthplace of the country's petroleum industry and a strategic transportation corridor. However, access to those assets and the income they generate is highly unequal. Only 4.5 percent of the value of petroleum and gas production stays in the region, and the predominant extractive industries do not provide employment or income for most of the population. What is more, severe environmental problems have significantly undercut productivity of key

This chapter was prepared under the leadership of Jairo Arboleda; Father Alejandro Angulo, director of CINEP, prepared a first draft.

activities such as fishing and peasant agriculture. Thus, despite the fact that the region's oil industry generates about US$2 billion annually, 70 percent of the population falls below the poverty line and 53 percent have unmet basic needs.

The region was settled only recently, seeing a major influx of population in the 1950s, and regional authorities have historically devoted limited attention to it. A majority of the population is rural, although 34 percent of the people live in two cities, Barrancabermeja and Aguachica. ECOPETROL—the national oil company—and the central government spend enormous amounts on security, yet violence continues to grow. In fact, Magdalena Medio can be seen as a microcosm of the actors and issues underlying Colombia's armed conflict between guerrillas and right-wing paramilitary units, with the army battling for control as the civilian population struggles to survive.

The Program for Development and Peace in Magdalena Medio originated with the Catholic Diocese of Barrancabermeja. Their network of community workers was seeking solutions to the region's growing poverty and violence, which national and local governments had been unable to address. The program, initiated in 1995, embodies a dynamic vision for community-led, comprehensive development, aiming to raise living standards and reduce violence by forging relationships among communities, NGOs, the business sector, government, and even armed actors. The program entails linking community, municipality, subregion, and region with national policies and institutions, and relies on a continuous learning approach to translate vision into action.

ORIGINS OF THE PROGRAM

The Catholic Church entrusted Magdalena Medio to the Jesuit Order in 1927 because the Church considered the region mission territory: it entailed a particularly difficult task. As part of their evangelizing activities, a group of young Jesuit priests carefully examined the living conditions of poor farmers and workers. In particular, the Center for Research and Popular Education (CINEP), a longtime Jesuit-based presence in the region, undertook such diagnostic work in the 1970s and 1980s in close collaboration with the Barrancabermeja Diocese, which declared its intention to work more actively and specifically to foster peace and social justice in Magdalena Medio.

CINEP investigators made specific efforts to identify the structural forces underlying armed conflict in the region, including social inequality and economic marginalization, and to formulate a realistic program to address both development and peace from a faith-based perspective. CINEP's approach to development resembles liberation theology in that it combines faith and social science: adherents apply technical investigation based on strong values and ethics to solve political and economic problems. CINEP also emphasizes building trust as a basic ingredient of peace. In Colombia, with its high levels of political and administrative corruption, this task is both critical and difficult.

In mid-1994 the Committee on Human Rights of ECOPETROL and the Oil Workers' Union (USO) proposed to involve CINEP as well as another well-respected and long-established Colombian NGO—the Association of Economists, Friends of the Country—in creating a program to address the growing violence. Representatives of the four entities worked for six months to identify the perverse dynamics that underlie the region's persistent and pervasive poverty and violence. One factor, they concluded, is administrative and political fragmentation. The region is composed of 29 municipalities in four departments (Antioquia, Santander, Bolivar, and Cesar). The resulting program aimed to overcome these barriers by testing and refining a participatory approach to development that strengthened a citizens' network and provided technical support and funding to community organizations to develop and implement specific projects they identified as priorities.

ECOPETROL's board of directors allocated US$500,000 to launch the program in February 1995, and the prestige and technical excellence of the convening powers convinced the central government to endorse the initiative as a pilot partnership between the public and private sectors and civil society. The National Planning Department formally requested World Bank support for the program in April 1996, and the Colombian government obtained a US$5 million Learning and Innovation Loan from the Bank[1] and US$1.25 million from ECOPETROL to finance the Magdalena Medio Regional Development Project. The project represented one of the World Bank's first lending operations in a new area: peace and development. In 1997, during a dialogue on the Bank's strategy for assisting Colombia, representatives of government and civil society identified peace as the number one development priority. The project dovetailed with the government's strategy of supporting regional and local initiatives to build social capital and address the causes of violence while initiating peace negotiations with armed groups.

THE PARTICIPATORY, FAITH-BASED APPROACH

A key lesson of the project—one highlighted by the Colombian government—is how a nonpublic entity can use public funds to lead regional development and build peace. The central government was poorly positioned to manage a participatory, community-led program effectively, as armed conflict had sown mistrust, fear, and polarization, and municipal governments were weak and controlled by interest groups, including armed actors. The regional government, for its part, had a record of neglecting the local municipalities. Thus, the program aimed to develop the capacity of the Consortium for Development and Peace Magdalena Medio (CDPMM)—an independent, faith-based entity—as a change agent and program manager. CDPMM's role in designing, leading, and managing the project was critical to the program's success, as the organization enjoyed strong credibility among stakeholders because its staff consistently displayed high levels of integrity, commitment, and professionalism.

Although the program's formal documents and contracts—which require the normal level of financial accountability and transparency—do not mention faith, it is an implicit underpinning and consistent with the Colombian notion of *ethos*, which relates religion and politics. The Bishop of Barrancabermeja chairs the program's board of directors, and CINEP's general secretary, a Jesuit priest, serves as the board's secretary. The fact that two religious individuals occupy the highest leadership positions has helped build a collaborative form of decisionmaking. Religious leaders enjoy high levels of prestige among the population, as evidenced by the fact that religious individuals and groups often mediate between the Colombian government and guerrilla groups. A team of promoters, most linked to the Social Pastoral of the Barrancabermeja Diocese, is at the heart of the program, parlaying its credibility to resolve conflicts amid complex economic and political interests.

This participatory approach proved effective in initiating a community-led process of creating a long-term vision for the region, strengthening its human and social capital, mobilizing resources and attracting investment, and improving basic services. The most striking achievement was the creation of 23 *nucleos* (small local centers) and 147 organizations involving nearly 9,000 people.

Funding for community initiatives generated immediate interest among citizen groups anxious to take concrete action to improve their situation. For small projects in isolated communities to exert a significant impact on development, however, they must link strategically with municipal, subregional, and regional development priorities. The *nucleo*, municipal proposal, and regional planning system provided those strategic links.

Community and producer organizations pursued 67 investment initiatives and were actively involved in an ambitious health program. Contrary to original expectations, most projects focused on productive activities (60 out of 67), with the remainder in education, institutional development, and peace and conflict resolution. Thus, the project established a solid basis to improve incomes and living standards. It also achieved significant immediate gains in health and education

Despite this record, the community-led process of transforming initial ideas into investment projects turned out to be difficult and time consuming. During the first two-and-a-half years of project implementation, few of the 60 productive initiatives fully entered the investment phase, partly because it took some time for participants to understand the project development process. CDPMM also began to favor more complex projects covering several municipalities, because those would have a greater impact on the region's economic and social development. The organization realized that complete feasibility studies are essential before investing in projects with higher technical requirements. Still, CDPMM considered three-quarters of the 67 initiatives, accounting for 94 percent of the funding, as worthy of further funding at the end of the project period.

The National Planning Department, ECOPETROL, the U.N. Development Programme, and the World Bank also gained invaluable experience in working together for common goals during this process.

COMMON VALUES

Faith and government interests have now forged an alliance that is benefi-
cial to both in this demanding region. This collaboration helped a group
of officials with expertise in both the technical and spiritual dimensions
of community development to come together. Underlying the CDPMM
are a set of ethical assumptions that act as a unifying force:

- *The concept of a Christian person.* Among the program's values, the most
  important are the dignity of life, the importance of human rights, and
  the goal of communities living together in a culture of peace and social
  inclusion. These values are reflected in the project's educational
  components, which have been implemented following the educational
  philosophy of Fe y Alegría, a Jesuit-based organization that manages
  elementary and high schools across Latin America (see chapter 14).
- *A common language.* All the key actors, including the bishop, the
  Program for Development and Peace director, the CINEP director, and
  members of Pastoral Social's dynamic unit, share a common religious
  and ethical vocabulary concerning social justice based largely on the
  teachings of the Catholic Church. This common framework facilitated
  consensus on initial strategies, ensured clarity and consistency of
  purpose, and reinforced the consortium's credibility.
- *The prestige of religion in Colombia.* In Colombia, religious leaders and
  institutions enjoy the confidence of most of the population, which
  regards them as uncontaminated by corruption and political
  maneuvering, unlike many private and political entities. Corruption is
  one of the region's gravest problems, and transparency is one of the
  program's strongest features.
- *Inspiration from higher values.* The engagement of faith leaders inspires
  greater commitment to social justice and equity among communities,
  linking spiritual and economic development as workers risk death daily.
- *A vision of the future.* Even if failures are likely, given the conflicted
  environment in which the program operates, participants persist. Such
  tenacity sustains the teams in the face of great obstacles. However, the
  teams must work constantly to minimize the sense of fatalism that
  inevitably surfaces in the face of the region's seemingly intractable
  problems.

Despite its critical importance to the program, the faith dimension also raises significant planning and management dilemmas, especially surrounding efforts to hire staff members and assess their performance. For example, program leaders may value loyalty and faith over competence and efficiency in recruiting participants—a form of management that may foster inefficiencies. PDPMM staff have shown phenomenal courage and conviction in fulfilling their duties in situations that threaten their own personal safety. However, these staff members may also regard performance assessments as unnecessary and reflecting a lack of trust within a group united by faith.

Leaders may find it difficult to negotiate compensation for staff who are seeking spiritual gratification as well as monetary income. Meanwhile, personnel who lack a faith motivation and who are seeking only a salary may undermine team strength and integration despite their technical expertise. Communities perceive a clear difference between staff members whose work reflects a lifelong commitment to social justice and those who are simply fulfilling an assignment.

Overall, the success of the Magdalena Medio project is clearly not due solely to the engagement of faith groups or the application of religious values. However, the strength of faith does seem to have overcome the threshold of terror, a favorite weapon of all warriors. And engaging people for whom faith and ethics serve as a foundation and motivation for achieving development goals has helped foster a strong sense of community trust and ownership. Although these attributes raise the issue of whether the program is replicable in other regions, the program's success suggests that faith dimensions in the Colombian context, at least, can serve as a strong spur to development in conflict areas. It is an appropriate ending that at the time this book goes to press, final preparations are under way for a new Peace and Development project, which will involve an expansion of the framework of the Magdalena Medio project to four additional conflict-affected regions of Colombia, in three of which religious leaders of the Catholic faith play a key role.

NOTE

1. This is a relatively new financial instrument for the World Bank that is designed to test innovative approaches on a small scale.

18

Sri Lanka: Delivering Aid and Building Partnerships amid Armed Conflict

The engagement of communities is critical to building peace in Sri Lanka, and it necessarily involves Sri Lanka's faith leaders and communities. This chapter explores two specific ventures in conflict areas where community development work and local consultation processes, supported by the World Bank among other development partners, have engaged faith communities. The project-specific description is set in the context of Sri Lanka's complex and turbulent history of conflict. The engagement of the faith communities is credited with helping to build much needed bridges and to bring a measure of hope in dark times, and the experience has highlighted concrete, often community-specific, issues linking faith and development agendas that need to be addressed.

THE CONFLICT

Sri Lanka's 20-year civil war, which has ravaged the small South Asian island and claimed some 65,000 lives, has long and deep roots dating

This chapter draws heavily on information provided by Mariana Todorova, former country director for the World Bank, and on internal World Bank reports on the projects described.

from the period of British colonialism. Like most domestic conflicts, Sri Lanka's is marked by complex ethnic, linguistic, and religious divides. The country's population of 19.4 million is split along four main ethnic and faith lines: some three-quarters of the people are Sinhalese, mainly Buddhist; less than one-fifth are Tamil, mainly Hindu; some 7 percent are Muslim; and about 5 percent are Christian. Occupied by the Portuguese in the sixteenth century and the Dutch in the seventeenth century, the island was ceded to the British in 1802. As Ceylon, it gained its independence in 1948, and changed its name to Sri Lanka in 1972.

Conflict originated during the Raj, when Christian missionaries established schools in predominantly Tamil regions of the country. The Tamil population developed proficiency in English—a significant advantage in securing public employment. The Sinhalese majority, in contrast, was far less integrated into the colonial administration and held far fewer official positions. After independence, in 1948, language-related issues became highly divisive and ethnic communities became increasingly polarized.

The political and ethnic polarization intensified during the run-up to the 1956 general election, when the Sri Lanka Freedom Party swept into power in all parts of the country except in the North and East. The party's success symbolized the resurgence of the forces of Sinhala Buddhist nationalism, while the Federal Party's success in the North and East represented the emergence of a new form of Tamil linguistic nationalism. In 1957, the Sinhalese majority, which controlled the government, established Sinhalese as the national language and Buddhism as the national religion, albeit while permitting other languages and religions. Tension between the Buddhist Sinhalese and the Hindu Tamils escalated during the 1960s and 1970s, and successive administrations rejected efforts by the Tamils to establish a federal form of government that would have recognized the autonomy of Tamil areas.

Extremist groups formed on both sides. Heavily Marxist political parties and extremist organizations of Buddhist monks operated among the Sinhalese, while the Liberation Tigers of Tamil Eelam (LTTE) effectively controlled and sought independence for the country's northern and eastern provinces even as more moderate Tamil groups continued to press for a federal system. By the mid-1980s, tensions between the Sinhalese majority and Tamil separatists had erupted in violence. Over 700,000 Tamil-speaking Sri Lankans who have fled abroad fund the LTTE from afar.

Perhaps the worst collective violence was in 1983, when Sinhalese mobs attacked the capital and 2,000 to 3,000 Tamils were murdered, although official records show a death toll of approximately 400. Spencer, a British anthropologist, described the 1983 riots as "the dark night of the collective soul."[1] Many were beaten, hacked, or even torched to death. Thousands of homes and buildings, including about 100 industrial plants and hundreds of shops and small trade establishments, were destroyed. The objective appeared to be the breaking of the economic backbone of the Tamils.

The initial response to the escalating conflict and the outbreak of violence by civil society institutions was to mobilize humanitarian relief operations. Local relief organizations in some cases worked with religious groups to provide food and other essential items to the refugee camps that had been established for internally displaced persons. Successive governments engaged in efforts to negotiate with the LTTE beginning in the early 1990s, but each effort was disrupted by new outbreaks of violence and terrorist attacks that counted a number of government authorities among their victims. The Norwegian government[2] began to facilitate peace talks in 2000, and in early 2002, after general elections that brought the opposition United National Front to power, the sides agreed to an uneasy truce.

Decades of civil strife have badly wounded Sri Lanka's economy and democratic institutions. Approximately 2.5 million people lived in areas of direct military activity, and along with the 65,000 killed, 800,000 have been internally displaced and 172,000 currently live in refugee camps. The northeast region was traditionally among the most productive in the country, but large numbers of families fled their lands, and social and physical infrastructure fell into a state of disrepair. In the poor, uneducated villages of the south, the burden of war sacrifice was perhaps the greatest, since they provided most of the 20,000 troops killed up to that time. With the start of peace talks, although the LTTE often obscured the voice of more moderate Tamils, the cease-fire generally allowed people to resume social and economic activities within their communities.

Amid this challenging and volatile context, the Sri Lankan government invited the World Bank to assist in two endeavors that entailed extensive consultation with civil society groups, including religious leaders. These included the Northeast Irrigated Agriculture Project (NEIAP), approved in December 1999; and the Framework for Relief, Rehabilitation, and Reconciliation (RRR), which addressed development in war-affected communities in the country's northern and eastern regions from September 1999 to June 2002. Whereas the RRR represents an overall framework to support both consultative, consensus-building processes and dialogue at the country and district levels (mainly in the north and east), NEIAP is more focused on community development. It is grounded in a participatory approach for specific communities to identify their needs and to identify future steps to rebuild their losses due to war.

THE NORTHEAST IRRIGATED AGRICULTURE PROJECT

The project set out to help conflict-affected communities reestablish at least a subsistence level of production and basic community services through agricultural and small-scale reconstruction activities. Communities prepare village development plans that reflect residents' needs and expectations, which government agencies then use to coordinate relief and rehabilitation programs. Organizers originally implemented the project in five of eight earmarked northeast districts as well as border villages of four neighboring provinces, and the project later expanded to all northeast districts, whether controlled by the government or the LTTE. Initial efforts were successful in building partnerships and networks and establishing organizational structures to coordinate and monitor projects.

However, delivering development assistance and building partnerships amid armed conflict proved challenging for central and local government agencies, participating communities, supporting NGOs, and the World Bank and its partner organizations, which have included the U.N. High Commission for Refugees (UNHCR) and the International Committee of the Red Cross (ICRC). Enthusiasm and commitment have helped overcome these barriers as well as participants' lack of experience in implementing a community-based approach. Partnering NGOs have helped villages and communities prepare social profiles and development plans, and these localities then took on the execution of small-scale civil works through a combination of voluntary labor and community-based contracts. UNHCR and ICRC helped to enhance communication among project managers, the Sri Lanka Army, and the World Bank. Most important, the government started to recognize the extent to which the village development plans offer vital sources of information about people's needs and expectations, and some government agencies began to rely on them to organize relief and rehabilitation programs.

The project involved the development of an interesting safeguard system for ensuring transparency and accountability. As part of this system, the president of Sri Lanka appointed the governor of the northeast province to oversee the project, and project managers hired private companies to conduct technical and financial audits and advise agencies on how to improve civil works and make financial transactions more transparent.

Sri Lanka Army commanders realized that development within areas under LTTE control was essential for building trust among governments, communities, and the LTTE. The central government therefore agreed to proceed with projects in many LTTE-controlled areas, allowing officials, government vehicles, and small quantities of construction materials to move into these regions. Since the cease-fire took hold after 2002, freer movement of people, goods, and vehicles sped up implementation, and LTTE development officials took responsibility for implementing and monitoring activities in the areas they controlled. The project was expected to reach some 40,000 people in 128 of 400 targeted communities in 2002, and an updated implementation plan encompassed all targeted districts, including severely affected Hindu, Tamil, Muslim, and Buddhist Sinhalese communities. By July 2003, project activities had included rehabilitation of 86 small irrigation schemes, enabling farmers to recommence agriculture and increase the land area farmed with ensured water supply by some 5,400 hectares; rehabilitation of 275 kilometers of roads; and the digging of over 200 wells for drinking water. As part of a livelihood support activities component, 132 village community centers were constructed and more than 6,500 women received small-scale, repayable funds to start up income-generating activities.

Religious leaders played a significant role in mobilizing communities and keeping the spirit and hope of peace alive during violent times, and were instrumental in establishing the Council for Peace and Goodwill, composed of members of the business and professional elite in the northern Jaffna district. The council helped conceptualize alternative approaches to implementing the project when hostilities and the lack of access to the peninsula posed major impediments for two years. Faith leaders also helped mobilize communities in the initial planning and organizational stage, not only in Jaffna but also in the northern and eastern districts, most often as respected members of NGOs.

The project brings hope to communities and builds bridges among parties enmeshed in armed conflict. The initiative is thus not only about rebuilding self-reliance and liberating war-affected people from poverty and subhuman conditions but also about building a foundation for reconciliation and peace.

A good example of NEIAP in action is the community of Nithiyanaga in Vavuniya district, described in the appendix to this chapter.

THE FRAMEWORK FOR RELIEF, REHABILITATION, AND RECONCILIATION

The RRR was initiated in September 1999 to address development issues in war-affected—mainly Tamil—communities in the north and east of Sri Lanka. The central government sought World Bank assistance in developing a consultative mechanism to bring together government, civil society, religious leaders, communities, and the donor community to improve relief, rehabilitation, and reconciliation. The Bank, the governments of the Netherlands and Canada, UNHCR, and the U.N. Development Programme, among others, helped fund the framework, intended to offer a consensus-building process for the entire country even while it focused on the north and east.

While the World Bank viewed this endeavor as largely uncharted territory involving delicate political sensitivities and significant risks amid armed conflict, it also saw the framework as a unique opportunity to support a consultative process to foster peace and development.

The Consortium of Humanitarian Agencies and the National Peace Council sponsored numerous district-level consultative workshops to address aid, institution building, development priorities, and reconciliation and peace building. The consortium is an association and network of national and international agencies working in and supporting work in Sri Lanka, and the council is a Sri Lankan organization dedicated to support a negotiated solution to the war. They both operate under the guidance of a steering committee, where the consultations convened government officials, donors, NGO representatives, and academics, and targeted the needs of specific groups such as ex-combatants, children, religious leaders, educators, and health specialists, forming a working committee for each. These working groups engaged in open and frank debate. The government presented interim recommendations from them—endorsed by the steering committee—at an international Development Forum in Paris in December 2000. Government officials and donor representatives discussed Sri Lanka's leading development issues at the forum, and a final framework was produced at the Development Forums in Colombo in June 2002. Military operations, elections, and changes in government have occurred since, but the Sri Lankan government has assumed ownership of the framework even as it has continued to evolve under the guidance of the steering committee.

LESSONS FROM THE RRR CONSULTATION PROCESS

Consultations among disparate groups posed both organizational and substantive challenges, as participants lacked confidence in their ability to forge consensus. However, the process ultimately helped cement social cohesion, laying a foundation for peace and prosperity.

Consultations aimed at religious groups—mainly Buddhist and Hindu—in particular revealed deep-seated needs and concerns, and inspired the following:

- Calls for religious tolerance without fear of harassment and discrimination, as clergy from different sects had been arrested, detained, and even murdered
- Calls for religious leaders to guide efforts to reestablish social trust within and among sects
- Calls for an interfaith approach to political divisions[3]
- Calls for religious leaders to help heal ethnic divides through education, especially among youth

- Calls to confront poverty and unemployment
- Calls from Buddhist, Christian, and Muslim representatives alike to confront drug abuse, alcoholism, and violence[4]
- Calls for the government to channel the "war budget" to underfunded educational and cultural programs[5]
- Concern among displaced Muslims that they are unable to practice their religion owing to conditions within refugee camps[6]
- Concern among religious leaders that a war levy and poorly performing economy had lowered their own living standards.

Recommendations emerging from the consultations included the following:

- Exposing and punishing attacks on clergy by separatist groups
- Encouraging interfaith dialogue through activities such as food services and medical outreach
- Establishing a national bilingual (Sinhalese and Tamil) training program for the public as well as religious leaders to address the language divide
- Reasserting the legitimate voice of faith groups in promoting and negotiating peace
- Calling on the central government to establish a domestic peace exchange program for young people through the Ministry of Education and the Ministry of Culture
- Calling on the central government to establish rehabilitation programs to address drug addiction and alcoholism among ex-combatants.[7]

The LTTE participated in the workshop process, receiving information, reports, and draft documents through NGOs. The government also invited a representative of the Tamil Rehabilitation Organization (TRO) to participate officially at the Colombo Forum. The TRO was formed in 1985 primarily as a self-help organization for the Tamil refugees in India at that time. Today its mission is to support Tamil people throughout the world and provide relief, rehabilitation, and development schemes for the people of northeast Sri Lanka. A representative from TRO was therefore crucial in understanding the sufferings of the Tamil people and contributing to the primary objective of the RRR, which is to rebuild the lives of the Sri Lankan people who had suffered from two decades of armed conflict.

Both World Bank projects were strengthened by the support of partnerships with faith-based organizations that had an understanding of the deep-rooted issues of conflict and were therefore able to open and promote dialogue between ethnic and religious groups.

APPENDIX. NEIAP IN ACTION IN A CONFLICT-AFFECTED COMMUNITY

After fighting in 1990, the entire Tamil-origin population of Nithiyanaga (Vavuniya district) was forced to leave. Nearly half fled to southern India, while the remaining 55 families—the owners of the 45 hectares of irrigated paddy lands in the village—relocated to the Madhu refugee camp or moved in with friends and relatives in the adjoining Mannar district. After 1997, these 55 farm families returned to their home community, but the war caused major disruption to their lives and livelihoods through damage to homes and the irrigation tank; destruction of farm equipment, livestock, and supplies; and breakdown of social links. Although there was government relief assistance to repair the homes and replace basic agricultural supplies, people were not able to cultivate their paddy lands, as there was no reliable source of water after the irrigation tank was damaged.

NEIAP engineers and social mobilizers came to the village in August 2000. Their initial efforts resulted in the revitalization, revalidation, or formulation of a number of community based organizations (CBOs)— the Farmers' Organization, Rural Development Society, Temple Society, and Women's Service Society. The villagers also formed a participatory action group (PAG) with 11 members selected from the CBOs (including two women) to lead the village rehabilitation and development efforts. Following a participatory needs assessment led by a social scientist, the community participated in a socioeconomic profiling process (village social profile—VSP) and identified priority needs and a strategy to fulfill these needs (village development plan—VDP). The VSP and VDP served as the basis for NEIAP assistance.

Under the leadership of the PAG and with the participation of the majority of community members, the village came a long way toward successfully rehabilitating the irrigation tank. A cadre of about 40 villagers (including women) worked at the site on weekends for four months to complete the civil works required as their up-front voluntary contribution. Following this, about 80 percent of the remaining civil works for tank rehabilitation were completed through a contract awarded to the Farmers' Organization. The PAG kept detailed records of attendance and financial transactions, including payments received, expenditures incurred (for example, for hiring farm tractors, purchasing material, and so forth), and daily wages for participating community members. The PAG expected a reasonable profit margin to be used (supplemented from other sources) for the after care of the irrigation tanks. The PAG is to serve as the vigilance group and an executive committee to oversee after care. As a next stage, the community would like to repair agricultural roads and community drinking water wells, their next two identified priorities.

In addition to the financial benefits from the employment opportunities created by this project, the families looked forward to a tank filled with water that would serve as a year-round source for domestic needs and allow them to cultivate the paddy lands in the coming agricultural season for the first time in 11 years.

NOTES

1. See Spencer 1990, p. 192.
2. The Norwegian government's lead in peace talks for Sri Lanka has historic roots but is above all linked to Norway's tradition of support for peace efforts.
3. In Sri Lanka, the different roles of the religions and the fact that Buddhism and Christianity are institutionalized religions (in comparison with Hinduism and Islam) conditions the way different religious leaders are affected, and respond to the war. Buddhist, Protestant, and Catholic clergy are to some extent engaged with the conflict. In contrast, Hindu leaders generally do not delve into the political aspects of conflict and war. Hindu leaders saw themselves as having virtually no community social role; rather, their work was defined by their caste (Brahmin) and as such, their societal roles could not exceed this definition.
4. Particularly in areas where temples are not present or have been destroyed. Representatives noted that temples play a large role in social activism, community outreach, information dissemination, and community development.

5. The government of Sri Lanka's FY98 military expenditure amounted to $US 719 million (which accounted for 4.2 percent of GDP) (Government of Sri Lanka 1999).

6. Since the outbreak of hostilities between the government and armed Tamil separatists in the mid-1980s, several hundred thousand Tamil civilians have fled the island. As of mid-1999, approximately 66,000 were housed in 133 refugee camps in southern India, another 40,000 lived outside the Indian camps, and more than 200,000 Tamils have sought refuge in the West.

7. Faith-based organizations have started local agricultural and vocational programs to train people in business management.

REFERENCES

Government of Sri Lanka. 1999. "Budget Review Report." Colombo.

Spencer, Jonathan. 1990. "Introduction, the Power of the Past." In Jonathan Spencer, ed., *Sri Lanka: History and the Roots of Conflict.* London: Routledge.

CHAPTER 19

"*Kacel pi Kuc*": Together for Peace in Uganda

One of Africa's most intractable conflicts continues to rage in the north of Uganda, with a specific religious group primarily responsible. Uganda's different faith groups have come together in different formations to seek a peaceful solution, to draw attention to and demand action on the conflict, and to support the communities devastated by the conflict. International institutions, including the World Bank, are finding a variety of promising ways to work with these faith-led coalitions at both community and national levels.

CONFLICT IN NORTHERN UGANDA

Since independence from the United Kingdom in 1962, Uganda has experienced a long series of wrenching civil conflicts. The current war in Acholiland, in northern Uganda, is fed by the Lord's Resistance Army (LRA), which has contested President Yoweri Museveni's rule since 1987. Backed by the Sudanese government, which resents Museveni's support of southern Sudanese liberation groups, the LRA has cut off all agricultural and commercial activities in the region, aiming to establish its own rule based on the Biblical Ten Commandments. The Uganda People's Defense Force has waged "Operation Iron Fist" against the LRA in the territory it controls in Uganda and southern Sudan since March 2002.

This case study is based on inputs from Godwin Hlatshwayo, institutional development and training consultant for the Northern Uganda Social Action Fund Project.

Fifteen years of conflict have imposed an enormous toll on the people of northern Uganda, severely exacerbating poverty by isolating communities from each other and from development partners. A vicious cycle of insecurity, governance problems, and capacity constraints has discouraged production and the delivery of social services. Where people once depended on cattle for income and security, stock has declined sharply. And violence against civilians and the abduction of many thousands of children forced to work as soldiers, porters, and sex slaves has destroyed families and communities.

To isolate civilians from the rebels and close off the north from the rest of the country, the government has created protected camps housing 460,000 displaced people, and peace-building efforts have therefore focused on reviving community cohesiveness. Several religious organizations have actively addressed the causes and consequences of civil strife in this region, among them the Acholi Religious Leaders' Peace Initiative (ARLPI) and the Mennonite Central Committee. The World Bank is also supporting the Northern Uganda Social Action Fund. This fund sponsors community-initiated projects that respond to natural and human-made disasters and deep economic problems in 18 districts, and it benefits from inputs from religious groups.

ACHOLI RELIGIOUS LEADERS' PEACE INITIATIVE

Organized in 1997, the ARLPI brings together leaders of the Catholic Church, the Anglican Church of Uganda, and Muslims to promote dialogue between the government and the LRA rebels. With 90 percent of the Acholi population belonging to one of the three faiths, the leaders have wielded their moral and religious authority, neutrality, and the organizational anchor of churches, parishes, and mosques to promote peace.[1] The group has held multifaith prayers for peace, lobbied for amnesty for the rebels, organized seminars on conflict resolution and trained volunteers, and provided local and regional mediation services. The intervention's guiding principle is that peace is a long-term group effort—hence the phrase *Kacel pi kuc*, or "together for peace."

The religious leaders view their collaboration as a major step in antisectarianism, not only in the north, but throughout Uganda. The group also aims to mobilize local and national leaders, NGOs, and the international community to achieve a mediated solution to the rebellion.

ARLPI began with discussions organized by Anglican and Catholic leaders in 1997 on common approaches to peace. The result was Joint Justice and Peace, which organized a prayer for peace by Christians and Muslims and condemned the government's policy of establishing protected camps. In March 1998, ARLPI presented "A Call for Peace and an End to Bloodshed in Acholiland," which recommended mediation among all the warring parties. This message of reconciliation legitimized the group both locally and nationally and helped engage local governments in peace initiatives.

The religious leaders appointed Bishop Onon Onweng to work with the U.N. Development Programme (UNDP) and other international agencies to secure financing for such initiatives, and UNDP Director Babatunde Thomas provided funds to ARLPI for workshops, meetings, and travel to establish contacts with the LRA and its allies. These efforts, under way since December 2000, convinced the Sudanese government to end support for the rebels.

THE MENNONITE CENTRAL COMMITTEE

A relief, service, and peace agency of the North American Mennonite and Brethren in Christ churches, the Mennonite Central Committee (MCC) first began working in Uganda following the Tanzanian invasion and overthrow of Idi Amin in 1979. MCC has played a major role in the Karamoja district in northern Uganda, where armed raids and cattle theft are common, by working through the Church of Uganda. The government of Uganda had asked the Jie, a local ethnic group, to turn in its guns, but the Jie refused. The resulting violent clashes with the Ugandan military destroyed 115 small villages and displaced thousands of families.

Through the Kotido Initiative for Peace, religious leaders collaborated with MCC and the Catholic Diocese to provide five truckloads of food, seed, and supplies worth US$20,570 to 1,000 Jie families from May to July 2002. MCC also funded the purchase by a local church group of oxen and farm implements to be used as a demonstration project for the surrounding community. MCC also provided emergency assistance to a local hospital contending with an Ebola epidemic, grants to an AIDS ministry, teachers for a vocational school, and a Trickle Up grant and loan program for low-income entrepreneurs. MCC also worked with ARLPI to organize community programs to prepare people for peace.

NORTHERN UGANDA SOCIAL ACTION FUND

With the support of a World Bank credit of US$100 million, approved in 2002, the Northern Uganda Social Action Fund was designed to mesh with a carefully elaborated national strategy for reducing poverty. That strategy includes investments that promote peace, enable the poor to raise their incomes,[2] and enhance communities' capacity to identify, set priorities, and plan systematically to meet their needs. The social fund thus exemplifies the World Bank's emerging framework for community-responsive development.

The five-year project includes four types of activities:

- Community development initiatives—small, discrete projects planned and managed by local elected committees
- Vulnerable group support—projects that respond to the needs of children and adults recovering from the effects of the war
- Community reconciliation and conflict management—activities that rely on both indigenous and modern knowledge to promote peaceful development and reduce conflict
- Institutions at the community, district, and national levels that develop local capacity to manage sustainable subprojects.

The fund's designers made special efforts to reflect lessons from other small-scale social funds in Africa, especially in conflict-affected regions. These lessons include the value of a pilot phase, the need to mobilize local resources and build local capacity, and the importance of autonomy, transparency, and accountability at district and community levels. The fund's activities therefore entail discussions with elected district assemblies and local councils as well as groups such as youth, women, and elders to elicit their environmental and social concerns.

The Interfaith Cooperation Circle Initiative of Uganda—linked to the United Religions Initiative, a global grassroots group dedicated to ending religious violence and creating cultures of peace, justice, and healing—is helping to oversee the fund's community reconciliation and conflict management activities. These include helping host communities reintegrate the child soldiers, ex-rebels, and war criminals who have disarmed and surrendered under the Amnesty Act of 2000, and enabling communities to resolve tribal conflicts over resources. These activities link to the broader, two-phase peace-building program in northern Uganda. Phase one will focus on designing, testing, and finalizing community peace-building efforts, while phase two will extend the projects to more districts and communities.

NOTES

1. Khadiagala 2001.
2. World Bank 2002.

REFERENCES

Khadiagala, Gilbert. 2001. "Greater Horn of Africa Peace Building Project: The Role of the Acholi Religious Leaders' Peace Initiative in Peace Building in Northern Uganda." Washington, D.C.: United States Agency for International Development.

World Bank. 2002. "Northern Uganda Social Action Fund Staff Appraisal Report." Africa Region. Washington, D.C.

20

Social Funds for Peace and Development in Conflict Regions of the Philippines

A peace accord between the Filipino government and the Moro National Liberation Front (MNLF) in September 1996 brought a resolution to over three decades of conflict in the Mindanao region of southern Philippines. The area, home to the country's largest concentration of Muslims, has since fluctuated from near peace to violent conflict. Many civil society organizations, including faith-based groups, have provided services to help rehabilitate the war-torn region, developing a variety of ways to work with international donors and development organizations.

THE CONFLICT

Established as the Sultanate of Sulu in 1450, the predominantly Muslim state of Mindanao fought the Spaniards for some 333 years and remained free until 1898, when the United States purchased the Philippine archipelago. In 1946, when the Republic of the Philippines again gained independence, the sultanate remained under the control of the central

This chapter is based on materials prepared by Richard Anson.

government in Manila. Between 1950 and 1960, the country encouraged immigration to the Mindanao region, known as the Land of Promise for its abundant resources. The resulting movement of Christians marginalized the native Lumads and the Moros, or Muslims, and new policies, tedious application processes, and formidable judicial procedures dispossessed many people of their lands.

Muslim evangelists in Mindanao led a resurgence of Islam in the 1960s. Heightened awareness of Islamic identity contributed to the social and cultural reawakening of the Moros, and mosques, *madaris* (Islamic schools), and Moro associations have since proliferated. This expanding civil society—built on perceived discrimination evidenced by the relatively slow pace of development in Muslim areas of Mindanao—fomented nationalist sentiment among the Moro population.

A series of events in the late 1960s and early 1970s further alienated Muslims. These included the Jabidah massacre of Muslim trainees by the Philippine military on Corregidor Island in March 1968, communal clashes between Muslims and Christians in which authorities often sided with Christians, and the gradual loss of Muslim lands to new settlers. The November 1971 elections, in which Christian politicians captured many provincial and municipal offices in traditionally Muslim areas, added fuel to the situation. The result was armed conflict.

By 1972, partisan political violence, generally divided along religious lines, gripped Mindanao and the Sulu Archipelago. The government's declaration of martial law and an order that all civilians surrender their guns sparked spontaneous rebellion among the Moros, who were suspicious of the government and had traditionally equated the right to carry arms with their religious heritage. Isolated uprisings rapidly spread in scope and size, and partisan Moro forces soon gathered under the loosely unified framework known as the MNLF.

Fighting for an independent Moro nation, the MNLF received outside support from the Organization of Islamic Conference, a union of Muslim nations. The military arm of the MNLF fielded some 30,000 armed fighters by 1973–75, when the conflict reached its peak. The Philippine government deployed its forces against the Moros, and the resulting casualties and destruction—both military and civilian—were heavy, with an estimated 50,000 people killed.

NEGOTIATIONS BEGIN

Meanwhile, the government announced economic aid programs and political concessions, and these—combined with a sharp decrease in the flow of arms from other countries—blunted the Moro movement. Dialogue between the government and the Moros began in late 1976, under the auspices of the Organization of Islamic Conference, and those talks led to the Tripoli Agreement, which provided a cease-fire and a plan for Moro autonomy. The government never fully implemented the peace agreement, however, and fighting broke out once again.

Low-level conflict continued for two more decades, as Moro refashioned itself into a broadly based and self-declared Islamic movement led by Islamic clerics. With the fall of the Marcos regime in 1985, Moro leaders organized mass demonstrations to petition the government for political autonomy for Philippine Muslims, and formed an Islamic political party to contest provincial elections. Abiding by her campaign pledge to promote national reconciliation, President Corazon Aquino initiated talks with the MNLF in 1986, but those eventually deadlocked over a proposal for an autonomous region, and the MNLF officially resumed its armed insurrection.

However, the government continued to press ahead with plans for Muslim autonomy without MNLF cooperation. Article 10 of the 1987 Philippines Constitution mandated that the new congress establish an Autonomous Region of Muslim Mindanao (ARMM). In a November 1989 plebiscite, only two Mindanao provinces, Maguindanao and Lanao del Sur, and two provinces in the Sulu Archipelago, Sulu and Tawitawi, opted to accept the government's autonomy measure. The government officially inaugurated the fragmented ARMM, with its own governor and unicameral legislature, in November 1990.

MOVEMENT TOWARD PEACE AND DEVELOPMENT

Despite the creation of the initial autonomous region, the MNLF remained dissatisfied with the government's concessions and, along with other opposition groups, pursued kidnappings, assassinations, and conflict with government forces. In 1992, President Fidel Ramos again initiated peace talks with the MNLF and ultimately signed a peace accord in September 1996. The two-part, four-year dynamic peace process that ensued made creative use of informal networks and multiple channels of communication.

The first component of this process—a three-year transition period—entailed creating a Special Zone of Peace and Development (SZOPAD), composed of 14 of Mindanao's 24 provinces and nine cities, as a precursor to an autonomous region. The agreement also called for establishing the Southern Philippines Council for Peace and Development (SPCPD) to manage peace-building and development efforts within SZOPAD. The SPCPD consisted of a chair, vice-chair, and three deputies—the latter representing Muslims, Christians, and native Lumads. A Consultative Assembly included SPCPD members, officials from the ARMM, members of the MNLF, and representatives from NGOs and other civil society organizations.

The creation of SZOPAD gave the international donor community access to long-neglected areas of the southern Philippines. The U.N. Development Programme, the European Union, the U.S. Agency for International Development, the Canadian International Development Agency, and the Australian Agency for International Development responded with assistance and rehabilitation programs. The World Bank also moved quickly to reach agreement on a loan for US$10 million to establish the SZOPAD Social Fund, designed to reintegrate the MNLF, the indigenous Lumad people, thousands of displaced people, and other marginalized groups into society. The SCPCD acted as lead agency for the fund, which supported small infrastructure programs such as farm-to-market roads, communal irrigation systems, potable water sources, and health and education facilities in the poorest, most conflict-affected areas. The fund allowed local stakeholders to choose priority projects and ensure fair allocation of resources.

The social fund took specific steps to engage religious communities as part of its overall efforts to contribute to peace and development in the southern Philippines, especially in majority-Muslim areas. The chair of SPCPD sits on the fund's board of directors. A survey financed by the World Bank's Post-Conflict Fund sought input from Muslim religious leaders and faith-based NGOs throughout the region. Some two-thirds of projects approved for funding have occurred in the autonomous region, as areas most affected by the conflict have the largest Muslim populations and could receive more funds. Nearly 43 percent of approved projects focused on education, most entailing construction of two- to three-room *madaris* for Muslim communities in Sulu, Palawan, and Zamboanga City. One objective was to add academic subjects to the *madari* curricula to prepare graduates for employment. The World Bank survey reported overall satisfaction with SZOPAD and a desire for more Bank help in training SCPCD members to administer funds.

FURTHER CONFLICT

The second phase of the 1996 peace accord entailed expanding the ARMM. However, the MNLF remained in conflict with the government, and the 1998 election of President Joseph Ejercito Estrada brought a declaration of "all-out war" against the insurgents. This conflict eventually displaced over 300,000 people.

In January 2001, following the impeachment of President Estrada, former Vice-President Gloria Macapagal-Arroyo almost immediately announced that her administration would pursue "all-out peace." To convince the MNLF to engage in peace talks, the Arroyo administration held a referendum to expand ARMM. However, former MNLF leader Nur Misuari, governor of the original ARMM, claimed that this unilateral action violated the timeline in the 1996 peace agreement, and after the government backed an opponent in elections, Misuari responded by reopening conflict with the MNLF. The Philippine military launched an aggressive counterattack, sending more than 6,000 soldiers to pursue Misuari and his estimated 600 fighters. The fighting displaced more than 20,000 civilians.

The Filipino government continued to battle both the MNLF and the Abu Sayyaf (a Muslim insurgency group) throughout much of 2001. The government and the MNLF signed a cease-fire agreement in June 2001, reinforced with guidelines for rehabilitating displaced people. However, at year's end the two sides were still working to implement the cease-fire, and conditions did not yet allow the 150,000 people still displaced in Mindanao to return. These farmers and villagers were sheltered in schools, mosques, chapels, or other public buildings, many with inadequate or nonexistent health facilities.

WORKING WITH INTERNALLY DISPLACED PERSONS

The World Bank Post-Conflict Fund—in collaboration with Community and Family Services International (CFSI), a Philippines-based social development organization with 20 years of domestic and international experience with uprooted persons—has since helped return and resettle some 6,759 families (33,550 persons) in five municipalities in Mindanao. These efforts entailed profiling communities, arranging site visits by the U.N. human rights commission, exploring income-generating opportunities, strengthening peace and education efforts, and expanding psychosocial services.

CFSI worked closely with recognized local leaders and volunteers—many of whom were faith leaders or active members of faith communities—to address these community needs. For example, the project organized and trained 70 volunteers known as *Sumpats*, a term that derives from the Maguindanaoan dialect and means "connecting with," in close consultation with recognized leaders. The *Sumpats* represent the ideal of local leaders who take responsibility for facilitating social development in war-affected communities.

The *Sumpats* also helped CFSI organize "information committees" to raise refugees' awareness of resources and ensure their access to service providers. Newly built *Pulangen* centers—typically hut-like structures made of indigenous materials and designed to reflect local tradition—serve as community meeting places. These centers, whose activities sometimes include prayer services and other faith-based pursuits, are important in helping reweave the social fabric.

CFSI continues to try to return displaced people safely to their homes while creating community ownership of the process. However, while many people displaced during the violence of 2000–2001 have been able to return to their homes, others have encountered reconstruction delays, land mines, and rebel presence in evacuated areas.

AN ENHANCED SOCIAL FUND

Because the SZOPAD Social Fund played a significant role in fostering peace and development in the region, attention turned early to possible continuation and expansion of the effort. The ARMM Social Fund for Peace and Development envisaged four goals. These include creating partnerships among stakeholders formerly on opposing sides, and generating both temporary and longer-term job opportunities, especially for women and out-of-school youth, sometimes by assisting micro-enterprises. The successor program aimed to enhance the access of poor, conflict-affected communities to medical and social services, and improve local governance and institutional capacity, with an emphasis on transparency and accountability.

Faith-based NGOs and other civil society organizations are expected to play a significant and continuing role in the development process in Mindanao, with the social fund a continuing instrument for channeling their energies to community-based works, underlying the basic objective of rebuilding social capital.

This reconstruction process is designed to promote inclusion, trust, and social cohesion by involving both communities and government agencies. The fund has engaged local leaders from Muslim, Christian, and indigenous Lumad communities; and many faith-based NGOs, as trusted entities in the post-conflict environment. Because religion has played a significant role in the conflict in Mindanao, community leaders and international observers alike believe it can and must play an even greater role in building peace and fostering development.

CHAPTER 21

Building Peace in Cambodia
Faith Initiatives 1992–2001

Some 700 orange-swathed monks and white-clad nuns and laypeople travel through former Khmer Rouge territory on an annual peace walk known as the Dhammayietra. A few hundred miles away in Battambang, the portico of a small building at a local *wat* (pagoda) is crammed with young, newly shaven monks who eagerly and painfully read about Gandhi in English, supervised by a former Jesuit brother. Around a table, government officials, police, community leaders, and monks meet to discuss a problem. An antigovernment demonstration in Phnom Penh turns ugly when police hunt down monks, arguing that they are too partisan to be authentic clergy.

These incidents are examples of "socially engaged Buddhism," a new form of nonviolent activism that has arisen in Cambodia since it reopened to the international community after U.N.–moderated elections in 1993. This new Buddhism is encouraging religious participation in the public sphere, particularly in building peace and mediating conflict. Engaged Buddhism attests to a fluid mixture of political forms and philosophies in an era of global cultural melange, as well as the rapid growth of a transnational interfaith peace movement no longer dominated by Christian interests.[1]

The initial draft of this chapter was prepared by Kathryn Poethig, Ph.D., St. Lawrence University, New York, in August 2002, as a step in assessing links between faith and development issues and institutions in Cambodia.

Since it embarked on its transition to democracy in 1992, after 15 years of Communist isolationism, Cambodia has seen a marked renewal of religious life and the participation of religious groups in the country's fledgling civil society. Religious pluralism in Cambodia includes revitalization of Cham (Islam), multiple Christian churches, and new Chinese religions. The return of former Buddhist refugees and a partnership between international faith-based NGOs and their local counterparts has encouraged Buddhists, especially, to help rebuild the strife-torn country.

CAMBODIAN BUDDHISM AND ITS "TRAGEDY OF HISTORY"

As a philosophy of liberation focusing on the mind, Buddhism is not known for its activism. While the religion rests on a strong philosophy of nonviolence, the means toward that end have not classically been political. "Socially engaged Buddhism," coined by the South Vietnamese monk Thich Nhat Hanh, refers to his order's commitment to a Buddhist basis for social action during the Vietnam war.[2] In the 1980s, Sulak Sivaraksa, an outspoken Thai lawyer, employed the term as a Buddhist critique of development strategies in Thailand.[3] By the mid-1990s, the International Network of Engaged Buddhists (INEB), with members in over 30 countries, were evidence of the vitality of this new form of contemporary activism.[4]

As in other countries, the significance of Buddhist-based movements in Cambodia can be understood only within 40 years of relations between the *sangha* (Buddhist clergy) and the state. *Sangha*–state relations have often been likened to a chariot requiring two wheels: both must turn harmoniously for the chariot to move smoothly. According to this philosophy, Buddhism attends to the moral and spiritual needs of the people while the state maintains the political sphere. On the community level, Cambodian social life is organized around the *wat*—the main site for meetings, rites of passage, and healing.[5] Young Cambodian men traditionally join the monkhood for the rainy season to gain merit (*bon*) for a better future life and "ripen" them into adulthood.

Although Cambodian monks instigated significant nationalist uprisings in the early 1900s, Khmer Buddhism, like Thailand's Buddhism, which has forged a close alliance between the state, monarchy, and *sangha*, has historically helped legitimate political authority.[6] As the foundation of the Khmer culture and way of life, Buddhism was a profound force in the Khmer revitalization.

Prince Sihanouk's attempt to forge a "Buddhist socialism" represented perhaps the most explicit political expression of the religion during the late 1950s and early 1960s.[7] Sihanouk's peculiar brand of Buddhist socialism was not Marxist: instead of eschewing private property, he argued that Buddhist socialism would inspire the wealthy to meritorious acts of charity. However, his espousal of this "middle path" was short-lived. By the end of the 1960s, Sihanouk had abandoned his socialist Buddhism, arguing that it was impossible for a small country like Cambodia to advocate nonviolence, neutrality, and compassion when harassed by superpowers intent on war.

With the support of the United States, General Lon Nol unseated Sihanouk in a bloodless coup in 1970 and exchanged Buddhist socialism for a "Buddhist holy war." Though government forces fought the Communist Khmer Rouge in the countryside, Lon Nol saw the real enemy as the Vietnamese. His virulent ethno-nationalism construed Khmer Buddhism as the spiritual basis of the war that would ultimately revive Cambodian prestige to the glories of Angkor, the vaunted ancient Khmer empire.

Lon Nol's Khmer Republic lasted until 1975, when the Khmer Rouge unfurled a radical Communist, antimodernist plan that destroyed the Cambodian economy, infrastructure, and social fabric while wiping out all signs of "corrupting" western capitalism. An estimated 2 million Cambodians died through execution, starvation, and disease; some 60,000 monks were forced to disrobe; and 3,000 *wats* were destroyed or converted to prisons in just four years. Invasion by Vietnam in 1979 ended the Khmer Rouge experiment but maintained a socialist agenda, replacing one cadre of Khmer Rouge with others who had sought the assistance of the new Vietnamese Socialist Republic.

The *sangha*'s rehabilitation was contingent on its compliance with the policies of the socialist state. Monks were urged to attend revolutionary training and reinterpret the teachings of Buddha to support Communist ideology and government policies. Any attempt to "sabotage the correct lines, subvert national and international solidarity and destroy the fruits of the Kampuchean people's revolution" would be punished.[8] Only men over the age of 50 could become monks, as a younger generation was denied the traditional route to community religious life. However, *wats* provided the vehicle for preserving Cambodian culture in diaspora communities throughout the West. By the mid-1980s, Cambodian Buddhism fused with nationalist anti-Communist factions, as refugee camps became staging grounds for anti-Vietnamese resistance forces.[9]

RETURNING TO BUDDHISM IN POST-SOCIALIST CAMBODIA

The weakened Buddhist *sangha* was a peripheral concern to the U.N. Transitional Authority (UNTAC), the architect of Cambodia's transition to democracy, which saw governance and infrastructure as the most pressing need. The first nod to Buddhism as a cultural resource for participatory democracy occurred during the development of UNTAC's human rights curriculum, which incorporated Buddhist tenets and sought to enlist monks in providing support.

Most of the fledgling human rights NGOs that emerged in Cambodia during the early 1990s reflected this merger of rights with Buddhist moral principles.[10] Of these groups, the most directly associated with the *sangha* was the Human Rights Training Project, initiated by a Cambodian-American. Although the project was short-lived, other human rights NGOs have continued to develop this curriculum in secondary and Buddhist schools.

The most dramatic expression of peacemaking, however, occurred outside the elaborate plans of U.N. advisers, state officials, and warring factions. In April 1992, over 100 monks, nuns, and international staff from Site II, the main Cambodian refugee camp in Thailand, walked over the border to symbolize that peace was returning to Cambodia "step by step." Although Cambodian and U.N. officials had given the walkers only grudging permission, the action was an astounding success, galvanizing both international and local support for a second walk that occurred the following year during elections. The "pilgrimage of truth" quickly became an annual event, with organizers housed in the Dhammayietra Center for Peace and Reconciliation in Phnom Penh.

THE DHAMMAYIETRA

The Dhammayietra was the only explicitly nonviolent response to entrenched factionalism in Cambodia's transition to democracy. Unlike the United Nations' plans and other official strategies for national reconstruction and reconciliation, the Dhammayietra Center aims to build a culture of peace through engaged Buddhist philosophy and practice. Its charismatic leader, Samdech Preah Maha Ghosananda, known as the Gandhi of Cambodia, teaches "peacemaking as the dharma"—a way of life embodied in mindful meditation.[11]

During the conflict between the Khmer Rouge and the government from 1993 to 1998, the Dhammayietra Center's annual walks promoted social messages sanctioned by the monks—peaceful elections, cessation of civil war, ecological balance, a ban on land mines. For two weeks in April or May, hundreds of nuns, monks, laypeople, and international supporters traversed some 300 kilometers through Cambodia's country-side, stopping at *wats* and planting Bodhi trees, the sacred tree of the Buddha. Each route was mapped so walkers would encounter those most affected by Cambodia's conflict. As the procession passed through small villages, thousands of Cambodians lined the roads, ready for the *tuk mon*—the blessing with lustral water.

One of the primary contributions of the Dhammayietra to post-social-ist Khmer Buddhism was the discipline and training of a new generation of monks. The young monks who joined the walk lacked self-discipline and tended to abuse the respect of villagers. Ven. Nhem Kim Teng, a senior monk of the walk, has noted that the young monks needed role models and training in the *dharma*. He maintains that "Maha Ghosananda is trying to bring back the things we have lost. Khmers used to be gentle, honest and forgiving. We would help each other in times of difficulty, speak respectfully... all those things we have lost because of the war and violence and destruction."[12] By the fourth walk, the Dhammayietra had developed an organizational structure, prewalk training, and a signed pledge that ensured more discipline among the walkers—and the *sangha*.

An interfaith partnership that included a Buddhist monk, a Jesuit brother, and a Jewish activist from Site II founded the Coalition for Peace and Reconciliation, the organizing body of the Dhammayietra. These activists consulted with the Bangkok office of the INEB and Nonviolence International to develop nonviolent workshops for the *sangha* on either side of the border. Since the group's inception, Japanese monks from Nipponzan Myohoji, an order dedicated to world peace, have accompanied the walk, and Maha Ghosananda's connections to engaged Buddhist leaders in the United States and around the world have given the Dhammayietra international visibility.

THE DHAMMAYIETRA'S PEACE WALKS MULTIPLY

While the Dhammayietra Center and the Coalition for Peace and Reconciliation were the primary institutions supporting faith-based peace work, other initiatives began to emerge in the mid-1990s, drawing on the symbolic power of the peace walk and its nonviolence training to respond to a rising climate of violence. The Forum for Peace through Love and Compassion, or *Mehta Thor*, for example, grew from a grenade attack that killed 20 and wounded 100 during a March 1997 rally held by opposition candidate Sam Rainsy outside the National Assembly.

The 23 NGOs most active in *Mehta Thor* and the Dhammayietra formed the Campaign to Reduce Violence through Peace on the Cambodian New Year in April 1997. A strategic planning conference in May to encourage peaceful conduct in the 1998 national elections attracted representatives from 70 organizations, including the Forum of the Poor in Thailand and the Peace Council in Sri Lanka.

Then, on July 5–6, 1997, a brief, violent coup in Phnom Penh upset the fragile coalition government, and officials fled the country as tanks rumbled down the streets and military personnel looted shops. In early August, Maha Ghosananda led monks, nuns, and laypersons from *wat Sampeou Meas* to the National Assembly, where they conducted a traditional ceremony and meditation as a call for peace. The group also issued statements to political officials, the United Nations, and the media asking for calm. Both actions took tremendous courage, as the political situation was highly charged.[13]

A challenge to the *sangha*'s presence in the peace walks occurred after the election, when opposition parties raised charges of voter fraud. A two-week nonviolent sit-in sparked a violent confrontation between the demonstrators and government forces. Monks were particularly visible in a series of protest marches calling for nonviolence on both sides. The government claimed they could not be "real monks" because their presence violated Buddhist precepts about the *sangha*'s participation in partisan politics, and police chased, beat, and defrocked monks. Ordered by the deputy of the National Police to "tell monks not to participate in protest and to root out demonstrators that may be hiding there," troops and antiterrorist police entered *wats* throughout the country to arrest targeted monks.[14] This event stunned national and international peace activists who had expressed confidence in the growing support for peace work in Cambodia. While the police did not harass the Dhammayietra Center, the government's violence shut down its peace activities.

With the final defections of the Khmer Rouge in 1999, new peace initiatives opened up in western Cambodia, the Khmer Rouge's last stronghold. At issue was how to draw these conflict-ridden areas into the national community without alienating the populace. Buddhism for Development, an NGO founded by former monk Mony Chenda and supported by the German Konrad Adenauer Foundation, has designed one of the most impressive projects trying to ensure that outcome. The NGO hosted a conference and provided publications on a Buddhist approach to reconciliation and reduction of small arms, particularly in the western Cambodia war zone. A popular item was a yellow umbrella distributed to monks with the dictum "Put down the gun, pick up the *Dharma*."

INITIATIVES WITH INTERNATIONAL FAITH-BASED NGOS

Not long after its emergence, the Dhammayietra found support in a small circle of primarily faith-based international NGOs—the Mennonite Central Committee (MCC), the American Friends Service Committee (AFSC), Church World Service, and Catholic Relief Services. These NGOs have not only offered consistent financial support but have joined the walks and provided organizational leadership for a faith-based, grassroots peace movement.[15]

As Christian "peace churches," the MCC and the AFSC arrived in Cambodia in 1979, when the rest of the international community was adhering to a hands-off policy owing to Vietnam's occupation of the country.[16] The two NGOs sponsored small-scale community development projects to aid in postwar reconstruction. After 1992, when the well-funded international development community arrived en masse, these smaller NGOs determined that they could not compete with large-scale ventures. According to an AFSC staff member, two Cambodian staff said: "Our biggest concern is violence in Cambodia and the need for people to resolve their conflicts, inner and outer. We'd like you to do something about peace."[17] Given their theological commitment to pacifism, MCC and AFSC therefore formed a Peace Partnership with the Dhammayietra Center to collaborate on conflict-reduction projects. This partnership, along with other religious NGOs, energetically supported the International Campaign to Ban Landmines in Cambodia.

One of the partnership's most successful endeavors has been the Small Arms Reduction project, an effort the Quakers have supported internationally. In 1998, the Peace Partnership convened 20 representatives from local and international NGOs to discuss the widespread use of arms in Cambodia. This meeting resulted in a feasibility study of arms reduction, while a working group developed a long-term, multifaceted campaign to accomplish that goal.

AFSC has also initiated a Local Capacities for Nonviolence Project that supports local peace-building efforts in conjunction with its community development programs. Judy Saumweber, project coordinator, notes that religion figures prominently in communities' understanding of how to build peace. "All the communities we work with are Buddhist, and when we ask them what they want to do to build peace . . . [they say] that they want to build Buddhism in their village."[18]

THE GRASSROOTS POWER OF RELIGION

Cambodia's religious sources for peace building remind organizers to attend to the "grassroots power of religion even when conflicts are not centered around religious animosities and even when the religious establishment is weak."[19] The new engaged Cambodian Buddhism introduced through transnational networks encouraged the *sangha* to consider new forms of religious participation in the public sphere. This participation has enlivened a new consciousness of religious citizenship that has tested the parameters of the *sangha*'s role in partisan politics.

While a number of initiatives—including the Dhammayietra—are now dormant, a loose network of NGOs interested in peace-based programs is addressing Khmer Rouge integration, election violence, and community development. International support for these peace initiatives has ranged from U.N. agencies to small, faith-based NGOs that have helped develop a grassroots Buddhist peace movement. Although not without tensions, the partnership between these international NGOs and their local counterparts has generally been positive. As competence in a range of peace-building activities grows in Cambodia, and new members of civil society and the international development community join in, they may well promote the local *sangha*'s involvement at the request of the community.

NOTES

1. See Arjun Apadurai, *Modernity at Large: Cultural Dimensions of Globalization* (Minneapolis: University of Minnesota Press, 1996), who writes on the dialectical process by which dominant ideologies integrate into local communities.

2. Thich Nhat Hanh became well known on both sides of the Pacific in the 1960s and 1970s for his nonviolence and radical neutrality, which earned him a nomination for the Nobel Peace Prize by Martin Luther King Jr. in 1967. For his work on interdependence, a significant contribution to contemporary philosophy of engaged Buddhism, see Thich Nhat Hanh, *Interbeing: Fourteen Guidelines for Engaged Buddhism* (Berkeley: Parallax Press, 1997). See also Christopher Queen and Sallie King, eds., *Engaged Buddhists: Buddhist Liberation Movements in Southeast Asia* (Albany: SUNY Press, 1996).

3. Sulak Sivaraksa is prolific. For an overview of his vision, see Sivaraksa, *Seeds of Peace: A Buddhist Vision of Renewing Society* (Berkeley: Parallax Press, 1993), and Donald Swearer, "Sulak Sivaraksa's Buddhist Vision for Renewing Society," in *Engaged Buddhists: Buddhist Liberation Movements in Southeast Asia*, pp. 195–235. David Chappell, Soka University of America, published a collection of tributes to Sivaraksa in 2003 on his 70th birthday.

4. There is a stimulating transnational interchange among engaged Buddhists. Recent books include Christopher Queen, ed., *Engaged Buddhism in the West* (Boston: Wisdom Publications, 2000); Christopher Queen, Prebisch, and Keown, eds., *Action Dharma: New Studies in Engaged Buddhism* (Richmond, Va: Curizon, 2001); and Udomittippong and Walker, eds., *Socially Engaged Bud-*

dhism for the New Millennium (Bangkok: Sathirakoses-Nagappradipa Foundation and Foundation for Children, 1999).

5. Ebihara 1971.

6. Tambiah 1976.

7. Chandler 1991.

8. Suksamran 1993, p 143.

9. The Research Center of Khmer Buddhist Association was established at Site II to reinvigorate Buddhist philosophy and integrate those teachings into the anti-Communist agenda. The center produced a journal that offered a Buddhist justification of the faction's nationalist platform for the inevitable "reconstruction" of Cambodia.

10. These include the most prominent human rights NGOs such as the Cambodian Human Rights Association, the Cambodian League for the Promotion and Defense of Human Rights, the Khmer Institute of Democracy, Human Rights Vigilance of Cambodia, and Human Rights and Community Outreach Projects.

11. See Samdech Preah Maha Ghosananda's collected *dharma* talks in Jane Mahoney and Philip Edmonds, eds., *Step by Step* (Berkeley: Parallax Press, 1992).

12. *Phnom Penh Post* 1993.

13. This information is drawn from McGrew 1998.

14. *Cambodia Daily* 1998. (See also Laura McGrew, "Buddhism and Beatings," *Phnom Penh Post*, October 20, 1998).

15. Sasse 1999.

16. See Cynthia Sampson and John Paul Lederach, *From the Ground Up: Mennonite Contributions to International Peacekeeping* (Oxford: Oxford University Press, 2000). For peace building among the Society of Friends, see the Web site of the Quaker United Nations Office: http://www.afsc.org/quno.htm.

17. Eva Mysliwiec, then a staff member at MCC, wrote *Punishing the Poor* (Oxford: OXFAM, 1988), a scathing denunciation of international isolation of Cambodia, and went on to found the influential Cambodian Resource Development Institute.

18. Judy Saumweber, personal communication, June 22, 2001.

19. Morris 2004.

REFERENCES

Cambodia Daily. 1998. "Police Target Activist Monks." September 10.

Chandler, David. 1991. *The Tragedy of Cambodian History: Politics, War, and Revolution Since 1945.* New Haven: Yale University Press.

Ebihara, May. 1971. *Svay: A Khmer Village in Cambodia,* Ph.D. dissertation. Department of Anthropology. Columbia University.

McGrew, Laura. 1998. "Building Peace in Cambodia, Step by Step: Cooperation to Reduce Violence for Peace." Unpublished manuscript. Phnom Penh.

Morris, Catherine. 2004. "Case Studies in Religion and Peacebuilding: Cambodia." In Harold Coward and Gordon Smith, eds., *Religion and Peacebuilding.* Albany, N.Y.: SUNY Press.

Phnom Penh Post. 1993. "Maha Ghosananda's Peace Revolution." July 16–29.

Sasse, Rolien. 1999. "A Long March to Peace: Evaluation of the Dhammayietra Center for Peace and Nonviolence 1993–1999." Phnom Penh: Dhammayietra Center. February/March.

Suksamran, Sombon. 1993. "Buddhism, Political Authority and Legitimacy in Thailand and Cambodia." In Trevor Ling, ed., *Buddhist Trends in Southeast Asia.* Singapore: Institute of Southeast Asian Studies.

Tambiah, Stanley. 1976. *World Conqueror and World Renouncer.* Cambridge, U.K.: Cambridge University Press.

22

The Community of Sant'Egidio

Its Role in Mediating Peace

The roots of the Community of Sant'Egidio, a Catholic lay association, date back to 1968, when a group of high school students, meeting in Rome to read the gospel, launched reading and writing programs for children of poor immigrants. Committed to serving the poor, the homeless, the sick, and needy foreigners, and to working for peace, Sant'Egidio has become an international movement, present in 70 countries, with a membership of about 40,000. All are volunteers, all unpaid, who share a common commitment to social justice and to working through spirituality to this end. Community activities are financed through voluntary contributions, sometimes supplemented by government funds. The Community works in a wide spectrum of countries, cultures, and religions, though it is clearly grounded in Roman Catholicism. This chapter outlines the Community's work and approach, with a focus on its peace-building activities. Chapter 10 describes Sant'Egidio's work on HIV/AIDS in Mozambique.

The Community's wide-ranging activities reflect today's complex patterns of poverty. The links between poverty and conflict emerge vividly through its experience, and thus are woven through its approach and work. Sant'Egidio has been noteworthy for its creative and tenacious

This chapter was prepared by Lucy Keough and Katherine Marshall in collaboration with the Community of Sant'Egidio; particular thanks go to Mario Giro, Community of Sant'Egidio.

pursuit of partnerships with a wide range of organizations—governmental, private sector, academic, community, lay, and secular—all within the framework of a network of communities in each country where it is active, that together Sant'Egidio calls a movement.

The organization's charitable works, activism on behalf of the marginalized, and initiatives in conflict resolution are rooted in its corporate spiritual identity as a community of prayer and fellowship. Community leaders describe themselves as friends and ascribe much of their success to their core philosophy of friendship and service. Sant'Egidio works in the very poorest communities, often finding itself in places where raging conflict and the absence of basic services make misery deeper still. Where government services are weak to nonexistent, organizations such as Sant'Egidio may represent the only source of basic health and education services. Some programs address emergency situations: aid to Afghani and Kosovar refugees (in which it collaborated with the World Bank, as described in this chapter), support for flood victims in Mozambique and Sudan, and for survivors of the 2001 earthquake in El Salvador. Other programs have specific development objectives, for example, the rehabilitation of a hospital destroyed in Guinea-Bissau's recent civil conflict (again in partnership with the World Bank), and the DREAM treatment program for HIV/AIDS patients in Mozambique (chapter 10). In all cases, the Community seeks to work in partnership and build capacities with project beneficiaries. Partnership, hope, and a strong sense of shared responsibility define the essence of the Community.

An important focus of the Community is ecumenical and interreligious dialogue, emphasizing the need for a prayer for peace. Sant'Egidio's annual international interreligious meetings have offered important opportunities to further what many see as a renewed desire in today's world (especially after September 11, 2001) for better comprehension between the great world religions. These meetings carry on the tradition of the major 1987 meeting of faith leaders led by the Pope in Assisi. The annual meetings are held in a different city of Europe each year (Palermo in 2002, Aachen in 2003, Milan in 2004). They culminate in a remarkable ceremony where each faith worships individually (symbolizing that interfaith dialogue is grounded in a deepening of individual faith), then moves in a procession to a central square, with faith groups meeting and exchanging greetings and embraces at each intersection. The gatherings conclude with a common declaration of commitment to peace and a symbolic lighting of candles by each faith leader.

Sant'Egidio combines its focus on peace with a continuing concern and advocacy for the very poor, and has gained a special status for its work in poor and conflict-ridden countries in different parts of the world. It is widely recognized for its deep commitment and its skill and experience. Sant'Egidio illustrates both what can be done and what needs to be done in some of the most destitute situations around the world. The organization has received numerous awards, including UNESCO's 1999 Félix Houphouët-Boigny Peace Prize,[1] in recognition of its work for peace through interfaith dialogue and understanding.

SANT'EGIDIO'S ROLE AS A PEACE MEDIATOR

Sant'Egidio sees conflict and poverty as closely linked to one another—in the words of Sant'Egidio's founder, Andrea Riccardi, "War is the mother of all poverty. War makes everybody poor, also the rich."[2] Through personal relationships and an active diplomacy based on friendship and an appreciation for and respect of different perspectives, the Community of Sant'Egidio has been active in peace efforts in Mozambique, Liberia, Lebanon, El Salvador, Guatemala, Romania, Albania, Armenia, the Horn of Africa, Algeria, and many other conflict situations. The Community works continuously to network and establish relationships with political, religious, and civil society actors at every level. Sant'Egidio is considered one of the most interesting examples of the ability of civil society to affect international situations and influence peace and reconciliation processes.[3] Former U.N. Secretary General Boutros Boutros-Ghali observed that the Community of Sant'Egidio had developed a technique that differed from those of the professional policymakers, but that was complementary to theirs. He ascribed the Community's technique to informal discretion, which converges with the official work of governments and of intergovernmental organizations.

Sant'Egidio sometimes operates as part of a two-track approach: government and professional diplomats lead the official discussions, while Sant'Egidio acts as a mediator in unofficial talks. In Burundi, the peace process had two diplomatic tracks—an official one, led by former Tanzanian President Julius Nyerere, and an unofficial one led by the Community. While Nyerere focused on the Arusha process (which brought together Hutu and Tutsi parties), Sant'Edigio attempted to intervene to suspend hostilities between government and rebel forces, thereby facilitating progress on the political dialogue. Some call such efforts a practical demonstration of the value of citizen diplomacy.

Sant'Egidio's work and the nature of its partnerships in the conflict countries of Mozambique and Albania offer two quite distinct experiences.

MOZAMBIQUE

Mozambique's civil war began in 1977, almost immediately after independence. Portugal relinquished power in 1974 to Frelimo, an independence movement founded in 1962 that had engaged for some years in an armed struggle for independence. Frelimo insisted that it was the sole legitimate representative of the Mozambican people. Once in power, Frelimo focused on eliminating Portuguese culture and government institutions, imposing a nationalist socialist authority, and concentrating virtually all power within a small circle of Frelimo senior hierarchy.[4]

Reflecting long-standing hostility toward the white minority rule in then-Rhodesia and South Africa, Frelimo was openly supportive of the Zimbabwean nationalist guerillas (ZANLA) in Rhodesia and the African National Congress (ANC) in South Africa. In response, Rhodesia supported the creation of Renamo (Mozambique National Resistance), a military right-wing resistance group opposed to the strict Marxist Frelimo regime. Following Rhodesian (Zimbabwean) independence in 1980, the apartheid state of South Africa continued to support Renamo with arms and financial assistance.[5] Renamo's political strength within Mozambique drew on discontent in the center and north of the country where Frelimo had tried to force the rural population into large collective farms. Its actions also entailed suppression of religious expression.

By the mid-1980s, all regions of Mozambique were gripped in civil war. With significant support from South Africa, Renamo was waging a fierce guerilla war, attacking villages and demolishing schools, bridges, hospitals, and roads. With a stated objective of constitutional reform and multiparty democracy, Renamo in practice undermined administrative and governmental institutions. During the bitter 17-year war, some 900,000 Mozambicans died, more than 3 million were driven from their homes, and half the total population of 16 million faced starvation.

The Catholic Church presence in Mozambique was affected by its strong historic association with Portuguese colonial interests. After independence, therefore, the Church sought to establish a new identity for itself, its actions including active efforts to promote black bishops and a renewed focus on assistance to the poor. Despite Frelimo's attempts to repress religious traditions, in many regions traditional religious beliefs and practices survived. Renamo, in contrast, sought to use religion as a political force. Playing heavily on Frelimo's Marxist philosophy, Renamo used traditional religion and Christianity in its efforts to win popular support.

Sant'Egidio's Relationship with Mozambique

Sant'Egidio's relationship with Mozambique started with the effort of Bishop Gonçalves, from the Portuguese city of Beira, who asked that Sant'Egidio intervene on behalf of Mozambican Catholics, who he believed were being marginalized and constrained in their expression of religious belief.

A significant point of contention between Frelimo and the Church centered on the return of Church property that had been nationalized. Sant'Egidio used its strong ties with the Italian government and with Enrico Berlinguer, head of the Italian Communist Party (PCI), who had extensive political and economic ties with Frelimo. Together they organized meetings between the leaders of PCI and Frelimo. Berlinguer offered to use his own moral authority and the weight of PCI to persuade Frelimo to remove restrictions against the practice of religion.[6] The combined result was that Sant'Egidio was able to establish a strong relationship with the Mozambique government and the Vatican, and the local Catholic leadership was strengthened in its negotiations with the government to settle property disputes. By the mid-1980s, Sant'Egidio had succeeded in establishing a serious dialogue with the state, while continuing its humanitarian assistance.

In parallel, Bishop Gonçalves had been working with Catholic communities and had established ties with Renamo. Through the Bishop, Sant'Egidio succeeded in developing relationships with Renamo as well as with the Frelimo government.

Mediations

Toward the late 1980s, partly as a result of efforts by Mozambican church leaders, Frelimo and Renamo agreed to engage in direct talks, but outside Mozambique. However, the question of who would serve as mediator in these talks was never fully resolved. A first, failed attempt took place in Malawi in June 1990. Shortly thereafter, Sant'Egidio organized exploratory talks in Rome, bringing the two parties together without referring to the issue of a mediator. Sant'Egidio also held out the prospect of financial and diplomatic support from the Italian government.

This meeting in Rome set the stage for the direct involvement of the Community in peace talks over an extended period (1990–92), as part of a complex effort involving neighboring countries and observers from the United States, France, the United Kingdom, and Portugal. Ultimately, these efforts were a significant factor contributing to the formulation of the Mozambique Peace Agreement in October 1992.

Sant'Egidio's initiative built both on its own good offices and the active participation of three African governments: Kenya, Malawi, and Zimbabwe. The role of the mediator was hotly contested, with Renamo preferring Kenya, and Frelimo, Zimbabwe; this nearly caused a stalemate. Finally it was decided that this function would be shared between Sant'Egidio and Italy, with Kenya advising Renamo delegates. Under U.N. leadership, a multicountry force was to be formed to guarantee implementation of any peace agreement.

Sant'Egidio thus succeeded in creating a political process based on dialogue on neutral ground in Rome, with strong adherence to the basic principles of pluralism and inclusiveness. The focus was squarely on peace, rather than victory. In the first formal meeting, Sant'Egidio secured agreement on two fundamental rules for the dialogue: both sides agreed not to use force as a means of securing their political goals, and they would emphasize issues that united rather divided them. Once the mediators assumed management of the negotiations process, they were able to hammer out an agenda that included the issues of Zimbabwean forces, political concerns, and a cease-fire.

Sant'Egidio's success in its role as mediator reflected its recognized integrity, honesty, and ability to act as an objective, honest broker. An unofficial neutral actor, with no agenda of its own, without any international power base, it was never forced into political positions that could have been the downfall of a more traditional mediator.[7] The Sant'Egidio team made interpersonal relationships central to their strategy of conflict resolution. They facilitated a process where the parties themselves were fully responsible for the peace process, drawing on the international community as necessary, as significant, but nonintrusive, actors in the process.

Sant'Egidio encouraged other players to be introduced into this peacemaking process, creating political latitude that was previously nonexistent. Mozambique's civil society was a strong component in this multiparty negotiation, through churches and religious communities. The Italian government was a key player; it hosted the peace talks and provided financial support and a role model of democracy. Sant'Egidio ensured that the U.S. government remained up-to-date on the talks and the United States offered technical expertise on military, legal, economic, and institutional issues in negotiations. These allowed for the successful mediation process. Chester Crocker noted that the strategic alliances in Mozambique demonstrated the benefits of engaging all external players to work together in both the negotiation phase, 1990–92, and the implementation phase, 1992–94.[8]

The ultimate peace accord was a political agreement, not a document of retributive justice; it included a successful exit strategy for the mediators and observers. The accord stipulated a cease-fire followed by a large-scale demobilization of troops and an electoral process that would take place one year later. Under this agreement the United Nations was assigned the responsibility of monitoring and coordinating the political, military, electoral, and humanitarian aspects of the General Peace Agreement.[9]

Results

The peace agreement was signed on October 4, 1992, with a cease-fire to take effect on October 16. A U.N. peacekeeping force of 7,500 arrived in mid-December to supervise demobilization, followed by 2,400 international observers to supervise elections on October 27–28, 1994.[10] The subsequent political leadership succeeded largely because its policies were framed in a context of reconciliation that was inclusive and open to structural institutional changes. The churches made a major contribution in the process of rehabilitating communities such that people were able to feel confident and secure in living and working together again.[11] Through the process of reconciliation and forgiveness, acknowledging and celebrating people's return, and through mechanisms that allowed people to put the war behind them, the churches played an active role in reaffirming the process of reconstruction and in assisting children and adults to rebuild their lives and to envisage a more hopeful future.

One element accounting for Sant'Egidio's success was its ability to establish trust with both Frelimo and Renamo, as well as with religious communities of Mozambique and other participants in the peace process. This was due to its nonpartisan social action for the common good and its continuous effort to understand each perspective on the conflict. It worked in collaboration with a variety of governmental, nongovernmental, cultural, and religious organizations and individuals, both inside and outside Mozambique. Finally, a shift in the goal from victory to peace secured popular support in Mozambique, both from local leaders and civil society, and the international community, and ultimately ensured this goal was not reversed.[12]

ALBANIA

Religious and ethnic tensions between Albanians and Serbs have deep roots. For generations, Kosovo, a province of the former Socialist Federal Republic of Yugoslavia, was disputed between Serbs and Albanians. Albanians claimed to be the original inhabitants, as descendants of the ancient Illyrians, who occupied this area even before the Roman Empire. Most Albanians are either Muslim or Roman Catholic. For the Serbs, meanwhile, Kosovo is the birthplace of Serbian nationalism; the defeat of Serbian forces there in 1389 by Turkish troops became emblematic of the fall of the Serbian empire, eventually leading to Turkish domination of the Balkans. The Serbs have thus asserted that Kosovo was the heart of its medieval kingdom through the middle ages, with few, if any, Albanians within the population. Serbs are Slavic in origin and in general follow the Serbian Orthodox Church. Religious enmities run especially high: "religious identity has been present constantly in the antagonisms that have fragmented the Balkans for centuries, setting neighbor against neighbor, Muslims against Orthodox Christians and Orthodox Christians against Western Christians."[13] From the late fourteenth century, since the time of Turkish rule, Kosovo has seen a steady stream of Albanian refugees. In the period following World War II, Kosovo's population was 90 percent Albanian.

In 1945, the Communist regime in socialist Yugoslavia dealt with national aspirations by creating a federation of six nominally independent republics—Croatia, Montenegro, Serbia, Slovenia, Bosnia-Herzegovina, and Macedonia. In Serbia, the two provinces of Kosovo and Vojvodina were given autonomous status in 1974, giving Kosovo almost the same rights as the other six republics. From the early 1990s onward, a series of conflicts consumed the republics, leading to the disintegration of Yugoslavia and the Dayton Agreement of 1995. When Serbian leader Slobodan Milosevic became president of Yugoslavia in 1989, he refused demands for Kosovo's independence, revoked the province's autonomous status, and installed military rule in its stead. As a result, the Albanians boycotted the state institutions and created a parallel government.

In 1998, nine years after the abolition of Kosovo's autonomy, the Kosovo Liberation Army, supported by the mainly ethnic Albanians, openly rebelled against Serbian rule, demanding the full status of a republic. In early 1998, Serb troops entered Kosovo and there was sporadic armed conflict in the area, which escalated to a full civil war later that same year. The North Atlantic Treaty Organization (NATO) organized a cease-fire on October 25, 1998, with a number of peace monitors deployed in the region. The cease-fire ended months later and the war resumed. This was followed by failed peace talks in Rambouillet, France, after which NATO began a bombing campaign in March 1999. Shortly afterward, refugees started fleeing Kosovo, having been forced out of their homes. At least

800,000 Kosovars fled the province, most of them ethnic Albanians who fled into impoverished Albania. The crisis in Kosovo should be seen in a regional context—the most recent outbreak of a longer-term regional crisis that erupted in the 1980s with the economic decline and breakup of the former Socialist Federal Republic of Yugoslavia.[14]

Albania's recent history is equally turbulent, characterized by a host of political and economic crises. Following relatively good progress from 1993 until 1996 in the transition to independence, subsequent reforms in governance and the financial sector were very slow, resulting in social and economic crisis in 1997, with hesitant economic recovery beginning again in 1998. As hostilities in Kosovo were escalating in 1998, Albania played an active role in promoting negotiations between the warring factions during the Rambouillet peace talks. But in 1999, the armed conflict reached new heights and the Albanian government and the international community were not prepared for the mass inflow of Kosovar Albanian refugees fleeing to Albania and other neighboring countries. As a result, Albanian budgetary expenditures were diverted to meet the needs for immediate assistance to this group, putting serious pressure on the state budget and crowding out resources for essential public functions at all levels of government.[15]

Sant'Egidio's History in Albania and Kosovo

Sant'Egidio had a presence in Albania for many years before the arrival of the refugees. It had organized projects defending religious liberty, helped renascent churches, created a dialogue with local Muslims, and provided medical and educational assistance, among other services. Sant'Egidio has also been present in Kosovo since 1996. In Kosovo it established strong ties with Ibrahim Rugova, the leader of the Democratic League of Kosovo, which allowed Sant'Egidio to take on a role in the reconciliation between Serbs and Albanians. Sant'Egidio chose to focus on education in the region because of the deplorable conditions in which students were studying and low participation rates. After the war of 1999, Sant'Egidio continued its efforts in the region, committing itself to assisting the fleeing Kosovar refugees, specifically in the area of Kukes, where the Community had been present since 1998.

In 1998, Sant'Egidio collaborated with the World Bank on a program to support education and health facilities in central Albania, aimed at responding to the region's enormous education and health needs that were exacerbated by the arrival of refugees from the north. Previous research by Sant'Egidio had shown a high drop-out rate among primary school students, and only 30 percent of the population in central Albania had access to clean water. As part of a broader program to assist Albania to respond to the Kosovo crisis,[16] the World Bank provided a grant of US$1 million under its Post-Conflict Fund. The project aimed to strengthen health and educational services in the districts of Shkoder, Lezhe, and Tropoje, increasing resources for school and drug supplies, and for training of local personnel, keeping in mind the unstable situation of the region and the need for support in these areas. The project consistently involved strong consultations and collaboration with local Albanian authorities. The project lasted 19 months and included four main component categories: health, education, infrastructure, and emergency measures.

Health

Sant'Egidio had been working specifically on health projects in this area since 1992 and extended its intervention to include the refugees from Kosovo. The project supported six health centers in the following service areas:

- Improving access to basic health services for all Albanian refugee children from Kosovo, through periodic visits to judge their state of health and growth and by training local staff in epidemiological surveillance
- Supplying essential drugs for needy patients, either in hospital or as outpatients, for both Albanian and Kosovar citizens
- Screening to evaluate malnutrition, training local staff in detecting nutritional deficiencies, and educating people in basic health and nutrition practice
- Supplying supplementary nutrition for cases of moderate or serious malnutrition
- Improving the transport systems for drug supplies (to health posts), for patients (needing to get to health clinics), and for health workers (to visit rural areas or refugee camps) with the provision of an ambulance and a second off-road vehicle.

These activities were carried out in collaboration with the district health authorities and local Albanian personnel working in public pediatric services. The consultation mechanism established at the start of the project included Albanian experts representing refugee-focused institutions, as well as local authorities who were responsible for components such as infrastructure, health, and education. These consultations were held through periodic steering committee meetings, and informal meetings and discussions throughout the various phases of the project. The process made possible more active participation by the Albanians, both in the identification of priorities and as a source of data for the initiatives that were being established.

Education

The project's education components, undertaken by Sant'Egidio to support and improve the educational facilities in the area, included the following:

- Establishing Schools of Peace to assist the children in camps who were not only threatened by health needs but also traumatized mentally from the violence. Using Kosovar teachers, this component reached more than 14 schools and more than 3,000 students, with hundreds of teachers also benefiting.
- Linking the Schools of Peace and the Country of the Rainbow, an international organization that works with minors in difficulty and attempts to encourage them to accept an educational path as a personal commitment.
- Providing support for existing schools in the districts for the integration of Kosovar students into the Albanian schools, with structural works to modernize the elementary school in the area, with all material and work purchased and contracted locally. The Community provided scholastic material to the students and teachers; supported summer schools for younger refugee children; and provided teacher training.

During the first phase of the intervention, November 1998 to March 1999, Sant'Egidio and the World Bank focused on the district of Lezhe because so many Kosovars had fled Kosovo in July and August to that area. The intervention focused primarily on minors, who represented a large proportion of the refugee population. Initial support concentrated on alleviating malnutrition among infants through distribution of food with high protein and calorie content.

The period from April to August 1999 was characterized by the first mass arrival of Kosovar refugees in Albania—UNHCR estimated about 40,000 in the district of Kukes-Has. During this period, support was offered to the Kukes in refugee camps that had arisen spontaneously and to the Albanian health services that had collapsed at Kukes. Sant'Egidio used funding to enhance the health clinic in Kukes, which was already working with the management assistance of Sant'Egidio. Based on the precarious situation in the impromptu camps, Sant'Egidio set up a special mobile medical unit to treat patients who could not be moved. Other international organizations were present in Kukes during the first days of the crisis, such as the International Medical Corps, the Italian Red Cross, Doctors without Borders, and UNICEF. In parallel with its substantial engagements in Kukes, Sant'Egidio continued its work in the Lezha district, where health and educational activities had been under way for years.

During September 1999 through June 2000 there was support for the reorganization of health and educational facilities after the conflict. There were activities of reconstruction and rehabilitation to assist Albania with the massive inflow of refugees. With the departure of the refugees there was a reduction in the aid that was coming into Albania, which left the health services in critical condition. During this phase the World Bank and Sant'Egidio identified priorities for the health services, focusing on maternal–infant care centers where the Community had been working since 1993.

Conclusion

The Albania program was marked by its success in staving off major potential health problems. It is also credited with restraining the discontent and tension between the local population and the refugees that was a real threat lying not far beneath the surface. Sant'Egidio's local knowledge and long-standing presence in the area allowed it to design well-honed, appropriate programs, suited to and based on locally available resources. The

Community's consistent efforts to cultivate solid relationships based on trust with local authorities and the beneficiary populations, both local and refugee, were major success factors. Synergy with the World Bank (which financed the project) helped make implementation more effective and efficient. The inclusion and collaboration with the local population as active participants was an important element of success: for instance, the project made extensive use of unemployed Albanian workers to implement various components. Sant'Egidio established a strong support network for the refugees, thereby creating a sense of solidarity within the refugee population.

NOTES

1. The Félix Houphouët-Boigny Peace Prize—created in 1989 and awarded by UNESCO annually—honors people, organizations, and institutions that have contributed significantly to the promotion, research, safeguarding, or maintaining of peace, mindful of the Charter of the United Nations and the Constitution of UNESCO. The prize is named after the first president of Côte d'Ivoire, Félix Houphouët-Boigny.

2. http://www.santegidio.org/en/pace/pace3.htm

3. *Community of Sant'Egidio and Peace,*
   http://www.santegidio.org/en/pace/pace1.htm

4. Walter 1999.

5. Contreras 1994.

6. Hume 1994, p. 17.

7. Bartoli 1999, p. 248.

8. Aall, Crocker, and Hampson 2001, p. 509.

9. Bennett 1995.

10. Cascon Case MOZ: Mozambique Civil War 1975-94, http://web.mit.edu/cascon/cases/case_moz.html

11. Gibbs 1994, p. 235.

12. Bartoli 1999, p. 251.

13. Robinson 2002, no page number.

14. World Bank 1999.

15. European Commission, World Bank, and IMF 1999.

16. The Post-Conflict Grant is a facility that provides limited amounts of grant funding in countries emerging from conflict that frequently do not have access to—or only very limited access to—more traditional forms of financ-

ing. Grant activities may be implemented by the country, another organization or, infrequently, by the Bank. A second Post-Conflict Grant of US$1 million in 2002 supported more intensive refugee support activities and assistance in strengthening NGOs to better equip them to assist in the administration of inflows of aid funds. An IDA grant of US$30 million supports the Public Sector Support Program. Several ongoing projects were restructured to support refugees.

REFERENCES

Aall, Pamela, Chester A. Crocker, Fen Osler Hampson. 2001. "Is More Better? The Pros and Cons of Multiparty Mediation." In Pamela Aall, Chester A. Crocker, Fen Osler Hampson, eds. *Turbulent Peace: The Challenges of Managing International Conflict*. Washington D.C.: USIP Press.

Bartoli, Andrea. 1999. "Mediating Peace in Mozambique: The Role of the Community of Sant'Egidio." In Pamela Aall, Chester A. Crocker, Fen Osler Hampson, eds. *Herding Cats: Multiparty Mediation in a Complex World*. Washington, D.C.: USIP Press.

Bennett, Jon. 1995. "Mozambique: Post-War Reconstruction and the LINK NGO Forum, 1987–94." In Jon Bennett, ed., *Meeting Needs: NGO Coordination in Practice*. London: Earthscan.

Contreras, Joseph. 1994. "Long Road Home." *Rolling Stone*. December 29.

European Commission, World Bank, and the IMF (International Monetary Fund). 1999. "The Impact of the Kosovo Conflict on Albania." Report for the Emergency Joint G-24/Consultative Group Meeting. Brussels. May 26.

Gibbs, Sara. 1994. "Post-War Social Reconstruction in Mozambique: Re-framing Children's Experience of Trauma and Healing." *Disasters* 18(3):268–76.

Hume, Cameron. 1994. "Ending Mozambique's' War: The Role of Mediation and Good Offices," Washington, D.C.: United States Institute of Peace.

Robinson, B. A. 2002. "Religious Aspects of the Yugoslavia-Kosovo Conflict." At Web site of Ontario Consultants on Religious Tolerance. Available at http://www.religioustolerance.org/war_koso.htm

Walter, Barbara F. 1999. "Designing Transitions from Civil War: Demobilization, Democratization, and Commitments to Peace." *International Security* 24(1):127–55.

World Bank. 1999. "World Bank Group Response to Post-Conflict Reconstruction in Kosovo, General Framework For an Emergency Assistance Strategy." Washington, D.C. Available at http://www.worldbank.org/html/extdr/kosovo/kosovo_st.htm

CHAPTER 23

Toward Conclusions
Covenants for Action

"All of life is interrelated. We are all caught in an inescapable network of mutuality, tied to a single garment of destiny. Whatever affects one directly affects all indirectly."

—Martin Luther King Jr.[1]

D evelopment is a complex process. For decades practitioners of varied backgrounds—from traditional development institutions to an array of faith communities and nongovernmental organizations, from large multilateral agencies to small grassroots groups and private institutions and individuals—have struggled to deepen our understanding of the kaleidoscope of factors that explain success stories and account for disappointments. Despite many noteworthy examples of success, there is, sadly, no set recipe, no silver bullet. What is incontrovertible, however, is the vital need for all participants to develop better listening and learning skills, to engage in wider partnerships, and to embrace new ideas and perspectives. As institutions, and as individuals, we need more humility, more patience, and greater understanding.

Given these needs, what observations can we draw from existing collaborative efforts between development and faith institutions, whether working to improve the quality of human life or advocating for peace? This volume highlights lessons from the breadth and depth of these joint efforts.

The stories illustrate the vast experience of faith communities across an array of sectors, from direct work with poor communities as critical providers of health and education, to vital roles in the Herculean struggle against the scourge of HIV/AIDS, to long-standing service as mediators of peace and reconciliation. Some of these stories recount cooperation between the worlds of faith and development, some tell of constructive criticism by faith communities of more traditional development actors, and some show how faith groups have gone it alone, working in juxtaposition with other partners but without formal bonds.

Heart, Mind, and Soul is intended to convey not only the need for broader and stronger partnerships but also the need for individuals and organizations—faith and development agents alike—to remain open to transformation. Development institutions come equipped with an armory of analytical tools and techniques, and rightly so. However, faith-based organizations tend to be much more "of the soil," as well as the soul. They tend to be grounded close to communities and focus more profoundly on human motivations and aspirations. The challenge is to bridge the all-too-frequent divide between these perspectives.

The implicit hypothesis is that better solutions will emerge from more dialogue and closer cooperation between faith and development organizations. An obvious question, therefore, is to what extent these examples help clarify and quantify the gains from such partnerships.

Each of the stories highlights the role and importance of heart, mind, and soul for faith and development institutions in their fight against poverty and for social justice, their work to fulfill the Millennium Development Goals (MDGs), and their search for global peace and security. The natural instinct is to focus on the separate roles of these key attributes, but experience underscores time and again how they are most effective when interacting.

In examining why not-for-profit Ugandan health providers choose to work for lower wages than other health providers, for example, economists Ritva Reinikka and Jakob Svensson lay out an empirical explanation to bolster a hunch—perhaps even faith—that the nonprofits place heart and soul at the fore. Reviewing the Poverty Reduction Strategy Papers (PRSPs) supported by the World Bank and the IMF, we see faith groups apply different concepts of time, space, welfare, and commitment to development that we might also call heart and soul. The Jesuits' centuries-old commitment to Colombia's Magdalena Medio region—today to maintaining the peace there—and the creative efforts of the Community of Sant'Egidio in so many countries speak directly from the heart with a strong dose of mind and hands; that is, practical experience. The stories of the extraordinary efforts by the Fe y Alegría Federation to bring quality education to Latin America's poorest communities and of the ATD Fourth World Movement to work with poor communities as partners provide a similar perspective. The Inter-American Development Bank ventured into new territory when, inspired by the horrific stories of the "new poor" devastated by the financial crisis in Argentina, it looked to new partners in the Jewish communities in Argentina and elsewhere to design new kinds of support. And the outreach by the U.N. Population Fund and Planned Parenthood Association of Ghana to faith groups anticipated their heart and soul while also tapping their appeal among adolescents and young adults.

The fundamental dimension to which we constantly return is action, reflected in our focus on a fourth element: the hands. That element rests on the foundation provided by the heart, mind, and soul, because—however well motivated these other aspects—without sound implementation we will see no progress in attacking world poverty, in fostering greater social and economic justice, and in entrenching global security and stability. The challenge is to infuse action with the inspiration, commitment, and passion provided by heart, mind, and soul.

This analysis returns us to the complexity of the struggle against poverty: the importance of appreciating differences as well as recognizing common goals, of maintaining the curiosity to explore different approaches and form new alliances, of the willingness to persist over extended periods, and of the courage to address difficult problems where they exist and when they recur.

LOOKING AHEAD: RETURNING TO WHERE WE STARTED, AND SEEING FOR THE FIRST TIME

> *"We shall not cease from exploration*
> *And the end of all our exploring*
> *Will be to arrive where we started*
> *And know the place for the first time."*
> —T.S. Eliot, *Four Quartets*

T.S. Eliot's insights have special relevance for the explorations that underlie this book. At the simplest level, this journey reminds us of how much we have yet to learn about the processes of development, and hence the need for continuing exploration and dialogue. The journey also vividly illustrates how much we can gain from reexamining our experiences with a new lens. The stories highlighted here weave a rich tapestry of engagement by very different organizations in similar areas, often with little initial knowledge of the motivations of others, their results, and the conclusions they drew from their experiences.

By pushing beyond the limits of our disciplines and vocabulary, and determining how to build upon past successes and learn from past failures, we can cross and re-cross the divides separating the worlds of development and religion. This effort will yield as much wisdom and insight as expanding our horizons in new directions.

The central purpose of this analysis has been to spur action. Among the many themes that have emerged, eight merit special consideration and pose specific questions for future exploration:

1. The MDGs *demand an ever wider array of creative partnerships and alliances.* One such example is support by the AVINA Foundation for Centro Magis—a project that aims to bring sound business practices to the passion of the Fe y Alegría educational movement in Latin America. The Aga Khan Foundation's work with *madrasa* preschools in East Africa reflects a similar creative partnership. However, in both instances the lessons of these experiences have yet to be reflected in mainstream development strategies. Realizing the MDGs will require forging many new nontraditional alliances.

2. The question of incentives is key to partnerships, particularly when, as is the case in the most interesting ones, the actors bring very different experiences and cultures to the table. What incentives can encourage *cross-cutting partnerships* between development and faith partners? That is, how do we move from "ships passing in the night" to genuine partners on the journey?

3. How can we make *better use of existing instruments* to translate rhetoric on such partnerships into action? Perhaps the most important tool for engaging civil society—including faith leaders and religious institutions—is the PRSPs. The framework of the MDGs offers another powerful basis for partnership and action. Development institutions

trying to expand access to education and health care are seeking wider engagement of nongovernmental partners at every level. Encouraging broad ownership of the results of such analyses warrants wider sharing of the debate using a wide variety of communication tools.

4. What steps can generate *unconventional dialogue* that attracts different perspectives and breaks down barriers? The Fez Colloquium offers a creative effort to address critical and sensitive issues around globalization, confronting very different viewpoints with one another against the backdrop of a vivid multicultural event. The experience has been that people communicate fresh ideas and learn at least what they do not know in such a setting. Such dialogue processes need focus, discipline, and sharing of results.

5. More systematic *appreciation and incorporation of the elements that faith traditions can bring to the development processes* would enrich the growing body of "lessons learned." Faith perspectives on poverty and the environment have already exerted many practical effects. Similar analysis of both common and different approaches by faith traditions to health and education would be invaluable.

6. Many faith organizations reveal a widespread *hunger for information and ways to share their experiences,* both among themselves and with development organizations. Information systems such as the Development Gateway[2] are one avenue for such sharing, as is the probing and systematic use of case studies.

7. The need to harness *differing perspectives regarding public accountability and the honest use of funds* is urgent. Corruption shapes public attitudes toward development assistance, but accountability mechanisms can be an uncomfortable topic among faith and development institutions, because they appear to question their reliance on trust. Faith–development alliances to foster transparency and implement clear and effective financial management and reporting systems are critical. Such an outcome occurred in Uganda, where publishing information on aid allocations yielded huge increases in the resources that actually reached their intended beneficiaries.

8. This volume's case studies in HIV/AIDS, health care more generally, and education highlight the potential for *joint advocacy* in alleviating poverty.

Many observers see today's globalized world at a crossroads. Unprecedented levels of information, communication, and financial capital offer extraordinary opportunities for tackling poverty, yet the breadth and depth of the problem and its links to global instability and terrorism suggest daunting challenges. Eliminating poverty and extending human dignity— that is, attaining the MDGs—will require an upsurge in the urgency with which we view these needs, as well as more active outreach to engage all actors, especially the faith communities, which have a special role to play.

Every one of the world's great faith traditions contains a core moral and ethical underpinning confirming that life should be just and fair— that every human being deserves respect and dignity. Enormous progress on these goals is possible, but we must mobilize faith-based energy and moral authority on the world stage if we hope to make them a reality.

NOTES

1. From "Letter from Birmingham Jail," April 16, 1963.

2. The Development Gateway (http://www.developmentgateway.org/node/ 190911/) is an independent not-for-profit organization that is designed to enable development, helping to build partnerships and information systems in developing countries that provide access to knowledge for development. It aims to exploit affordable information and communication technologies that were previously unavailable to increase knowledge sharing; enhance development effectiveness; improve public sector transparency; and build local capacity to empower communities.

Selected Bibliography

The word *processed* describes informally reproduced works that may not be commonly available through libraries.

Belshaw, Deryke, Robert Calderisi, Christopher Sugden, eds. 2001. *Faith in Devel opment: Partnership between the World Bank and the Churches of Africa.* London: Regnum Press.

Braybrooke, Marcus. 1992. *Pilgrimage of Hope: One Hundred Years of Global Interfaith Dialogue.* London: SCM Press.

Centre for Research on Islamic and Malay Affairs (RIMA) and the World Bank. 2003. *Asian Interfaith Dialogue: Perspectives on Religion, Education and Social Cohesion.* Singapore and Washington, D.C.

Chappell, David, ed. 2003. *Socially Engaged Spirituality: Essays in Honor of Sulak Sivaraksa on his 70th Birthday.* Bangkok: Sathirakoses-Nagapradipa Foundation.

Eade, Deborah, ed. 2002. *Development and Culture: Selected Essays from Development in Practice.* Oxford, U.K.: OXFAM.

Edwards, Michael. 2004. *Civil Society.* Cambridge, U.K.: Polity Press.

Gibbs, Charles, and Sally Mahe. 2004. *Birth of a Global Community: Appreciative Inquiry in Action.* Bedford Heights, Ohio: Lakeshore Communications, Inc.

Harper, S. 2000. *The Lab, the Temple and the Market: Reflections at the Intersection of Science, Religion and Development.* Ottawa: Kumarian.

Johnston, Douglas, and Cynthia Sampson, eds. 1994. *Religion: The Missing Dimension of Statecraft.* New York: Oxford University Press.

Kliksberg, Bernardo. 2003. *Social Justice: A Jewish Perspective.* Washington, D.C.: Geffen Books.

Kliksberg, Bernardo, Amartya Sen, and Joseph Stiglitz. 2002. *Etica y Desarrollo: la Relacion Marginada.* Washington, D.C.: Ateneo.

Knox, Geoffrey, ed. 2002. *Religion and Public Policy at the UN*. Washington, D.C.: Religion Counts.

Kung, Hans. 2002. *World Religions, Universal Peace, Global Ethic*. Tübingen, Germany: Institute for Global Ethics.

———. 2002. *Declaration Toward a Global Ethic*. Tübingen, Germany: Institute for Global Ethics. Available at www.weltethos.org.

Marshall, Katherine. 2001. "Development and Religion: A Different Lens on Development Debates." *Peabody Journal of Education* 76(3&4):339–75.

Marshall, Katherine, and Richard Marsh, eds. 2003. *Millennium Challenges for Faith and Development Institutions*. Washington, D.C.: World Bank.

Narayan, Deepa, ed. *Empowerment and Poverty Reduction: A Sourcebook*. Washington, D.C.: World Bank.

Narayan, Deepa, Raj Patel, Kai Schafft, Anne Rademacher, and Sarah Kock-Schulte. 2000. *Voices of the Poor: Can Anyone Hear Us?* New York: Oxford University Press.

Palmer, Martin, with Victoria Finlay. 2003. *Faith in Conservation: New Approaches to Religions and the Environment*. Washington, D.C.: World Bank.

Peccoud, Dominique, ed. 2004. *Philosophical and Spiritual Perspectives on Decent Work*. Geneva: International Labour Office.

Ryan, W. F. 1995. *Culture, Spirituality and Economic Development: Opening a Dialogue*. Ottawa: Canadian International Development Research Centre.

———. 2001. *The Lab, the Temple and the Market: Expanding the Conversation*. Ottawa: Canadian International Development Research Centre.

UNFPA (United Nations Population Fund). 2004. *Culture Matters—Working with Communities and Faith-based Organizations: Case Studies from Country Programmes*. New York.

UNICEF (United Nations Children's Fund). 2003. *What Religious Leaders Can Do About HIV-AIDS*. New York.

World Bank. 2004. *Poverty Reduction Strategy Sourcebook*. Washington, D.C. Processed.

World Faiths Development Dialogue. 1999. *Poverty and Development: An Interfaith Perspective*. Oxford, U.K.

———. 2001. *Cultures, Spirituality and Development*. Oxford, U.K.

World Faiths Development Dialogue Web site: www.wfdd.org.uk

Index